1999 SUPPI

MW01103936

CONSTITUTIONAL LAW
THE AMERICAN CONSTITUTION
CONSTITUTIONAL RIGHTS AND LIBERTIES

Eighth Editions

By
Yale Kamisar
Clarence Darrow Distinguished University Professor of Law,
University of Michigan

Jesse H. Choper
Earl Warren Professor of Public Law,
University of California, Berkeley

Steven H. Shiffrin
Professor of Law,
Cornell University

Richard H. Fallon, Jr.
Professor of Law,
Harvard University

AMERICAN CASEBOOK SERIES®

WEST GROUP

ST. PAUL, MINN., 1999

COPYRIGHT © 1996 By WEST PUBLISHING CO.
COPYRIGHT © 1997, 1998 By WEST GROUP
COPYRIGHT © 1999 By WEST GROUP
                    610 Opperman Drive
                    P.O. Box 64526
                    St. Paul, MN 55164–0526
                    1–800–328–9352

ISBN 0–314–24052–7

*TEXT IS PRINTED ON 10% POST
CONSUMER RECYCLED PAPER*

Preface

This Supplement contains significant developments that have occurred since March 1, 1996—the "cut-off" date of the principal books.

The editorial style of this Supplement follows that of the principal books. In designating the places in the principal books at which the supplementary material is to be inserted, the following abbreviations have been used:

Constitutional Law: Cases, Comments & Questions—CON LAW

The American Constitution: Cases & Materials—AMER CON

Constitutional Rights & Liberties: Cases & Materials—RTS & LIB

Chapter and section titles from the principal books have been reproduced in this Supplement to facilitate identification of the material to be inserted.

YALE KAMISAR
JESSE H. CHOPER
STEVEN H. SHIFFRIN
RICHARD H. FALLON, JR.

July, 1999

*

Table of Contents

Table of Cases

The principal cases are in bold type. Cases cited or discussed in the text are roman type. References are to pages. Cases cited in principal cases and within other quoted materials are not included.

*

1999 SUPPLEMENT TO
CONSTITUTIONAL LAW
THE AMERICAN CONSTITUTION
CONSTITUTIONAL RIGHTS
AND LIBERTIES

Eighth Editions

✳

NATURE AND SCOPE OF
JUDICIAL REVIEW

CONGRESSIONAL REGULATION
OF JUDICIAL POWER

CON LAW: P. 47, at end of note 3(b)

Felker v. Turpin, 518 U.S. 651, 116 S.Ct. 2333, 135 L.Ed.2d 827 (1996), per Rehnquist, C.J., unanimously rejected a constitutional challenge to a federal statute withdrawing the Court's appellate jurisdiction in a category of habeas corpus cases involving "successive" petitions. In a concurring opinion, Souter, J., joined by Stevens and Breyer, JJ., reserved the question whether the statute might be held unconstitutional as applied to subsequent cases if, in practice, it stopped the Court from reviewing "divergent interpretations" of a federal statute.

CON LAW: PP. 47–48, at end of footnote d

The Court followed *Yerger*'s interpretive principle that implied repeals of Supreme Court appellate jurisdiction should be disfavored in *Felker v. Turpin*, 518 U.S. 651, 116 S.Ct. 2333, 135 L.Ed.2d 827 (1996). Per Rehnquist, C.J., the Court held, 9–0, that a statute withdrawing its certiorari jurisdiction in certain habeas cases had not affected its authority to review the case before it upon a petition for an original writ of habeas corpus under 28 U.S.C. §§ 2241 and 2254. As in *McCardle*, the availability of an alternative mechanism for the Court to exercise jurisdiction "obviate[d]" any constitutional challenge to the jurisdiction-limiting legislation under Article III, § 2.

NATIONAL LEGISLATIVE POWER

APPLYING NATIONAL POWERS TO STATE GOVERNMENTS: INTERGOVERNMENTAL IMMUNITIES

STATE IMMUNITY FROM FEDERAL REGULATION

CON LAW: P. 158, after note 3
AMER CON: P. 132, after note 3

PRINTZ v. UNITED STATES

521 U.S. 898, 117 S.Ct. 2365, 138 L.Ed.2d 914 (1997).

JUSTICE SCALIA delivered the opinion of the Court.

The question presented in these cases is whether certain interim provisions of the Brady Handgun Violence Prevention Act, [a detailed federal scheme governing the distribution of firearms,] commanding state and local law enforcement officers to conduct background checks on prospective handgun purchasers and to perform certain related tasks, violate the Constitution.

[T]he Brady Act purports to direct state law enforcement officers to participate, albeit only temporarily, in the administration of a federally enacted regulatory scheme. Regulated firearms dealers are required to forward Brady Forms not to a federal officer or employee, but to the CLEOs ["chief law enforcement officers"], whose obligation to accept those forms is implicit in the duty imposed upon them to make "reasonable efforts" within five days to determine whether the sales reflected in the forms are lawful. While the CLEOs are subjected to no federal requirement that they prevent the sales determined to be unlawful (it is perhaps assumed that their state-law duties will require prevention or apprehension), they are empowered to grant, in effect, waivers of the federally prescribed 5-day waiting period for handgun purchases by notifying the gun dealers that they have no reason to believe the transactions would be illegal.

The petitioners here object to being pressed into federal service, and contend that congressional action compelling state officers to execute federal laws is unconstitutional. Because there is no constitutional text speaking to this precise question, the answer to the CLEOs' challenge must be sought in historical understanding and practice, in the structure of the Constitution, and in the jurisprudence of this Court.

[The Court concluded that the relevant historical practice tends to negate Congress' power to impose federal responsibilities on state officers without the States' consent. "[E]nactments of the early Congresses [contain] no evidence of an assumption that the Federal Government may command the States' executive power in the absence of a particularized constitutional authorization," such as the Extradition Clause of Art IV, Sec. 2. The "early laws establish, at most, that the

Constitution was originally understood to permit imposition of an obligation on state judges to enforce federal prescriptions, insofar as those prescriptions related to matters appropriate for the judicial power." Finally, there is "an absence of executive-commandeering statutes [in] our later history as well, at least until very recent years."

[The dissents disputed each of these points, as well as the meaning of *The Federalist* Nos. 27 and 44. STEVENS, J., concluded: "[T]he majority's opinion consists almost entirely of arguments against the substantial evidence weighing in opposition to its view; the Court's ruling is strikingly lacking in affirmative support. Absent even a modicum of textual foundation for its judicially crafted constitutional rule, there should be a presumption that if the Framers had actually intended such a rule, at least one of them would have mentioned it."]

* * * We turn next to consideration of the structure of the Constitution * * *. We have set forth the historical record in more detail elsewhere, see *New York v. United States,* and need not repeat it here. It suffices to repeat the conclusion: "The Framers explicitly chose a Constitution that confers upon Congress the power to regulate individuals, not States." * * *

This separation of the two spheres is one of the Constitution's structural protections of liberty. [The] power of the Federal Government would be augmented immeasurably if it were able to impress into its service—and at no cost to itself—the police officers of the 50 States.

[F]ederal control of state officers would [also] have an effect upon [the] separation and equilibration of powers between the three branches of the Federal Government itself. The Constitution does not leave to speculation who is to administer the laws enacted by Congress; the President, it says, "shall take Care that the Laws be faithfully executed," personally and through officers whom he appoints. [The] Brady Act effectively transfers this responsibility to thousands of CLEOs in the 50 States, who are left to implement the program without meaningful Presidential control (if indeed meaningful Presidential control is possible without the power to appoint and remove). [T]he power of the President would be subject to reduction, if Congress could act as effectively without the President as with him, by simply requiring state officers to execute its laws.[12] * * *

Finally, and most conclusively in the present litigation, we turn to the prior jurisprudence of this Court. * * *

The Government contends that *New York* is distinguishable on the following ground: unlike the "take title" provisions invalidated there, the background-check provision of the Brady Act does not require state legislative or executive officials to make policy. [But executive] action that has utterly no policymaking component is rare, particularly at an executive level as high as a jurisdiction's chief law-enforcement officer. Is it really true that there is no policymaking involved in deciding, for example, what "reasonable efforts" shall be expended to conduct a background check? It may well satisfy the Act for a CLEO to direct that (a) no background checks will be conducted that divert personnel time from pending felony investigations, and (b) no background check will be permitted to

---

12. There is not, as the dissent believes, "tension" between the proposition that impressing state police officers into federal service will massively augment federal power, and the proposition that it will also sap the power of the Federal Presidency. It is quite possible to have a more powerful Federal Government that is, by reason of the destruction of its Executive unity, a less efficient one. The dissent is correct that control by the unitary Federal Executive is also sacrificed when States voluntarily administer federal programs, but the condition of voluntary state participation significantly reduces the ability of Congress to use this device as a means of reducing the power of the Presidency.

consume more than one-half hour of an officer's time. [Is] this decision whether to devote maximum "reasonable efforts" or minimum "reasonable efforts" not preeminently a matter of policy? It is quite impossible, in short, to draw the Government's proposed line at "no policymaking," and we would have to fall back upon a line of "not too much policymaking." How much is too much is not likely to be answered precisely; and an imprecise barrier against federal intrusion upon state authority is not likely to be an effective one.

Even assuming, moreover, that the Brady Act leaves no "policymaking" discretion with the States, we fail to see how that improves rather than worsens the intrusion upon state sovereignty. Preservation of the States as independent and autonomous political entities is arguably less undermined by requiring them to make policy in certain fields than [by] "reduc[ing] [them] to puppets of a ventriloquist Congress." * * *

The Government also maintains that requiring state officers to perform discrete, ministerial tasks specified by Congress does not violate the principle of *New York* because it does not diminish the accountability of state or federal officials. This argument fails even on its own terms. By forcing state governments to absorb the financial burden of implementing a federal regulatory program, Members of Congress can take credit for "solving" problems without having to ask their constituents to pay for the solutions with higher federal taxes. And even when the States are not forced to absorb the costs of implementing a federal program, they are still put in the position of taking the blame for its burdensomeness and for its defects. Under the present law, for example, it will be the CLEO and not some federal official who stands between the gun purchaser and immediate possession of his gun. And it will likely be the CLEO, not some federal official, who will be blamed for any error (even one in the designated federal database) that causes a purchaser to be mistakenly rejected.

[The] Brady Act, the dissent asserts, is different [from] *New York* because the former is addressed to individuals—namely CLEOs—while the latter were directed to the State itself. That is certainly a difference, but it cannot be a constitutionally significant one. While the Brady Act is directed to "individuals," it is directed to them in their official capacities as state officers; it controls their actions, not as private citizens, but as the agents of the State. * * *

Finally, the Government puts forward a cluster of arguments that can be grouped under the heading: "The Brady Act serves very important purposes, is most efficiently administered by CLEOs during the interim period, and places a minimal and only temporary burden upon state officers." * * * Assuming all the mentioned factors were true, they might be relevant if we were evaluating whether the incidental application to the States of a federal law of general applicability excessively interfered with the functioning of state governments. See, e.g., *Fry; Usery.* But where, as here, it is the whole object of the law to direct the functioning of the state executive, and hence to compromise the structural framework of dual sovereignty, such a "balancing" analysis is inappropriate.[17] [We] conclude categorically, as we concluded categorically in *New York*:

17. The dissent observes that "Congress could require private persons, such as hospital executives or school administrators, to provide arms merchants with relevant information about a prospective purchaser's fitness to own a weapon," and that "the burden on police officers [imposed by the Brady Act] would be permissible if a similar burden were also imposed on private parties with access to relevant data." That is undoubtedly true, but it does not advance the dissent's case. The Brady Act does not merely require CLEOs to report information in their private possession. It requires them to provide information that belongs to the State and is available to them only in their official capacity; and to conduct investigations

"The Federal Government may not compel the States to enact or administer a federal regulatory program." * * *

JUSTICE O'CONNOR, concurring.

[T]he Court appropriately refrains from deciding [whether] purely ministerial reporting requirements imposed by Congress on state and local authorities pursuant to its Commerce Clause powers are similarly invalid. See, e.g., 42 U.S.C. § 5779(a) (requiring state and local law enforcement agencies to report cases of missing children to the Department of Justice).[a] The provisions invalidated here, however, which directly compel state officials to administer a federal regulatory program, utterly fail to adhere to the design and structure of our constitutional scheme.[b]

JUSTICE STEVENS, with whom JUSTICE SOUTER, JUSTICE GINSBURG, and JUSTICE BREYER join, dissenting. * * *

These cases do not implicate the more difficult questions associated with congressional coercion of state legislatures addressed in *New York*. Nor need we consider the wisdom of relying on local officials rather than federal agents to carry out aspects of a federal program, or even the question whether such officials may be required to perform a federal function on a permanent basis. The question is whether Congress, acting on behalf of the people of the entire Nation, may require local law enforcement officers to perform certain duties during the interim needed for the development of a federal gun control program. * * *

Indeed, since the ultimate issue is one of power, we must consider its implications in times of national emergency. Matters such as the enlistment of air raid wardens, the administration of a military draft, the mass inoculation of children to forestall an epidemic, or perhaps the threat of an international terrorist, may require a national response before federal personnel can be made available to respond. If the Constitution empowers Congress and the President to make an appropriate response, is there anything in the Tenth Amendment, "in historical understanding and practice, in the structure of the Constitution, [or] in the jurisprudence of this Court," that forbids the enlistment of state officers to make that response effective? More narrowly, what basis is there in any of those sources for concluding that it is the Members of this Court, rather than the elected representatives of the people, who should determine whether the Constitution contains the unwritten rule that the Court announces today? * * *

Unlike the First Amendment, which prohibits the enactment of a category of laws that would otherwise be authorized by Article I, the Tenth Amendment [confirms] the principle that the powers of the Federal Government are limited to those affirmatively granted by the Constitution, but it does not purport to limit the scope or the effectiveness of the exercise of powers that are delegated to Congress. Thus, the Amendment provides no support for a rule that immunizes local officials from obligations that might be imposed on ordinary citizens.[2] * * *

in their official capacity, by examining databases and records that only state officials have access to. In other words, the suggestion that extension of this statute to private citizens would eliminate the constitutional problem posits the impossible.

a. The Court commented that "federal statutes [which] require only the provision of information to the Federal Government, do not involve the precise issue before us [here]."

b. The concurring opinion of Thomas, J., who joined the Court's opinion, is omitted.

2. Recognizing the force of the argument, the Court suggests that this reasoning is in error because—even if it is responsive to the submission that the Tenth Amendment roots the principle set forth by the majority today—it does not answer the possibility that the Court's holding can be rooted in a "principle of state sovereignty" mentioned nowhere in the constitutional text. As a ground for invalidat-

There is not a clause, sentence, or paragraph in the entire text of the Constitution of the United States that supports the proposition that a local police officer can ignore a command contained in a statute enacted by Congress pursuant to an express delegation of power enumerated in Article I. * * *

Recent developments demonstrate that the political safeguards protecting Our Federalism are effective. The majority expresses special concern that were its rule not adopted the Federal Government would be able to avail itself of the services of state government officials "at no cost to itself." But this specific problem of federal actions that have the effect of imposing so-called "unfunded mandates" on the States has been identified and meaningfully addressed by Congress in recent legislation.[18] * * *

Perversely, the majority's rule seems more likely to damage than to preserve the safeguards against tyranny provided by the existence of vital state governments. By limiting the ability of the Federal Government to enlist state officials in the implementation of its programs, the Court creates incentives for the National Government to aggrandize itself. In the name of State's rights, the majority would have the Federal Government create vast national bureaucracies to implement its policies.[b]

JUSTICE BREYER, with whom JUSTICE STEVENS joins, dissenting.

[T]he United States is not the only nation that seeks to reconcile the practical need for a central authority with the democratic virtues of more local control. At least some other countries, facing the same basic problem, have found that local control is better maintained through application of a principle that is the direct opposite of the principle the majority derives from the silence of our Constitution. The federal systems of Switzerland, Germany, and the European Union, for example, all provide that constituent states, not federal bureaucracies, will themselves implement many of the laws, rules, regulations, or decrees enacted by the central "federal" body. * * *

Of course, we are interpreting our own Constitution, [but] their experience may nonetheless cast an empirical light on the consequences of different solutions to a common legal problem. * * *

ing important federal legislation, this argument is remarkably weak. The majority's further claim that, while the Brady Act may be legislation "necessary" to Congress' execution of its undisputed Commerce Clause authority to regulate firearms sales, it is nevertheless not "proper" because it violates state sovereignty, is wholly circular and provides no traction for its argument. [Our] ruling in *New York* that the Commerce Clause does not provide Congress the authority to require States to enact legislation—a power that affects States far closer to the core of their sovereign authority— does nothing to support the majority's unwarranted extension of that reasoning today.

18. The majority also makes the more general claim that requiring state officials to carry out federal policy causes states to "tak[e] the blame" for failed programs. The Court cites no empirical authority to support the proposition. [This] concern is vastly overstated. Unlike state legislators, local government executive officials routinely take action in response to a variety of sources of authority: local ordi-

nance, state law, and federal law. It doubtless may therefore require some sophistication to discern under which authority an executive official is acting, just as it may not always be immediately obvious what legal source of authority underlies a judicial decision. [But] the majority's rule neither creates nor alters this basic truth. The problem is of little real consequence in any event, because to the extent that a particular action proves politically unpopular, we may be confident that elected officials charged with implementing it will be quite clear to their constituents where the source of the misfortune lies. These cases demonstrate the point. Sheriffs Printz and Mack have made public statements, including their decisions to serve as plaintiffs in these actions, denouncing the Brady Act.

b. Souter, J.'s separate dissent, noting that "in deciding these cases, which I have found closer than I had anticipated, it is *The Federalist* that finally determines my position," is omitted.

DISTRIBUTION OF FEDERAL POWERS: SEPARATION OF POWERS

PRESIDENTIAL ACTION AFFECTING "CONGRESSIONAL" POWERS

CON LAW: P. 178, at the end of note 2(b)

AMER CON: P. 146, at the end of note 2(b)

Cf. *Minnesota v. Mille Lacs Band of Chippewa Indians,* ___ U.S. ___, 119 S.Ct. 1187, 143 L.Ed.2d 270 (1999) (finding no valid source of authority for an 1850 executive order purporting to require the removal of Chippewa Indians from lands ceded to the United States by an 1837 treaty).

CON LAW: P. 181, after note 6

AMER CON: P. 149, after note 6

7. *Line item veto.* Congress dramatically overhauled the structure established by the Congressional Budget and Impoundment Control Act by enacting the Line Item Veto Act of 1996, which delegated to the President substantially unrestricted authority to "cancel" certain spending and tax benefit measures after he has signed them into law. But the Court held the Line Item Veto Act unconstitutional in *Clinton v. New York,* 524 U.S. 417, 118 S.Ct. 2091, 141 L.Ed.2d 393 (1998), which appears below as a principal case.

CONGRESSIONAL ACTION AFFECTING "PRESIDENTIAL" POWERS

DELEGATION OF RULEMAKING POWER

CON LAW: P. 182, at end of note 1

Compare *Loving v. United States,* 517 U.S. 748, 116 S.Ct. 1737, 135 L.Ed.2d 36 (1996). The Court, per Kennedy, J., held unanimously, on the assumption that its death penalty jurisprudence applied to courts-martial, that it was constitutionally permissible for Congress to delegate to the President responsibility for prescribing aggravating factors warranting capital sentences. Because the assigned duties were "interlinked" with the President's constitutional powers as commander in chief, Congress, which had already defined the underlying capital offense, was not required to supply the President with "further guidance" concerning aggravating factors.[a]

a. Scalia, J., joined by O'Connor, J., concurring in part and concurring in the judgment, declined to join a part of the majority opinion treating English history as a source of relevant separation-of-powers principles in this case. Thomas, J., concurred in the judgment only.

CON LAW: P. 189, after note 5
AMER CON: P. 155, after note 5

THE LINE ITEM VETO

CLINTON v. NEW YORK

524 U.S. 417, 118 S.Ct. 2091, 141 L.Ed.2d 393 (1998).

Justice Stevens delivered the opinion of the Court.

[The Line Item Veto Act, which took effect on January 1, 1997, gives the President the power to "cancel in whole" three types of provisions that have been enacted by Congress and signed into law: "(1) any dollar amount of discretionary budget authority; (2) any item of new direct spending; or (3) any limited tax benefit." After a suit by members of Congress challenging the constitutionality of the Act was dismissed for lack of standing in *Raines v. Byrd*, p. 129 of this Supplement, the President exercised his "line item veto" to nullify the two provisions involved in this case: a section of the Balanced Budget Act of 1997 that waived the federal government's statutory authority to seek recoupment of as much as $2.6 billion in taxes that the State of New York had levied against Medicare providers, and a section of the Taxpayers Relief Act of 1997, which authorized favorable tax treatment of certain parties selling food processing facilities to farmers' cooperatives.]

It is undisputed that the New York case involves an "item of new direct spending" and that the [other] involves a "limited tax benefit" as those terms are defined in the Act. It is also undisputed that each of those provisions had been signed into law pursuant to Article I, § 7, of the Constitution before it was canceled.

The Act requires the President to adhere to precise procedures whenever he exercises his cancellation authority. [He] must [also] determine, with respect to each cancellation, that it will "(i) reduce the Federal budget deficit; (ii) not impair any essential Government functions; and (iii) not harm the national interest." Moreover, he must transmit a special message to Congress notifying it of each cancellation within five calendar days.

A cancellation takes effect upon receipt by Congress of the special message from the President. If, however, a "disapproval bill" pertaining to a special message is enacted into law, the cancellations set forth in that message become "null and void." The Act sets forth a detailed expedited procedure for the consideration of a "disapproval bill," but no such bill was passed for [the] cancellations involved in these cases. A majority vote of both Houses is sufficient to enact a disapproval bill. The Act does not grant the President the authority to cancel a disapproval bill, but he does, of course, retain his constitutional authority to veto such a bill.

With respect to both an item of new direct spending and a limited tax benefit, the cancellation prevents the item "from having legal force or effect."

[There] are important differences between the President's "return" of a bill pursuant to Article I, § 7, and the exercise of the President's cancellation authority pursuant to the Line Item Veto Act. The constitutional return takes place before the bill becomes law; the statutory cancellation occurs after the bill becomes law. The constitutional return is of the entire bill; the statutory cancellation is of only a part. Although the Constitution expressly authorizes the President to play a role in the process of enacting statutes, it is silent on the subject of unilateral Presidential action that either repeals or amends parts of duly enacted statutes.

There are powerful reasons for construing constitutional silence on this profoundly important issue as equivalent to an express prohibition. The procedures governing the enactment of statutes set forth in [Article] I were the product of the great debates and compromises that produced the Constitution itself. [Our] first President understood the text of the Presentment Clause as requiring that he either "approve all the parts of a Bill, or reject it in toto." What has emerged in these cases from the President's exercise of his statutory cancellation powers, however, are truncated versions of two bills that passed both Houses of Congress. They are not the product of the "finely wrought" procedure that the Framers designed.

[Relying] primarily on *Field v. Clark* [CON LAW p. 178, AMER CON p. 146], the Government contends that the cancellations were [not repeals or vetoes in the constitutional sense, but] merely exercises of discretionary authority granted to the President by the Balanced Budget Act and the Taxpayer Relief Act read in light of the previously enacted Line Item Veto Act. [In] *Field*, the Court upheld the constitutionality of the Tariff Act of 1890. That statute contained a "free list" of almost 300 specific articles that were exempted from import duties[, but] directed the President to suspend [the] exemption for sugar, molasses, coffee, tea, and hides "whenever, and so often" as he [determined] that any country producing and exporting those products imposed duties on the agricultural products of the United States that he deemed to be "reciprocally unequal and unreasonable * * *."

[But there are] three critical differences between the power to suspend the exemption from import duties and the power to cancel portions of a duly enacted statute. First, the exercise of the suspension power was contingent upon a condition that did not exist when the Tariff Act was passed: the imposition of "reciprocally unequal and unreasonable" import duties by other countries. In contrast, the exercise of the cancellation power within five days after the enactment of the Balanced Budget and Tax Reform Acts necessarily was based on the same conditions that Congress evaluated when it passed those statutes. Second, under the Tariff Act, when the President determined that the contingency had arisen, he had a duty to suspend; in contrast, [the Line Item Veto Act] did not qualify his discretion to cancel or not to cancel. Finally, whenever the President suspended an exemption under the Tariff Act, he was executing the policy that Congress had embodied in the statute. In contrast, whenever the President cancels an item of new direct spending or a limited tax benefit he is rejecting the policy judgment made by Congress and relying on his own policy judgment.

The Government's reliance upon other tariff and import statutes [that] contain provisions similar to the one challenged in *Field* is unavailing for the same reasons. [In addition, the] cited statutes all relate to foreign trade, and this Court has recognized that in the foreign affairs arena, the President has "a degree of discretion and freedom from statutory restriction which would not be admissible were domestic affairs alone involved." More important, when enacting the statutes discussed in *Field*, Congress itself made the decision to suspend or repeal the particular provisions at issue upon the occurrence of particular events subsequent to enactment, and it left only the determination of whether such events occurred up to the President. The Line Item Veto Act authorizes the President himself to effect the repeal of laws, for his own policy reasons, without observing the procedures set out in Article I, § 7. The fact that Congress intended such a result is of no moment. Although Congress presumably anticipated that the President might cancel some of the items in the Balanced Budget Act and in the Taxpayer Relief Act, Congress cannot alter the procedures set out in Article I, § 7, without amending the Constitution.[40]

Neither are we persuaded by the Government's contention that the President's authority to cancel new direct spending and tax benefit items is no greater than his traditional authority to decline to spend appropriated funds. [The] critical difference between this statute and all of its predecessors [is] that unlike any of them, this Act gives the President the unilateral power to change the text of duly enacted statutes.

[Because] we conclude that the Act's cancellation provisions violate Article I, § 7, [we] find it unnecessary to consider [whether] the Act [impermissibly delegates lawmaking authority to the President].

Justice Kennedy, concurring.

[To] say the political branches have a somewhat free hand to reallocate their own authority would seem to require acceptance of two premises: first, that the public good demands it, and second, that liberty is not at risk. The former premise is inadmissible. The Constitution's structure requires a stability which transcends the convenience of the moment. The latter premise, too, is flawed. Liberty is always at stake when one or more of the branches seek to transgress the separation of powers. Separation of powers was designed to implement a fundamental insight: concentration of power in the hands of a single branch is a threat to liberty. [If] a citizen who is taxed has the measure of the tax or the decision to spend determined by the Executive alone, without adequate control by the citizen's Representatives in Congress, liberty is threatened.

Justice Breyer, with whom Justice O'Connor and Justice Scalia join as to Part III, dissenting.

III.   [When] the President "canceled" the two appropriation measures now before us, he did not repeal any law nor did he amend any law. He simply followed the law, leaving the statutes, as they are literally written, intact.

To understand why one cannot say, literally speaking, that the President has repealed or amended any law, imagine how the provisions of law before us might have been, but were not, written. Imagine that the canceled New York health care tax provision at issue here [had said]:

Section One. Taxes [that] were collected by the State of New York from a health care provider before June 1, 1997 and for which a waiver of provisions [requiring payment] have been sought [are] deemed to be permissible health care related taxes [provided] however that the President may prevent the just-mentioned provision from having legal force or effect if he determines x, y and z.

---

40. The Government argues that the Rules Enabling Act, 28 U.S.C. § 2072(b), permits this Court to "repeal" prior laws without violating Article I, § 7. Section 2072(b) provides that this Court may promulgate rules of procedure for the lower federal courts and that "all laws in conflict with such rules shall be of no further force or effect after such rules have taken effect." See *Sibbach v. Wilson & Co.*, [CON LAW p. 184 n.19, AMER CON p. 150 n.19] (stating that the procedural rules that this Court promulgates, "if they are within the authority granted by Congress, repeal" a prior inconsistent procedural statute). In enacting § 2072(b), however, Congress expressly provided that laws inconsistent with the procedural rules promulgated by this Court would automatically be repealed upon the enactment of new rules in order to create a uniform system of rules for Article III courts. As in the tariff statutes, Congress itself made the decision to repeal prior rules upon the occurrence of a particular event—here, the promulgation of procedural rules by this Court.

(Assume x, y and z to be the same determinations required by the Line Item Veto Act).

Whatever a person might say, or think, about the constitutionality of this imaginary law, [one] could not say that a President who "prevents" the deeming language from "having legal force or effect" has either repealed or amended this particular hypothetical statute. Rather, the President has exercised the power it explicitly delegates to him. He has executed the law, not repealed it.

It could make no significant difference to this linguistic point were the italicized proviso to appear, not as part of what I have called Section One, but, instead, at the bottom of the statute page, say referenced by an asterisk, with a statement that it applies to every spending provision in the act next to which a similar asterisk appears. And that being so, it could make no difference if that proviso appeared, instead, in a different, earlier-enacted law, along with legal language that makes it applicable to every future spending provision picked out according to a specified formula. But, of course, this last-mentioned possibility is this very case.

[Because] one cannot say that the President's exercise of the power the Act grants is, literally speaking, a "repeal" or "amendment," the fact that the Act's procedures differ from the Constitution's exclusive procedures for enacting (or repealing) legislation is beside the point. The Act itself was enacted in accordance with these procedures, and its failure to require the President to satisfy those procedures does not make the Act unconstitutional.

IV. Because I disagree with the Court's holding of literal violation, I must consider whether the Act nonetheless violates Separation of Powers principles.

[One] cannot say that the Act "encroaches" upon Congress' power, when Congress retained the power to insert, by simple majority, into any future appropriations bill, into any section of any such bill, or into any phrase of any section, a provision that says the Act will not apply.

[Nor] can one say the Act's grant of power "aggrandizes" the Presidential office. The grant is limited to the context of the budget. It is limited to the power to spend, or not to spend, particular appropriated items, and the power to permit, or not to permit, specific limited exemptions from generally applicable tax law from taking effect.

[The] "nondelegation" doctrine [raises] a more serious constitutional obstacle here. [The] Constitution permits only those delegations where Congress "shall lay down by legislative act an intelligible principle to which the person or body authorized to [act] is directed to conform." [The standards in the Act] are broad. But this Court has upheld standards that are equally broad, or broader. See, e.g., *National Broadcasting Co. v. United States*, 319 U.S. 190, 63 S.Ct. 997, 87 L.Ed. 1344 (1943) (upholding delegation to Federal Communications Commission to regulate broadcast licensing as "public interest, convenience, or necessity" require).

[Like] statutes delegating power to award broadcast television licenses, [the] Act is aimed at a discrete problem: namely, a particular set of expenditures within the federal budget. [Second], like the award of television licenses, the particular problem involved—determining whether or not a particular amount of money should be spent or whether a particular dispensation from tax law should be granted a few individuals—does not readily lend itself to a significantly more specific standard. [Third], in insofar as monetary expenditure (but not "tax expenditure") is at issue, the President acts in an area where history helps to justify the discretionary power that Congress has delegated. [Congress] has frequently delegated the President the authority to spend, or not to spend, particular sums of money.

[The] "limited tax benefit" question [is] more difficult. [But this] Court has upheld tax statutes [involving tariffs] that delegate to the President the power to change taxes under very broad standards. [These] statutory delegations [have often involved] a duty on imports, which is a tax [that] in the last century was as important then as the income tax is now, for it provided most of the Federal Government's revenues.

[I] recognize that the Act before us is novel. [But the] Constitution, in my view, authorizes Congress and the President to try novel methods in this way.

JUSTICE SCALIA, with whom JUSTICE O'CONNOR joins, and with whom JUSTICE BREYER joins as to Part III, concurring in part and dissenting in part.

III. [Although the Court should rule that there is no party before it with standing to challenge the President's authority to cancel a "limited tax benefit,"] I agree [that] the New York appellees have standing to challenge the President's cancellation of [an] "item of new direct spending."

Article I, § 7 of the Constitution obviously prevents the President from canceling a law that Congress has not authorized him to cancel. But that is not this case. [Article I, § 7] no more categorically prohibits the Executive reduction of congressional dispositions in the course of implementing statutes that authorize such reduction, than it categorically prohibits the Executive augmentation of congressional dispositions in the course of implementing statutes that authorize such augmentation—generally known as substantive rulemaking.

[I] turn, then, to [whether] Congress's authorizing the President to cancel an item of spending [violates the non-delegation doctrine by giving] him a power that our history and traditions show must reside exclusively in the Legislative Branch. [Insofar] as the degree of political, "law-making" power conferred upon the Executive is concerned, there is not a dime's worth of difference between Congress's authorizing the President to cancel a spending item, and Congress's authorizing money to be spent on a particular item at the President's discretion. And the latter has been done since the Founding of the Nation. From 1789–1791, the First Congress made lump-sum appropriations for the entire Government— "sums not exceeding" specified amounts for broad purposes. From a very early date Congress also made permissive individual appropriations, leaving the decision whether to spend the money to the President's unfettered discretion.

[The] short of the matter is this: Had the Line Item Veto Act authorized the President to "decline to spend" any item of spending contained in the Balanced Budget Act of 1997, there is not the slightest doubt that authorization would have been constitutional. The title of the Line Item Veto Act, which was perhaps designed to simplify for public comprehension, or perhaps merely to comply with the terms of a campaign pledge, has succeeded in faking out the Supreme Court. The President's action it authorizes in fact is not a line-item veto and thus does not offend Art. I, § 7; and insofar as the substance of that action is concerned, it is no different from what Congress has permitted the President to do since the formation of the Union.

CONTROL OVER APPOINTMENT AND
REMOVAL OF OFFICERS

CON LAW: P. 204, at the end of note 3

AMER CON: P. 166, at the end of note 2

(c) EDMOND v. UNITED STATES, 520 U.S. 651, 117 S.Ct. 1573, 137 L.Ed.2d 917 (1997), upheld the authority of the Secretary of Transportation to appoint civilian members of the Coast Guard Court of Criminal Appeals, which hears appeals from courts martial. The Court, per SCALIA, J., reasoned that Coast Guard Court of Criminal Appeals judges were "inferior" officers, subject to appointment by heads of departments, because they were supervised by the Judge Advocate General, who could remove them without cause, and by the Court of Appeals for the Armed Forces, which has appellate jurisdiction over Coast Guard Court of Criminal Appeals judgments: "Generally speaking, the term 'inferior officer' connotes a relationship with some higher ranking officer or officers below the President: Whether one is an inferior officer depends upon whether he has a superior."

Is the rationale of *Edmond*, as advanced by Scalia, J., consistent with *Morrison v. Olson*, from which Scalia, J., dissented? Who is the independent counsel's "superior"?

EXECUTIVE PRIVILEGE AND IMMUNITY

CON LAW: P. 219, at the end of note 5

AMER CON: P. 175, at the end of note 5

CLINTON v. JONES, 520 U.S. 681, 117 S.Ct. 1636, 137 L.Ed.2d 945 (1997). Paula Jones, a former Arkansas state employee, filed a civil suit against President Bill Clinton, seeking damages for acts allegedly committed while Clinton was governor of Arkansas. More specifically, Jones alleged that then-Governor Clinton arranged for her to be brought to a suite in a hotel, where he had just addressed a conference for which Jones provided staff support, and made " 'abhorrent' sexual advances that she vehemently rejected." Claiming that defending the suit would interfere with his performance of the presidential office, Clinton sought to have the suit dismissed without prejudice, and the statute of limitations tolled, until the expiration of his term.

The Court, per STEVENS, J., unanimously rejected Clinton's claims and held that the suit could go forward, notwithstanding the holding of *Nixon v. Fitzgerald* that the President is absolutely immune from suits for civil damages based on official Presidential acts. "[Clinton's] principal submission—that 'in all but the most exceptional cases,' the Constitution affords the President temporary immunity from civil damages litigation arising out of events that occurred before he took office—cannot be sustained. [The] principal rationale for affording certain public servants immunity from suits for money damages arising out of their official acts" is to "enabl[e] such officials to perform their designated functions effectively without fear that a particular decision may give rise to personal liability. [This] reasoning provides no support for an immunity for unofficial conduct [including conduct occurring before Clinton became President].

"Petitioner's strongest argument * * * relies on separation of powers principles. [He] contends that this particular case—as well as the potential additional litigation that [it] may spawn—may impose an unacceptable burden on the

President's time and energy, and thereby impair the effective performance of his office. [But this] predictive judgment finds little support in either history or the relatively narrow compass of the issues raised in this particular case. [In] the more than 200 year history of the Republic, only three sitting Presidents have been subjected to suits for their private actions. [It therefore] seems unlikely that a deluge of such litigation will ever engulf the Presidency. As for the case at hand, if properly managed by the District Court, it appears to us highly unlikely to occupy any substantial amount of petitioner's time.

"[Of] greater significance, petitioner errs by presuming that interactions between the Judicial Branch and the Executive, even quite burdensome interactions, necessarily rise to the level of constitutionally forbidden impairment of the Executive's ability to perform its constitutionally mandated functions. [We] have long held that when the President takes official action, the Court has the authority to determine whether he has acted within the law. [E.g., *Youngstown*.] [If] the Judiciary may severely burden the Executive Branch by reviewing the legality of the President's official conduct, and if it may direct appropriate process to the President himself [e.g., United States v. Nixon], it must follow that the federal courts have power to determine the legality of his unofficial conduct."

Having found that Clinton lacked any constitutional immunity from Jones' suit, the Court went on to consider whether "a stay of either trial or discovery might be justified [in the discretion of the District Court] by considerations that do not require the recognition of any constitutional immunity. The District Court has broad discretion to stay proceedings as an incident to its power to control its own docket [and] potential burdens on the President [are] appropriate matters for the District Court to evaluate in its management of the case. The high respect that is owed to the Office of the Chief Executive [is] a matter that should inform the conduct of the entire proceeding, including the timing and scope of discovery."

Nonetheless, "the proponent of a stay bears the burden of establishing its need." And so far there was "nothing in the record to enable a judge to assess the potential harm that may ensue from scheduling the trial promptly after discovery is concluded."

BREYER, J., concurred in the judgment only. He agreed "that the Constitution does not automatically grant the President an immunity from civil lawsuits based upon his private conduct." But "once the President sets forth and explains a conflict between judicial proceeding and public duties, [the] Constitution permits a judge to schedule a trial in an ordinary civil damages action [only] within the constraints of a constitutional principle—a principle that forbids a federal judge in such a case to interfere with the President's discharge of his public duties." Breyer, J., was less "sanguine" than the majority that permitting suits against sitting Presidents would not lead to a proliferation of such actions and the threat of significant impositions on the President's time. He therefore thought that "ordinary case-management principles are unlikely to prove sufficient" and would make clear that the Constitution does "not grant a single judge more than a very limited power to second guess a President's reasonable determination (announced in open court) of his scheduling needs, nor could [the Constitution] permit the issuance of a trial scheduling order that would significantly interfere with the President's discharge of his duties."

STATE POWER TO REGULATE

CASES AND DOCTRINE

CON LAW: P. 244, at the end of note 3
AMER CON: P. 190, at the end of note 3

CAMPS NEWFOUND/OWATONNA, INC. v. TOWN OF HARRISON, 520 U.S. 564, 117 S.Ct. 1590, 137 L.Ed.2d 852 (1997), held that a Maine statute providing a general property tax exemption for charitable institutions, but withholding the exemption from charitable institutions operated principally for the benefit of non-residents, violates the Commerce Clause. The tax was challenged by the operators of a summer camp for children of the Christian Science faith, about 95% of whose campers are not Maine residents. Dividing 5–4, the Court, per STEVENS, J., viewed the tax as facially discriminatory against interstate commerce. The camp was selling a product that included "in part the natural beauty of Maine itself"; the statute created a financial incentive for the camp and other charitable institutions to prefer state residents over out-of-staters. Reasoning that the statute would be virtually per se illegal as applied to for-profit activities, Stevens, J., saw no reason to make an exception for not-for-profit organizations.

The majority rejected the argument that the "discriminatory tax exemption [at issue] is, in economic reality, no different from a discriminatory subsidy of those charities that cater principally to local needs" and should therefore be upheld. "Assuming, arguendo, that [a] direct subsidy benefitting only those nonprofits serving principally Maine residents would be permissible, our cases do not sanction a tax exemption serving similar ends. [E.g., *New Energy Co. of Indiana v. Limbach.*]"

SCALIA, J., joined by Rehnquist, C.J., and Thomas and Ginsburg, JJ., dissented. "[T]he provision at issue here is [narrowly] designed [to] compensate or subsidize those organizations that contribute to the public fisc by dispensing public benefits the state might otherwise provide." So understood, the statute did not facially discriminate against interstate commerce; any effect on interstate commerce was "indirect." In any event, the selective exemption was "supported by such traditional and important state interests that it survives scrutiny [even] under the 'virtually per se rule of invalidity.'" Alternatively, the state interests would support recognition of a " 'domestic charity' exception [to] the negative Commerce Clause."

THOMAS, J., joined by Scalia, J., and in part by Rehnquist, C.J., argued in a separate dissent that the Court should "abandon" its negative Commerce Clause jurisprudence. He suggested that the Court had developed its doctrine partly in response to the perception that it was "necessary to check [discriminatory] state measures contrary to the perceived spirit, if not the actual letter, of the Constitution." Rather than continuing with "policy-laden decisionmaking" that is unsupported by the constitutional text, the Court should consider whether there is not a textual prohibition against certain forms of discriminatory taxation in the Import–

15

Export Clause, Art. I, § 10, cl. 2, which provides that "[n]o state shall, without the Consent of Congress, lay any Imposts or Duties on Imports or Exports." Although the Court found this provision applicable only to foreign trade in *Woodruff v. Parham*, 75 U.S. (8 Wall.) 123 (1869), Thomas, J., argued that *Woodruff* "was, in all likelihood, wrongly decided" and ought to be reconsidered. Because the Import–Export Clause would not plausibly forbid the property tax at issue, the constitutional challenge should be rejected.

————

Ohio imposes general sales and use taxes on natural gas purchases from all sellers, except regulated utilities that meet the state's definition of a "natural gas company." Does the differential treatment of sales by regulated utilities, all of which are in-state entities, and other "marketers," many from other states, violate the Commerce Clause? In GENERAL MOTORS CORP. v. TRACY, 519 U.S. 278, 117 S.Ct. 811, 136 L.Ed.2d 761 (1997), the Court, per SOUTER, J., held that it does not: regulated utilities and other sellers are sufficiently different to warrant different treatment; the former serve "captive" markets of small consumers that the latter cannot reach and are subject to a variety of regulatory obligations—including obligations to provide costly services—that the latter are not. Even insofar as regulated gas companies and unregulated "marketers" compete for the same, non-captive customers (such as large corporations), "a number of reasons support a decision to give greater weight to the captive market and the local utilities' singular role in serving it" and thus to treat the disparity of tax treatment as constitutionally permissible. "First and most important, we must recognize an obligation to proceed cautiously lest we imperil the delivery by regulated [gas companies] of [gas and services] to the noncompetitive captive market. Second, as a court we lack the expertness and the institutional resources necessary to predict the effects of judicial intervention invalidating Ohio's tax scheme on the utilities' capacity to serve this captive market."

STEVENS, J., dissenting, would have upheld the challenged tax scheme as applied to sales of "bundled" gas and services in non-competitive, captive markets but not as applied to the competitive market for sales of "unbundled" gas to large customers.

INTERSTATE PRIVILEGES AND IMMUNITIES CLAUSE

CON LAW: P. 279, after note 2

AMER CON: P. 212, after note 2

In LUNDING v. NEW YORK STATE TAX APPEALS TRIBUNAL, 522 U.S. 287, 118 S.Ct. 766, 139 L.Ed.2d 717 (1998), the Court invalidated a New York statute that effectively denied non-resident taxpayers a state income tax deduction for alimony payments that was available to resident taxpayers. The 6–3 majority, per O'CONNOR, J., found that the state had advanced no justification for the disparate treatment adequate to satisfy the applicable standard, which it stated as follows: "[W]hen confronted with a challenge under the Privileges and Immunities Clause to a law distinguishing between residents and nonresidents, a State may defend its position by demonstrating that '(i) there is a substantial reason for the difference in treatment; and (ii) the discrimination practiced against nonresidents bears a substantial relationship to the State's objective.' " Ginsburg, J., joined by Rehnquist, C.J., and Kennedy, J., dissented.

THE EFFECT OF FEDERAL REGULATION: PREEMPTION

CON LAW: P. 286, at end of note 5

The Court again divided about the scope of an express preemption clause in MEDTRONIC, INC. v. LOHR, 518 U.S. 470, 116 S.Ct. 2240, 135 L.Ed.2d 700 (1996). A section of the Medical Device Amendments of 1976 provides that no state may establish or maintain "any requirement" that "is different from, or in addition to," any requirement of the Federal Food, Drug, and Cosmetic Act. In an opinion by STEVENS, J.,[a] a five-member majority agreed that application of the preemption clause should be informed by "the assumption that the historic police powers of the States were not to be superseded by the Federal Act unless that was the clear and manifest purpose of Congress." Writing only for a plurality on this point, Justice Stevens further found that state common law liability rules would "rare[ly,]" if ever, be specific enough in their application to particular medical devices to count as preempted "requirements" within the meaning of the federal statute. BREYER, J., concurring, thought that common law rules would be preempted "requirements" in some cases, but agreed that the particular common law rules in issue—imposing liability for the design and sale of a faulty heart pacemaker—were not "different from, or in addition to" any sufficiently specific federal requirements for the preemption clause to be triggered. In reaching their conclusions, both Stevens and Breyer, JJ., gave substantial weight to the interpretations expressed in regulations promulgated by the federal Food and Drug Administration.

O'CONNOR, J., joined by Rehnquist, C.J., and Scalia and Thomas, JJ., argued in partial dissent that substantive state liability standards for negligent manufacture and failure to warn were preempted; agency regulations suggesting the contrary deserved no deference. O'Connor, J., agreed with the majority, however, that plaintiffs' defective design claims were not in addition to or different from any applicable federal regulations and that state liability rules establishing standards identical or parallel to applicable federal standards also escaped preemption.

---

a. The opinion of Stevens, J., was joined in its entirety by Kennedy, Souter, and Ginsburg, JJ., and in part by Breyer, J., who also concurred entirely in the judgment.

SUBSTANTIVE PROTECTION OF ECONOMIC INTERESTS

ORIGINS OF SUBSTANTIVE DUE PROCESS

CON LAW: P. 325, at end of note 3
AMER CON: P. 224 end of note 3
RTS & LIB: P. 56, at end of note 3

However, does the Court's reliance on the privileges and immunities clause of the fourteenth amendment in *Saenz v. Roe*, discussed at pp. 54, 128 of this Supplement, signal that this long-ignored provision may become a new source of protection for individual rights?

"TAKING" OF PROPERTY INTERESTS

"TAKING" THROUGH REGULATION

CON LAW: P. 362, after note 9 add new notes
AMER CON: P. 253, after note 8 add new notes

Violation of the Takings Clause vs. violations of due process. Consider EASTERN ENTERPRISES v. APFEL, 524 U.S. 498, 118 S.Ct. 2131, 141 L.Ed.2d 451 (1998): As a signatory to various coal wage agreements executed between 1947 and 1964, petitioner Eastern Enterprises (Eastern) made substantial contributions to funds providing health benefits to miners and their dependents. In 1965 Eastern ceased its coal mining operations (transferring these operations to a subsidiary). Thus, Eastern neither participated in negotiations nor agreed to make contributions in connection with benefit plans established under agreements made in the 1970s, agreements suggesting for the first time an industry commitment to the funding of lifetime health benefits for both retirees and their family members.[a]

The decline in coal production, the retirement of a generation of miners, and rapid acceleration in health care caused serious financial problems for the 1950 and 1974 Benefit Plans. As more coal operators abandoned the Benefit Plans, the remaining signatories were forced to absorb the increasing cost of covering retirees left behind by existing employers. Ultimately Congress passed the Coal Industry Retiree Health Benefit Act of 1992 (Coal Act), providing for benefits to retirees by merging the 1950 and 1974 Benefit Plans into a new fund (Combined Fund) financed by annual premiums assessed against "signatory coal operators," i.e., coal operators that signed any agreement requiring contributions to the 1950 or 1974 Benefit Plans. The Commissioner of Social Security assigned Eastern the

---

a. Although Eastern's subsidiary continued mining coal until 1987, according to the plurality opinion by O'Connor, J., "Eastern's liability under the Act bears no relationship to [the] ownership of [its subsidiary]; the Act assigns Eastern responsibility for benefits relating to miners that Eastern itself, not [its subsidiary], employed, while [the subsidiary] would be assigned the responsibility for any miners that it had employed."

obligation for Combined Fund premiums respecting some 1,000 retired miners who had worked for the company before 1966. Eastern responded by suing the Commissioner, as well as the Combined Fund, asserting that the Coal Act violated both substantive due process and the Takings clause.

Although a 5–4 majority struck down the Coal Act as applied to Eastern, the justices making up the majority disagreed over the basis for the Act's invalidation. O'CONNOR, J., joined by Rehnquist, C.J., and Scalia and Thomas JJ., concluded that forcing Eastern "to bear the expense of lifetime health benefits for miners based on [the company's] activities decades before those benefits were promised" violated the Takings Clause.[b] She recognized that prior decisions "make clear that Congress has considerable leeway to fashion economic legislation, including the power to affect contractual commitments between private parties," but maintained that the Court's decisions left open the possibility that legislation might violate the Takings Clause "if it imposes severe retroactive liability on a limited class of parties that could not have anticipated the liability, and the extent of that liability is substantially disproportionate to the parties' experience. [The] Coal Act's allocation scheme, as applied to Eastern, presents such a case." When, continued the plurality opinion, a legislative solution to a problem "singles out certain employers to bear a burden that is substantial in amount, based on the employers' conduct far in the past, and unrelated to any commitment that the employers made or to any injury they caused, the governmental action implicates fundamental principles of fairness underlying the Taking Clause."[c]

Concurring in the judgment and dissenting in part, KENNEDY, J., rejected the O'Connor plurality's Takings Clause analysis. He concluded that the Coal Act "must be invalidated as contrary to essential due process principles, without regard to the Takings Clause." The Clause does not apply, he maintained, because the challenged Act "regulates the former mine owner without regard to property. It does not operate upon or alter an identified property interest, and is not applicable to or measured by a property interest. [The] law simply imposes an obligation to perform an act, the payment of benefits. The statute is indifferent as to how the regulated entity elects to comply or the property it uses to do so. To the extent it affects property interests, it does so in a manner similar to many laws; but until today, none were thought to constitute takings."

"Although we have been hesitant to subject economic legislation to due process scrutiny as a general matter" observed Kennedy, J., "the Court has given careful consideration to due process challenges to legislation with retroactive effects. As today's plurality opinion notes, for centuries our law has harbored a singular distrust of retroactive statutes. [The] Court's due process jurisprudence reflects this distrust. [It] is no accident that the primary retroactivity precedents upon which today's plurality opinion relies in its takings analysis were grounded in due process."

b. At one point O'Connor, J., noted that the Constitution "expresses concern with retroactive laws through several of its provisions, including the Ex Post Facto and Takings Clauses." Although Thomas, J., joined O'Connor, J.'s opinion in full, he wrote separately to emphasize that the Ex Post Facto Clause even more clearly than the Takings Clause "reflects the principle that 'retrospective laws are, indeed, generally unjust.'" Although the Court had long ago considered the Ex Post Facto clause to apply only in the criminal context, Justice Thomas expressed a willingness to re-consider these precedents in order to "determine whether a retroactive civil law that passes muster under our current Taking Clause jurisprudence is nevertheless unconstitutional under the Ex Post Facto Clause."

c. Because of its determination that the Coal Act's allocation scheme violates the Takings Clause as applied to Eastern, the plurality saw no need to address Eastern's due process claim. It noted, however, that "this Court has expressed concerns about using the Due Process clause to invalidate economic legislation."

Kennedy, J., acknowledged that the Court had upheld the imposition of liability on former employers based on past employment relationships, but "the statutes at issue were remedial, designed to impose an 'actual measurable cost of [the employer's] business' which the employer had been able to avoid in the past. *Usery v. Turner Elkhorn Mining Co.* [The] Coal Act, however, does not serve this purpose. Eastern was once in the coal business and employed many of the beneficiaries, but it was not responsible for their expectation of lifetime health benefits or for the perilous financial condition of the 1950 and 1974 Plans which put the benefits in jeopardy. [This] case is far outside the bounds of retroactivity permissible under our law."

When one takes into account Breyer, J.'s dissenting opinion, Kennedy, J.'s view of the appropriate constitutional provision in a case such as this commands a majority of the Court. Although BREYER, J., joined by Stevens, Souter and Ginsburg, JJ., thought the Coal Act constitutional, "as a preliminary matter" he agreed with Justice Kennedy that "the plurality views this case through the wrong legal lens." The Takings Clause does not apply, maintained Breyer, because "[t]he 'private property' upon which the Clause traditionally has focused is a specific interest in physical or intellectual property." However, the instant case involves not such an interest "but an ordinary liability to pay money, and not to the government, but to third parties."

"Insofar as the plurality avoids reliance upon the Due Process Clause for fear of resurrecting *Lochner* and related doctrines of 'substantive due process,'" continued Breyer, J., "that fear is misplaced. [To] find that the Due process Clause protects against this kind of fundamental unfairness—that it protects against an unfair allocation of public burdens through this kind of specially arbitrary retroactive means—is to read the Clause in light of a basic purpose: the fair application of law. [It] is not to resurrect long-discredited substantive notions of 'freedom of contract.'"

However, Breyer, J., did *not* consider it "fundamentally unfair to require Eastern to make future payments for health care costs of retired miners and their families, on the basis of Eastern's past association with these miners." For one thing the liability imposed upon Eastern "extends only to miners whom Eastern itself employed." Moreover, "the record shows that pre–1965 statements and other conduct led management to understand, and labor legitimately to expect, that health care benefits for retirees and their dependents would continue to be provided." Finally, "Eastern continued to obtain profits from the coal mining industry long after 1965, for it operated a wholly-owned coal-mining subsidiary [until] the late 1980s."[d]

Is interest earned in client funds that is paid to foundations financing legal services for low-income individuals the "private property" of the client for purposes of the Takings Clause? Texas, like 48 other states, has adopted an Interest on Lawyers Trust Account (IOLTA) program. Under these programs an attorney who receives client funds must place them in a separate, interest-bearing, federally authorized account upon determining that the funds could not reasonably be expected to earn interest for the client or that any interest which might be earned is unlikely to be sufficient to offset the cost of establishing and maintaining the account. IOLTA interest income is paid to foundations that finance legal services

---

d. In a separate dissent, Stevens, J., joined by Souter, Ginsburg and Breyer, JJ. emphasized that "there was an implicit understanding on both sides of the bargaining table that the operators would provide the miners with lifetime health benefits. It was this understanding that kept the mines in operation and enabled Eastern to earn handsome profits before it transferred its coal business to a wholly-owned subsidiary."

for low-income persons. In PHILLIPS v. WASHINGTON LEGAL FOUNDATION, 524 U.S. 156, 118 S.Ct. 1925, 141 L.Ed.2d 174 (1998), a 5–4 majority, per REHNQUIST, C.J., held that the interest earned on client funds held in IOLTA accounts is the "private property" of the client for Takings Clause purposes. However, the Court "express[ed] no view as to whether these funds have been 'taken' by the States" nor "the amount of 'just compensation,' if any, due respondents."

"Because the Constitution protects rather than creates property interests," observed the Court, "the existence of a property interest is determined by reference to 'existing rules or understandings that stem from an independent source such as state law.'" The firmly embedded and widely held view that "interest follows principal" applies in Texas.

Dissenting, SOUTER, J., joined by Stevens, Ginsburg and Breyer, JJ., maintained that "the Court's limited enquiry has led it to announce an essentially abstract proposition [that] may ultimately turn out to have no significance in resolving the real issue, [which] is whether [the IOLTA] scheme violated the Takings Clause":

"The Court recognizes three distinct issues implicated by a takings claim: whether the interest asserted by the plaintiff is property, whether the government has taken that property, and whether the plaintiff has been denied just compensation for the taking. [By addressing] only the first of these questions [the Court has] postponed consideration of the most salient fact relied upon by petitioners in contesting [the] Fifth Amendment claim: that the respondent client would effectively be barred from receiving any net interest on his funds subject to the state IOLTA rule by the combination of an unchallenged federal banking state and regulation [and other rules]. If it should turn out that within the meaning of the Fifth Amendment, the IOLTA scheme had not taken the property recognized today, or if it should turn out that the 'just compensation' for any taking was zero, then there would be no practical consequence for purposes of the Fifth Amendment in recognizing a client's property right in the interest in the first place; any such recognition would be an inconsequential abstraction."

In a separate dissent, Breyer, J., joined by Stevens, Souter and Ginsburg, JJ., criticized the Court's use of the truism that "interest follows principal": "The Question Presented is whether 'interest earned on client trust funds' [which] would 'not earn interest' in the absence of a special 'IOLTA program' amounts to a 'property interest of the client or lawyer' for purposes [of the] Takings Clause. [The] truism [that 'interest follows the principal'] does not help because the Question Presented assumes circumstances that differ dramatically from those in which interest is ordinarily at issue. Ordinarily, principal is capable of generating interest for whoever holds it. Here, by the very terms of the question, we must assume that (because of pre-existing federal law) the client's principal could not generate interest without IOLTA intervention. That is to say, the client could not have had an expectation of receiving interest without intervention. [Thus] the question is whether 'interest,' *earned only as a result of IOLTA rules* and earned upon otherwise *barren* client principal, 'follows principal.'"

PROTECTION OF INDIVIDUAL RIGHTS: DUE PROCESS, THE BILL OF RIGHTS, AND NONTEXTUAL CONSTITUTIONAL RIGHTS

THE NATURE AND SCOPE OF FOURTEENTH AMENDMENT DUE PROCESS; APPLICABILITY OF THE BILL OF RIGHTS TO THE STATES

BODILY EXTRACTIONS: ANOTHER LOOK AT THE "DUE PROCESS" AND "SELECTIVE INCORPORATION" APPROACHES

CON LAW: P. 385, after note 3

AMER CON: P. 269, after note 3

RTS & LIB: P. 116, after note 3

4. The "shocks-the-conscience" test and substantive due process claims. Applying the "shocks-the-conscience" test first articulated in the *Rochin* case, SACRAMENTO v. LEWIS, 523 U.S. 833, 118 S.Ct. 1708, 140 L.Ed.2d 1043 (1988), held, per SOUTER, J., that a police officer did not violate substantive due process by causing death through "reckless indifference" to, or "reckless disregard" for, a person's life in a high-speed automobile chase of a speeding motorcyclist. (The chase resulted in the death of the motorcyclist's passenger when the police car skidded into the passenger after the cycle had tipped over). In such circumstances, concluded the Court, "only a purpose to cause harm unrelated to the legitimate object of arrest will satisfy the element of arbitrary conduct shocking to the conscience, necessary for a due process violation [and for police liability under 42 U.S.C. § 1983]."

The Court recalled that it had held in *Graham v. Connor*, 490 U.S. 386, 109 S.Ct. 1865, 104 L.Ed.2d 443 (1989), that "where a particular amendment provides an explicit textual source of constitutional protection against a particular sort of government behavior, that Amendment, not the more generalized notion of substantive due process, must be the guide for analyzing [claims of substantive due process violations]." But the "more-specific-provision" rule of *Graham* did not bar respondents' lawsuit because neither the high-speed chase of the motorcycle nor the accidental killing of the motorcycle passenger constituted a Fourth Amendment "seizure." (Such a "seizure" occurs only when there is a governmentally caused termination of an individual's freedom of movement *through means intentionally applied.*") The Court then addressed respondents' substantive due process claim:

"Since the time of our early explanations of due process, we have understood the core of the concept to be protection against arbitrary action * * *. Our cases dealing with abusive executive action have repeatedly emphasized that only the

22

most egregious official conduct can be said to be 'arbitrary in the constitutional sense' * * *.

"[F]or half a century now we have spoken of the cognizable level of executive abuse of power as that which shocks the conscience. We first put the test this way in *Rochin* * * *. In the intervening years we have repeatedly adhered to *Rochin*'s benchmark.* * * Most recently, in *Collins v. Harker Heights,* 503 U. S. 115, 112 S. Ct. 1061, 117 L.Ed. 2d 261 (1992), we said again that the substantive component of the Due Process Clause is violated by executive action only when it 'can properly be characterized as arbitrary, or conscience shocking, in a constitutional sense.' "

The Court emphasized that much turns on the particular context in which the executive misconduct arises. Thus, in a prison custodial situation, when the state has rendered an individual unable to care for himself, and at the same time fails to provide for his basic needs, "the point of the conscience-shocking is reached" when injuries are produced by reckless or grossly negligent executive conduct. On the other hand, "deliberate indifference does not suffice for constitutional liability (albeit under the Eighth Amendment) even in prison circumstances when a prisoner's claim arises not from normal custody but from response to a violent disturbance." Continued the Court:

"Like prison officials facing a riot, the police on an occasion calling for fast action have obligations that tend to tug against each other. Their duty is to restore and maintain lawful order, while not exacerbating disorder more than necessary to do their jobs. They are supposed to act decisively and to show restraint at the same moment, and their decisions have to be made 'in haste, under pressure, and frequently without the luxury of a second chance.' [A] police officer deciding whether to give chase must balance on one hand the need to stop a suspect and show that flight from the law is no way to freedom, and, on the other, the high-speed threat to everyone within stopping range, be they suspects, their passengers, other drivers, or bystanders.

"To recognize a substantive due process violation in these circumstances when only mid-level fault has been shown [i.e., something more than simple negligence, but something less than intentional misconduct] would be to forget that liability for deliberate indifference to inmate welfare rests upon the luxury enjoyed by prison officials of having time to make unhurried judgments, upon the chance for repeated reflection, largely uncomplicated by the pulls of competing obligations. When such extended opportunities to do better are teamed with protracted failure even to care, indifference is truly shocking. But when unforeseen circumstances demand an officer's instant judgment, even precipitate recklessness fails to inch close enough to harmful purpose to spark the shock that implicates 'the large concerns of the governors and the governed.' Just as a purpose to cause harm is needed for Eighth Amendment liability in a riot case, so it ought to be needed for Due Process liability in a pursuit case. Accordingly, we hold that high-speed chases with no intent to harm suspects physically or to worsen their legal plight do not give rise to liability under the Fourteenth Amendment, redressible by an action under § 1983. * * * Regardless whether Smith's behavior offended the reasonableness held up by tort law or the balance struck in law enforcement's own codes of sound practice, it does not shock the conscience * * *."[a]

a. Kennedy, J., joined by O'Connor, J. joined the opinion of the Court, but also wrote separately. They "share[d] Justice Scalia's concerns about using the phrase 'shocks the conscience' in a manner suggesting that it is a self-defining test." The phrase, they observed,

Concurring in the judgment, SCALIA, J., joined by Thomas, J. would not have decided the case by applying the "shocks-the-conscience" test but "on the ground that respondents offer no textual or historical support for their alleged due process right." The concurring Justices maintained that in *Washington v. Glucksberg,* p. 27 of this Supplement (upholding a criminal prohibition against physician-assisted suicide), "the Court specifically rejected the method of substantive-due-process analysis employed by Justice Souter in that case, which is the very same method employed by Justice Souter in his opinion for the Court today." Scalia, J., continued:

"Adhering to our decision in *Glucksberg,* rather than ask whether the police conduct here at issue shocks my unelected conscience, I would ask whether our Nation has traditionally protected the right respondents assert.* * * I agree with the Court's conclusion that [respondents' complaint] asserts a substantive right to be free from 'deliberate or reckless indifference to life in a high-speed automobile chase aimed at apprehending a suspected offender.' Respondents provide no textual or historical support for this alleged due process right, [and] I would 'decline to fashion a new due process right out of thin air.' Nor have respondents identified any precedential support. Indeed, precedent is to the contrary * * *.

"[To] hold, as respondents urge, that all government conduct deliberately indifferent to life, liberty, or property, violates the Due Process Clause would make 'the Fourteenth Amendment a font of tort law to be superimposed upon whatever systems may already be administered by the States.' [If] the people [of] California would prefer a system that renders police officers liable for reckless driving during high-speed pursuits, '[t]hey may create such a system [by] changing the tort law of the State in accordance with the regular lawmaking process.' For now, they prefer not to [do so]. It is the prerogative of a self-governing people to make that legislative choice. [For] judges to overrule [the] democratically adopted policy judgment [of the people of California and their elected representatives] on the ground that it shocks *their* consciences is not judicial review but judicial governance."

"has the unfortunate connotation of a standard laden with subjective assessments. In that respect, it must be viewed with considerable skepticism."

CONSTITUTIONAL–CRIMINAL PROCEDURE

POLICE INTERROGATION AND CONFESSIONS

Can Congress "Repeal" Miranda?

AMER CON: P. 403, add to discussion of § 3501

Concurring in *Davis v. United States* (1994) (p. 415 n. a of AMER CON), SCALIA J., sharply criticized the Justice Department's "repeated refusal to invoke § 3501," a refusal that has "caused the federal judiciary to confront a host of '*Miranda*' issues that might be entirely irrelevant under federal law." Scalia, J. also maintained that because § 3501 "is a provision of law directed *to the courts*, reflecting the people's assessment of the proper balance to be struck [in this area], we shirk our duty if we systematically disregard that statutory command simply because the Justice Department declines to remind us of it."

Scalia, J.'s comments probably encouraged two conservative legal groups, the Washington Legal Foundation and the Safe Streets Coalition, to attack *Miranda*. Led by Paul Cassell, a Utah Law School professor who has become the nation's leading critic of *Miranda*, these groups repeatedly urged the federal courts to inject § 3501 into their cases.

In *United States v. Dickerson*, 166 F.3d 667 (4th Cir. 1999), the Washington Legal Foundation and the Safe Streets Coalition finally achieved some success. Although the dissenting judge protested that the ruling was made "without the benefit of any briefing in opposition" and "against the express wishes of the Department of Justice," a 2–1 majority of a panel of the U.S. Court of Appeals for the Fourth Circuit ruled that the pre-*Miranda* voluntariness test set forth in § 3501, rather than the famous *Miranda* case, governs the admissibility of confessions in the federal courts. Therefore, the district court had erred when it had suppressed a voluntary confession simply because it was obtained in violation of *Miranda*.

The reasoning of the Fourth Circuit may be summarized quite briefly: Congress has the power to "overrule" rules of evidence and procedure that are not required by the Constitution. The *Miranda* rules are not constitutionally required; they are only "prophylactic" rules designed to implement or reinforce the underlying constitutional right. Therefore, § 3501 is a valid exercise of Congressional authority to override judicially created rules not part of the Constitution.

But see Yale Kamisar, *Confessions, Search and Seizure and the Rehnquist Court*, 34 Tulsa L.J. 465, 471–72 (1999): "A 'prophylactic' rule is not a dirty word. Sometimes such rules are necessary and proper. The privilege against self-incrimination, no less than other constitutional rights, needs 'breathing space.' And prophylactic rules may be the best way to provide it.

"*Miranda* is based on the realization that case-by-case determination of the 'voluntariness' of a confession in light of the totality of the circumstances was severely testing the capacity of the judiciary and that institutional realities warranted a conclusive presumption that a confession obtained under certain conditions and in the absence of certain safeguards was compelled. The pre-*Miranda* 'voluntariness' test was too mushy, subjective, and unruly to provide suspects with adequate protection. And it was too time-consuming to administer. As Justice Hugo Black expressed it during the oral arguments in *Miranda*, 'If you are going to determine the admissibility of a confession each time on the circumstances [if] the Court will take them one by one [it] is more than we are capable of doing.'

"In 1966, after years of struggling with the 'voluntariness' test, a majority of the Supreme Court had arrived at the same conclusion—the traditional test for the admissibility of confessions was woefully inadequate and simply unworkable. Something else was needed, something easier to administer. That 'something else' turned out to be *Miranda*. Under any sensible approach to constitutional interpretation, the Supreme Court must be allowed to take into account its own fact-finding limitations.

"Establishing presumptions and prophylactic rules is inherent in the art of judging—in the effort to make constitutional rights more meaningful. The Fourth Circuit panel that decided *Dickerson* did a lot more than try to deal *Miranda* a fatal blow. Its approach to constitutional decision-making restricts the ability of the Rehnquist Court—and every Court—to interpret constitutional provisions in light of institutional realities."

THE RIGHT OF "PRIVACY" (OR "AUTONOMY" OR "PERSONHOOD")

CRITICISM OF *BOWERS v. HARDWICK*

CON LAW: P. 527, after note 7 add new note

AMER CON: P. 601, after note 5 add new note

RTS & LIB: P. 433, after note 7 add new note

8. *Are Romer and Hardwick reconcilable?* Compare *Hardwick* with *Romer v. Evans*, p. 119 of this Supplement, holding that a voter-initiated state constitutional amendment prohibiting state or local governments from acting to protect the status of persons based on their "homosexual, lesbian or bisexual orientation" violates the Equal Protection Clause: "[I]n making a general announcement that gays and lesbians shall not have any particular protections from the law," the amendment inflicts injuries on them "that outrun and belie any legitimate justifications that may be claimed for it"; "it is a classification of persons undertaken for its own sake, something the Equal Protection Clause does not permit." The 6–3 majority did not mention *Hardwick*, but the dissent did. It maintained that the majority had "contradict[ed]" *Hardwick* and "place[d] the prestige of this institution behind the proposition that opposition to homosexuality is as reprehensible as racial or religious bias." Do you share the *Romer* dissenters' view of the Court's holding? Why (not)?

THE "RIGHT TO DIE"

IS THERE A CONSTITUTIONAL RIGHT TO PHYSICIAN–ASSISTED SUICIDE?

CON LAW: P. 542, delete pp. 542–50 and substitute following

AMER CON: P. 615, delete pp. 615–23 and substitute following

RTS & LIB: P. 447, delete pp. 447–55 and substitute following

WASHINGTON v. GLUCKSBERG

521 U.S. 702, 117 S.Ct. 2258, 138 L.Ed.2d 772 (1997).

CHIEF JUSTICE REHNQUIST delivered the opinion of the Court.

The question presented in this case is whether Washington's prohibition against "caus[ing]" or "aid[ing]" a suicide offends the Fourteenth Amendment to the United States Constitution. We hold that it does not.

[Respondents, four physicians who declare they would assist terminally ill, suffering patients in ending their lives if not for Washington's assisted-suicide ban, along with three gravely ill patients, who have since died, and Compassion in Dying, a nonprofit organization that counsels people considering physician-assisted suicide, sought a declaration that Washington's statute is, on its face, unconstitutional. Respondents] asserted "the existence of a liberty interest protected by the Fourteenth Amendment which extends to a personal choice by a mentally competent, terminally ill adult to commit physician-assisted suicide." Relying primarily on *Casey* and *Cruzan,* the District Court agreed and concluded that Washington's assisted suicide ban is unconstitutional because it "places an undue burden on the exercise of [that] constitutionally protected liberty interest."[5]

A panel of the Court of Appeals for the Ninth Circuit reversed, emphasizing that "[i]n the two hundred and five years of our existence no constitutional right to aid in killing oneself has ever been asserted and upheld by a court of final jurisdiction." The Ninth Circuit reheard the case en banc, reversed the panel's decision [8–3], and affirmed the District Court. Like the District Court, the Court of Appeals emphasized our *Casey* and *Cruzan* decisions. The court [concluded] that "the Constitution encompasses a due process liberty interest in controlling the time and manner of one's death—that there is, in short, a constitutionally-recognized 'right to die.'" After "[w]eighing and then balancing" this interest against Washington's various interests, the court held that the State's assisted-suicide ban was unconstitutional "as applied to terminally ill competent adults who wish to hasten their deaths with medication prescribed by their physicians." * * *

We begin, as we do in all due-process cases, by examining our Nation's history, legal traditions, and practices. In almost every State—indeed, in almost every western democracy—it is a crime to assist a suicide. The States' assisted-suicide bans are not innovations. Rather, they are longstanding expressions of the States' commitment to the protection and preservation of all human life. * * * Indeed, opposition to and condemnation of suicide—and, therefore, of

5. The District Court determined that *Casey's* "undue burden" standard, not the standard from *United States v. Salerno,* 481 U.S. 739, 107 S.Ct. 2095, 95 L.Ed.2d 697 (1987) (requiring a showing that "no set of circumstances exists under which the [law] would be valid"), governed the plaintiffs' facial challenge to the assisted-suicide ban.

assisting suicide—are consistent and enduring themes of our philosophical, legal, and cultural heritages.

More specifically, for over 700 years, the Anglo–American common-law tradition has punished or otherwise disapproved of both suicide and assisting suicide.

[For] the most part, the early American colonies adopted the common-law approach. [Over] time, however, [the] colonies abolished [the] harsh common-law penalties [such as forfeiture of the suicide's property. However,] the movement away from the common law's harsh sanctions did not represent an acceptance of homicide, [but] reflected the growing consensus that it was unfair to punish the suicide's family for his wrongdoing.

[That] suicide remained a grievous, though nonfelonious, wrong is confirmed by the fact that colonial and early state legislatures and courts did not retreat from prohibiting assisting suicide. [And] the prohibitions against assisted suicide never contained exceptions for those who were near death. [In] this century, the [American Law Institute's] Model Penal Code also prohibited "aiding" suicide, prompting many States to enact or revise their assisted-suicide bans. The Code's drafters observed that "the interests in the sanctity of life that are represented by the criminal homicide laws are threatened by one who expresses a willingness to participate in taking the life of another, even though the act may be accomplished with the consent, or at the request, of the suicide victim."

Though deeply rooted, the States' assisted-suicide bans have in recent years been reexamined and, generally, reaffirmed. Because of advances in medicine and technology, Americans today are increasingly likely to die in institutions, from chronic illnesses. Public concern and democratic action are therefore sharply focused on how best to protect dignity and independence at the end of life, with the result that there have been many significant changes in state laws and in the attitudes these laws reflect. Many States, for example, now permit "living wills," surrogate health-care decisionmaking, and the withdrawal or refusal of life-sustaining medical treatment. At the same time, however, voters and legislators continue for the most part to reaffirm their States' prohibitions on assisting suicide.

The Washington statute at issue in this case was enacted in 1975 as part of a revision of that State's criminal code. Four years later, Washington passed its Natural Death Act, which specifically stated that the "withholding or withdrawal of life-sustaining treatment [shall] not, for any purpose, constitute a suicide" and that "[n]othing in this chapter shall be construed to condone, authorize, or approve mercy killing * * *." In 1991, Washington voters rejected a ballot initiative which, had it passed, would have permitted a form of physician-assisted suicide. Washington then added a provision to the Natural Death Act expressly excluding physician-assisted suicide.

California voters rejected an assisted-suicide initiative similar to Washington's in 1993. On the other hand, in 1994, voters in Oregon enacted, also through ballot initiative, that State's "Death With Dignity Act," which legalized physician-assisted suicide for competent, terminally ill adults. Since the Oregon vote, many proposals to legalize assisted-suicide have been and continue to be introduced in the States' legislatures, but none has been enacted. And just last year, Iowa and Rhode Island joined the overwhelming majority of States explicitly prohibiting assisted suicide. Also, on April 30, 1997, President Clinton signed the Federal Assisted Suicide Funding Restriction Act of 1997, which prohibits the use of federal funds in support of physician-assisted suicide.

Thus, the States are currently engaged in serious, thoughtful examinations of physician-assisted suicide and other similar issues. For example, New York State's Task Force on Life and the Law—an ongoing, blue-ribbon commission composed of doctors, ethicists, lawyers, religious leaders, and interested laymen— was convened in 1984 and commissioned with "a broad mandate to recommend public policy on issues raised by medical advances." Over the past decade, the Task Force has recommended laws relating to end-of-life decisions, surrogate pregnancy, and organ donation. After studying physician-assisted suicide, however, the Task Force unanimously concluded that "[l]egalizing assisted suicide and euthanasia would pose profound risks to many individuals who are ill and vulnerable. [T]he potential dangers of this dramatic change in public policy would outweigh any benefit that might be achieved."

Attitudes toward suicide itself have changed, [but] our laws have consistently condemned, and continue to prohibit, assisting suicide. Despite changes in medical technology and notwithstanding an increased emphasis on the importance of end-of-life decision-making, we have not retreated from this prohibition. Against this backdrop of history, tradition, and practice, we now turn to respondents' constitutional claim.

The Due Process Clause guarantees more than fair process, and the "liberty" it protects includes more than the absence of physical restraint. [The] Clause also provides heightened protection against government interference with certain fundamental rights and liberty interests. In a long line of cases, we have held that, in addition to the specific freedoms protected by the Bill of Rights, the "liberty" specially protected by the Due Process Clause includes the rights to marry, to have children, to direct the education and upbringing of one's children, to marital privacy, to use contraception, to bodily integrity, and to abortion. We have also assumed, and strongly suggested, that the Due Process Clause protects the traditional right to refuse unwanted lifesaving medical treatment. *Cruzan.*

But we "ha[ve] always been reluctant to expand the concept of substantive due process because guideposts for responsible decisionmaking in this unchartered area are scarce and open-ended." By extending constitutional protection to an asserted right or liberty interest, we, to a great extent, place the matter outside the arena of public debate and legislative action. We must therefore "exercise the utmost care whenever we are asked to break new ground in this field," lest the liberty protected by the Due Process Clause be subtly transformed into the policy preferences of the members of this Court.

Our established method of substantive-due-process analysis has two primary features: First, we have regularly observed that the Due Process Clause specially protects those fundamental rights and liberties which are, objectively, "deeply rooted in this Nation's history and tradition." * * * Second, we have required in substantive-due-process cases a "careful description" of the asserted fundamental liberty interest. * * *

Justice Souter, relying on Justice Harlan's dissenting opinion in *Poe v. Ullman,* would largely abandon this restrained methodology, and instead ask "whether [Washington's] statute sets up one of those 'arbitrary impositions' or 'purposeless restraints' at odds with the Due Process Clause of the Fourteenth Amendment."[17] In our view, however, the development of this Court's substan-

---

17. In Justice Souter's opinion, Justice Harlan's *Poe* dissent supplies the "modern justification" for substantive-due-process review. But although Justice Harlan's opinion has often been cited in due-process cases, we have never abandoned our fundamental-rights-based

tive-due-process jurisprudence, described briefly above, has been a process where-by the outlines of the "liberty" specially protected by the Fourteenth Amend-ment—never fully clarified, to be sure, and perhaps not capable of being fully clarified—have at least been carefully refined by concrete examples involving fundamental rights found to be deeply rooted in our legal tradition. This approach tends to rein in the subjective elements that are necessarily present in due-process judicial review. In addition, by establishing a threshold require-ment—that a challenged state action implicate a fundamental right—before re-quiring more than a reasonable relation to a legitimate state interest to justify the action, it avoids the need for complex balancing of competing interests in every case.

Turning to the claim at issue here, the Court of Appeals stated that "[p]roper-ly analyzed, the first issue to be resolved is whether there is a liberty interest in determining the time and manner of one's death" or, in other words, "[i]s there a right to die?" Similarly, respondents assert a "liberty to choose how to die" and a right to "control of one's final days," and describe the asserted liberty as "the right to choose a humane, dignified death" and "the liberty to shape death." As noted above, we have a tradition of carefully formulating the interest at stake in substantive-due-process cases. For example, although *Cruzan* is often described as a "right to die" case, we were, in fact, more precise: we assumed that the Constitution granted competent persons a "constitutionally protected right to refuse lifesaving hydration and nutrition." [The] Washington statute at issue in this case prohibits "aid[ing] another person to attempt suicide" and, thus, the question before us is whether the "liberty" specially protected by the Due Process Clause includes a right to commit suicide which itself includes a right to assis-tance in doing so.

We now inquire whether this asserted right has any place in our Nation's traditions. Here, as discussed above, we are confronted with a consistent and almost universal tradition that has long rejected the asserted right, and continues explicitly to reject it today, even for terminally ill, mentally competent adults. To hold for respondents, we would have to reverse centuries of legal doctrine and practice, and strike down the considered policy choice of almost every State.

[Respondents] contend, however, that the liberty interest they assert *is* consistent with this Court's substantive-due-process line of cases, if not with this Nation's history and practice. Pointing to *Casey* and *Cruzan*, respondents read our jurisprudence in this area as reflecting a general tradition of "self-sovereign-ty" and as teaching that the "liberty" protected by the Due Process Clause includes "basic and intimate exercises of personal autonomy." According to respondents, our liberty jurisprudence, and the broad, individualistic principles it reflects, protects the "liberty of competent, terminally ill adults to make end-of-life decisions free of undue government interference." The question presented in this case, however, is whether the protections of the Due Process Clause include a right to commit suicide with another's assistance. With this "careful description" of respondents' claim in mind, we turn to *Casey* and *Cruzan*. * * *

analytical method. Just four Terms ago, six of the Justices now sitting joined the Court's opinion in *Reno v. Flores,* 507 U.S. 292, 113 S.Ct. 1439, 123 L.Ed.2d 1 (1993); *Poe* was not even cited. And in *Cruzan,* neither the Court's nor the concurring opinions relied on *Poe;* rather, we concluded that the right to refuse unwanted medical treatment was so rooted in our history, tradition, and practice as to re-quire special protection under the Fourteenth Amendment. True, the Court relied on Justice Harlan's dissent in *Casey,* but, as *Flores* dem-onstrates, we did not in so doing jettison our established approach. Indeed, to read such a radical move into the Court's opinion in *Casey* would seem to fly in the face of that opinion's emphasis on stare decisis.

Respondents contend that in *Cruzan* we "acknowledged that competent, dying persons have the right to direct the removal of life-sustaining medical treatment and thus hasten death" and that "the constitutional principle behind recognizing the patient's liberty to direct the withdrawal of artificial life support applies at least as strongly to the choice to hasten impending death by consuming lethal medication."

[The] right assumed in *Cruzan,* however, was not simply deduced from abstract concepts of personal autonomy. Given the common-law rule that forced medication was a battery, and the long legal tradition protecting the decision to refuse unwanted medical treatment, our assumption was entirely consistent with this Nation's history and constitutional traditions. The decision to commit suicide with the assistance of another may be just as personal and profound as the decision to refuse unwanted medical treatment, but it has never enjoyed similar legal protection. Indeed, the two acts are widely and reasonably regarded as quite distinct. In *Cruzan* itself, we recognized that most States outlawed assisted suicide—and even more do today—and we certainly gave no intimation that the right to refuse unwanted medical treatment could be somehow transmuted into a right to assistance in committing suicide.

Respondents also rely on *Casey.* [The] Court of Appeals, like the District Court, found *Casey* " 'highly instructive' " and " 'almost prescriptive' " for determining " 'what liberty interest may inhere in a terminally ill person's choice to commit suicide' ": "Like the decision of whether or not to have an abortion, the decision how and when to die is one of 'the most intimate and personal choices a person may make in a lifetime,' a choice 'central to personal dignity and autonomy.' " Similarly, respondents emphasize the statement in *Casey* that: "At the heart of liberty is the right to define one's own concept of existence, of meaning, of the universe, and of the mystery of human life. Beliefs about these matters could not define the attributes of personhood were they formed under compulsion of the State."

By choosing this language, the Court's opinion in *Casey* described, in a general way and in light of our prior cases, those personal activities and decisions that this Court has identified as so deeply rooted in our history and traditions, or so fundamental to our concept of constitutionally ordered liberty, that they are protected by the Fourteenth Amendment. [That] many of the rights and liberties protected by the Due Process Clause sound in personal autonomy does not warrant the sweeping conclusion that any and all important, intimate, and personal decisions are so protected, and *Casey* did not suggest otherwise.

The history of the law's treatment of assisted suicide in this country has been and continues to be one of the rejection of nearly all efforts to permit it. That being the case, our decisions lead us to conclude that the asserted "right" to assistance in committing suicide is not a fundamental liberty interest protected by the Due Process Clause. The Constitution also requires, however, that Washington's assisted-suicide ban be rationally related to legitimate government interests. This requirement is unquestionably met here. As the court below recognized, Washington's assisted-suicide ban implicates a number of state interests.

First, Washington has an "unqualified interest in the preservation of human life." *Cruzan.* The State's prohibition on assisted suicide, like all homicide laws, both reflects and advances its commitment to this interest.

[The] Court of Appeals also recognized Washington's interest in protecting life, but held that the "weight" of this interest depends on the "medical condition and the wishes of the person whose life is at stake." Washington, however, has rejected this sliding-scale approach and, through its assisted-suicide ban, insists that all persons' lives, from beginning to end, regardless of physical or mental condition, are under the full protection of the law. [As] we have previously affirmed, the States "may properly decline to make judgments about the 'quality' of life that a particular individual may enjoy," *Cruzan*. This remains true, as *Cruzan* makes clear, even for those who are near death.

Relatedly, all admit that suicide is a serious public-health problem, especially among persons in otherwise vulnerable groups. [Those] who attempt suicide— terminally ill or not—often suffer from depression or other mental disorders. [But research indicates] that many people who request physician-assisted suicide withdraw that request if their depression and pain are treated. The New York Task Force, however, expressed its concern that, because depression is difficult to diagnose, physicians and medical professionals often fail to respond adequately to seriously ill patients' needs. Thus, legal physician-assisted suicide could make it more difficult for the State to protect depressed or mentally ill persons, or those who are suffering from untreated pain, from suicidal impulses.

The State also has an interest in protecting the integrity and ethics of the medical profession. [The] American Medical Association, like many other medical and physicians' groups, has concluded that "[p]hysician-assisted suicide is fundamentally incompatible with the physician's role as healer." [And] physician-assisted suicide could, it is argued, undermine the trust that is essential to the doctor-patient relationship by blurring the time-honored line between healing and harming.

[Next,] the State has an interest in protecting vulnerable groups—including the poor, the elderly, and disabled persons—from abuse, neglect, and mistakes. The Court of Appeals dismissed [this] concern, [but we] have recognized [the] real risk of subtle coercion and undue influence in end-of-life situations. *Cruzan*. Similarly, the New York Task Force warned that "[l]egalizing physician-assisted suicide would pose profound risks to many individuals who are ill and vulnerable. [The] risk of harm is greatest for the many individuals in our society whose autonomy and well-being are already compromised by poverty, lack of access to good medical care, advanced age, or membership in a stigmatized social group." [If] physician-assisted suicide were permitted, many might resort to it to spare their families the substantial financial burden of end-of-life health-care costs.

The State's interest here goes beyond protecting the vulnerable from coercion; it extends to protecting disabled and terminally ill people from prejudice, negative and inaccurate stereotypes, and "societal indifference." The State's assisted-suicide ban reflects and reinforces its policy that the lives of terminally ill, disabled, and elderly people must be no less valued than the lives of the young and healthy, and that a seriously disabled person's suicidal impulses should be interpreted and treated the same way as anyone else's.

Finally, the State may fear that permitting assisted suicide will start it down the path to voluntary and perhaps even involuntary euthanasia. [The] Court of Appeal's decision, and its expansive reasoning, provide ample support for the State's concerns. The court noted, for example, that the "decision of a duly appointed surrogate decision maker is for all legal purposes the decision of the patient himself"; that "in some instances, the patient may be unable to self-administer the drugs [and] administration by the physician [may] be the only way the patient may be able to receive them"; and that not only physicians, but also family members and loved ones, will inevitably participate in assisting suicide. Thus, it turns out that what is couched as a limited right to "physician-assisted suicide" is likely, in effect, a much broader license, which could prove extremely difficult to police and contain.[23] Washington's ban on assisting suicide prevents such erosion.

This concern is further supported by evidence about the practice of euthanasia in the Netherlands. The Dutch government's own [1990 study] suggests that, despite the existence of various reporting procedures, euthanasia in the Netherlands has not been limited to competent, terminally ill adults who are enduring physical suffering, and that regulation of the practice may not have prevented abuses in cases involving vulnerable persons, including severely disabled neonates and elderly persons suffering from dementia. * * * Washington, like most other States, reasonably ensures against this risk by banning, rather than regulating, assisting suicide.

We need not weigh exactingly the relative strengths of these various interests. They are unquestionably important and legitimate, and Washington's ban on assisted suicide is at least reasonably related to their promotion and protection. We therefore hold that [the challenged Washington statute] does not violate the Fourteenth Amendment, either on its face or "as applied to competent, terminally ill adults who wish to hasten their deaths by obtaining medication prescribed by their doctors."[24] * * *

Throughout the Nation, Americans are engaged in an earnest and profound debate about the morality, legality, and practicality of physician-assisted suicide. Our holding permits this debate to continue, as it should in a democratic society. * * *

JUSTICE O'CONNOR, concurring.*

[The] Court frames the issue in this case as whether the Due Process Clause of the Constitution protects a "right to commit suicide which itself includes a right to assistance in doing so," and concludes that our Nation's history, legal traditions, and practices do not support the existence of such a right. I join the Court's opinions because I agree that there is no generalized right to "commit suicide." But respondents urge us to address the narrower question whether a

23. Justice Souter concludes that "[t]he case for the slippery slope is fairly made out here, not because recognizing one due process right would leave a court with no principled basis to avoid recognizing another, but because there is a plausible case that the right claimed would not be readily containable by reference to facts about the mind that are matters of difficult judgment, or by gatekeepers who are subject to temptation, noble or not." We agree that the case for a slippery slope has been made out, [but] we also recognize the reasonableness of the widely expressed skepticism about the lack of a principled basis for confining the right. See Brief for United States as Amicus Curiae ("Once a legislature abandons a categorical prohibition against physician-assisted suicide, there is no obvious stopping point) * * *.

24. Justice Stevens states that "the Court does conceive of respondents' claim as a facial challenge—addressing not the application of the statute to a particular set of plaintiffs before it, but the constitutionality of the statute's categorical prohibition. . . ." We emphasize that we today reject the Court of Appeals'

specific holding that the statute is unconstitutional "as applied" to a particular class. Justice Stevens agrees with this holding, but would not "foreclose the possibility that an individual plaintiff seeking to hasten her death, or a doctor whose assistance was sought, could prevail in a more particularized challenge." Our opinion does not absolutely foreclose such a claim. However, given our holding that the Due Process Clause of the Fourteenth Amendment does not provide heightened protection to the asserted liberty interest in ending one's life with a physician's assistance, such a claim would have to be quite different from the ones advanced by respondents here.

* Justice Ginsberg concurs in the Court's judgments substantially for the reasons stated in this opinion. Justice Breyer joins this opinion except insofar as it joins the opinion of the Court.

[Justice O'Connor's opinion also constitutes her concurring opinion in the companion case of *Vacco v. Quill.*]

mentally competent person who is experiencing great suffering has a constitutionally cognizable interest in controlling the circumstances of his or her imminent death. I see no need to reach that question in the context of the facial challenges to the New York and Washington laws at issue here. [The] parties and *amici* agree that in these States a patient who is suffering from a terminal illness and who is experiencing great pain has no legal barriers to obtaining medication, from qualified physicians, to alleviate that suffering, even to the point of causing unconsciousness and hastening death. In this light, even assuming that we would recognize such an interest, I agree that the State's interests in protecting those who are not truly competent or facing imminent death, or those whose decisions to hasten death would not truly be voluntary, are sufficiently weighty to justify a prohibition against physician-assisted suicide.

Every one of us at some point may be affected by our own or a family member's terminal illness. There is no reason to think the democratic process will not strike the proper balance between the interests of terminally ill, mentally competent individuals who would seek to end their suffering and the State's interests in protecting those who might seek to end life mistakenly or under pressure. As the Court recognizes, States are presently undertaking extensive and serious evaluation of physician-assisted suicide and other related issues. In such circumstances, "[the] challenging task of crafting appropriate procedures for safeguarding * * * liberty interests is entrusted to the 'laboratory' of the States [in] the first instance." *Cruzan* (O'Connor, J., concurring) (citing *New State Ice Co. v. Liebmann* (1932)).

In sum, there is no need to address the question whether suffering patients have a constitutionally cognizable interest in obtaining relief from the suffering that they may experience in the last days of their lives. There is no dispute that dying patients in Washington and New York can obtain palliative care, even when doing so would hasten their deaths. The difficulty in defining terminal illness and the risk that a dying patient's request for assistance in ending his or her life might not be truly voluntary justifies the prohibitions on assisted suicide we uphold here.

JUSTICE STEVENS, concurring in the judgments.[a]

[The] morality, legality, and practicality of capital punishment have been the subject of debate for many years. In 1976, this Court upheld the constitutionality of the practice in cases coming to us from Georgia, Florida, and Texas. In those cases we concluded that a State does have the power to place a lesser value on some lives than on others; there is no absolute requirement that a State treat all human life as having an equal right to preservation. Because the state legislatures had sufficiently narrowed the category of lives that the State could terminate, and had enacted special procedures to ensure that the defendant belonged in that limited category, we concluded that the statutes were not unconstitutional on their face. In later cases coming to us from each of those States, however, we found that some applications of the statutes were unconstitutional.

Today, the Court decides that Washington's statute prohibiting assisted suicide is not invalid "on its face," that is to say, in all or most cases in which it might be applied. That holding, however, does not foreclose the possibility that some applications of the statute might well be invalid. * * *

History and tradition provide ample support for refusing to recognize an open-ended constitutional right to commit suicide. Much more than the State's

---

a. This opinion also constitutes Justice Stevens's concurring opinion in *Vacco v. Quill.*

paternalistic interest in protecting the individual from the irrevocable consequences of an ill-advised decision motivated by temporary concerns is at stake. There is truth in John Donne's observation that "No man is an island." [The] value to others of a person's life is far too precious to allow the individual to claim a constitutional entitlement to complete autonomy in making a decision to end that life. Thus, I fully agree with the Court that the "liberty" protected by the Due Process Clause does not include a categorical "right to commit suicide which itself includes a right to assistance in doing so."

But just as our conclusion that capital punishment is not always unconstitutional did not preclude later decisions holding that it is sometimes impermissibly cruel, so is it equally clear that a decision upholding a general statutory prohibition of assisted suicide does not mean that every possible application of the statute would be valid.

[The *Cruzan* Court] assumed that the interest in liberty protected by the Fourteenth Amendment encompassed the right of a terminally ill patient to direct the withdrawal of life-sustaining treatment. [That] assumption [was] supported by the common-law tradition protecting the individual's general right to refuse unwanted medical treatment. [However,] [g]iven the irreversible nature of her illness and the progressive character of her suffering, Nancy Cruzan's interest in refusing medical care was incidental to her more basic interest in controlling the manner and timing of her death. * * * I insist that the source of Nancy Cruzan's right to refuse treatment was not just a common-law rule. Rather, this right is an aspect of a far broader and more basic concept of freedom that is even older than the common law. This freedom embraces, not merely a person's right to refuse a particular kind of unwanted treatment, but also her interest in dignity, and in determining the character of the memories that will survive long after her death.

[Thus,] the common-law right to protection from battery, which included the right to reject medical treatment in most circumstances, did not mark "the outer limits of the substantive sphere of liberty" that supported the Cruzan family's decision to hasten Nancy's death. *Casey.* [Whatever] the outer limits of the concept may be, it definitely includes protection for matters "central to personal dignity and autonomy." *Casey.*

[The] *Cruzan* case demonstrated that some state intrusions on the right to decide how death will be encountered are also intolerable. The now-deceased plaintiffs in this action may in fact have had a liberty interest even stronger than Nancy Cruzan's because, not only were they terminally ill, they were suffering constant and severe pain. Avoiding intolerable pain and the indignity of living one's final days incapacitated and in agony is certainly "[a]t the heart of [the] liberty [to] define one's own concept of existence, of meaning, of the universe, and of the mystery of human life."

[Although] there is no absolute right to physician-assisted suicide, *Cruzan* makes it clear that some individuals who no longer have the option of deciding whether to live or to die because they are already on the threshold of death have a constitutionally protected interest that may outweigh the State's interest in preserving life at all costs. The liberty interest at stake in a case like this differs from, and is stronger than, both the common-law right to refuse medical treatment and the unbridled interest in deciding whether to live or die. It is an interest in deciding how, rather than whether, a critical threshold shall be crossed.

The state interests supporting a general rule banning the practice of physician-assisted suicide do not have the same force in all cases. First and foremost of these interests is the " 'unqualified interest in the preservation of human life,' " which is equated with " 'the sanctity of life' " * * * Properly viewed, however, this interest is not a collective interest that should always outweigh the interests of a person who because of pain, incapacity, or sedation finds her life intolerable, but rather, an aspect of individual freedom.

[Allowing] the individual, rather than the State, to make judgments " 'about the "quality" of life that a particular individual may enjoy' " does not mean that the lives of terminally-ill, disabled people have less value than the lives of those who are healthy. Rather, it gives proper recognition to the individual's interest in choosing a final chapter that accords with her life story, rather than one that demeans her values and poisons memories of her. See Brief for Bioethicists as Amici Curiae; see also Ronald Dworkin, *Life's Dominion* 213 (1993). * * *

Similarly, the State's legitimate interests in preventing suicide, protecting the vulnerable from coercion and abuse, and preventing euthanasia are less significant in this context. I agree that the State has a compelling interest in preventing persons from committing suicide because of depression, or coercion by third parties. But the State's legitimate interest in preventing abuse does not apply to an individual who is not victimized by abuse, who is not suffering from depression, and who makes a rational and voluntary decision to seek assistance in dying. * * *

Relatedly, the State and *amici* express the concern that patients whose physical pain is inadequately treated will be more likely to request assisted suicide. Encouraging the development and ensuring the availability of adequate pain treatment is of utmost importance; palliative care, however, cannot alleviate all pain and suffering. [An] individual adequately informed of the care alternatives thus might make a rational choice for assisted suicide. For such an individual, the State's interest in preventing potential abuse and mistake is only minimally implicated.

The final major interest asserted by the State is its interest in preserving the traditional integrity of the medical profession. The fear is that a rule permitting physicians to assist in suicide is inconsistent with the perception that they serve their patients solely as healers. But for some patients, it would be a physician's refusal to dispense medication to ease their suffering and make their death tolerable and dignified that would be inconsistent with the healing role. [Furthermore,] because physicians are already involved in making decisions that hasten the death of terminally ill patients—through termination of life support, withholding of medical treatment, and terminal sedation—there is in fact significant tension between the traditional view of the physician's role and the actual practice in a growing number of cases.[12]

[Unlike] the Court of Appeals, I would not say as a categorical matter that these state interests are invalid as to the entire class of terminally ill, mentally competent patients. I do not, however, foreclose the possibility that an individual plaintiff seeking to hasten her death, or a doctor whose assistance was sought, could prevail in a more particularized challenge. Future cases will determine whether such a challenge may succeed.

12. I note that there is evidence that a significant number of physicians support the practice of hastening death in particular situations. A survey published in the New England Journal of Medicine, found that 56% of responding doctors in Michigan preferred legalizing assisted suicide to an explicit ban. In a survey of Oregon doctors, 60% of the respond-ing doctors supported legalizing assisted suicide for terminally ill patients. Another study showed that 12% of physicians polled in Washington State reported that they had been asked by their terminally ill patients for prescriptions to hasten death, and that, in the year prior to the study, 24% of those physicians had complied with such requests. * * *

[There] remains room for vigorous debate about the outcome of particular cases that are not necessarily resolved by the opinions announced today. How such cases may be decided will depend on their specific facts. In my judgment, however, it is clear that the so-called "unqualified interest in the preservation of human life" is not itself sufficient to outweigh the interest in liberty that may justify the only possible means of preserving a dying patient's dignity and alleviating her intolerable suffering.

JUSTICE SOUTER, concurring in the judgment.

[The] question is whether the statute sets up one of those "arbitrary impositions" or "purposeless restraints" at odds with the Due Process Clause of the Fourteenth Amendment. *Poe v. Ullman* (Harlan, J., dissenting). I conclude that the statute's application to the doctors has not been shown to be unconstitutional, but I write separately to give my reasons for analyzing the substantive due process claims as I do, and for rejecting this one.

[In] their brief to this Court, [the four physicians who brought this challenge to the Washington statute] claim not that they ought to have a right generally to hasten patients' imminent deaths, but only to help patients who have made "personal decisions regarding their own bodies, medical care, and, fundamentally, the future course of their lives," and who have concluded responsibly and with substantial justification that the brief and anguished remainders of their lives have lost virtually all value to them. Respondents fully embrace the notion that the State must be free to impose reasonable regulations on such physician assistance to ensure that the patients they assist are indeed among the competent and terminally ill and that each has made a free and informed choice in seeking to obtain and use a fatal drug.

In response, the State argues that the interest asserted by the doctors is beyond constitutional recognition because it has no deep roots in our history and traditions. But even aside from that, without disputing that the patients here were competent and terminally ill, the State insists that recognizing the legitimacy of doctors' assistance of their patients as contemplated here would entail a number of adverse consequences that the Washington Legislature was entitled to forestall. The nub of this part of the State's argument is not that such patients are constitutionally undeserving of relief on their own account, but that any attempt to confine a right of physician assistance to the circumstances presented by these doctors is likely to fail.

First, the State argues that the right could not be confined to the terminally ill. Even assuming a fixed definition of that term, the State observes that it is not always possible to say with certainty how long a person may live. It asserts that "[t]here is no principled basis on which [the right] can be limited to the prescription of medication for terminally ill patients to administer to themselves" when the right's justifying principle is as broad as " 'merciful termination of suffering' " (citing Yale Kamisar, *Are Laws Against Assisted Suicide Unconstitutional?,* Hastings Center Report 32, 36–37 (May–June 1993)). Second, the State argues that the right could not be confined to the mentally competent, observing that a person's competence cannot always be assessed with certainty, and suggesting further that no principled distinction is possible between a competent patient acting independently and a patient acting through a duly appointed and competent surrogate. Next, according to the State, such a right might entail a right to or at least merge in practice into "other forms of life-ending assistance," such as euthanasia. Finally, the State believes that a right to physician assistance could not easily be distinguished from a right to assistance from others, such as friends, family, and other health-care workers. The State thus argues that recognition of the substantive due process right at issue here would jeopardize the lives of others outside the class defined by the doctors' claim, creating risks of irresponsible suicides and euthanasia, whose dangers are concededly within the State's authority to address.

[The] persistence of substantive due process in our cases points to the legitimacy of the modern justification for such judicial review found in Justice Harlan's dissent in *Poe*,[4] [while] the acknowledged failures of some of these cases point with caution to the difficulty raised by the present claim.

[Justice Harlan's *Poe* dissent] is important for three things that point to our responsibilities today. The first is Justice Harlan's respect for the tradition of substantive due process review itself, and his acknowledgment of the Judiciary's obligation to carry it on. For two centuries American courts, and for much of that time this Court, have thought it necessary to provide some degree of review over the substantive content of legislation under constitutional standards of textual breadth. [This] enduring tradition of American constitutional practice is, in Justice Harlan's view, nothing more than what is required by the judicial authority and obligation to construe constitutional text and review legislation for conformity to that text. * * *

Following the first point of the *Poe* dissent, on the necessity to engage in the sort of examination we conduct today, the dissent's second and third implicitly address those cases, already noted, that are now condemned with virtual unanimity as disastrous mistakes of substantive due process review. The second of the dissent's lessons is a reminder that the business of such review is not the identification of extratextual absolutes but scrutiny of a legislative resolution (perhaps unconscious) of clashing principles, each quite possibly worthy in and of itself, but each to be weighed within the history of our values as a people. It is a comparison of the relative strengths of opposing claims that informs the judicial task, not a deduction from some first premise. Thus informed, judicial review still has no warrant to substitute one reasonable resolution of the contending positions for another, but authority to supplant the balance already struck between the contenders only when it falls outside the realm of the reasonable.

[Justice Harlan's] approach calls for a court to assess the relative "weights" or dignities of the contending interests, and to this extent the judicial method is familiar to the common law. Common law method is subject, however, to two important constraints in the hands of a court engaged in substantive due process review. First, such a court is bound to confine the values that it recognizes to those truly deserving constitutional stature, either to those expressed in constitutional text, or those exemplified by "the traditions from which [the Nation] developed," or revealed by contrast with "the traditions from which it broke." *Poe* (Harlan, J., dissenting).

[The] second constraint, again, simply reflects the fact that constitutional review, not judicial lawmaking, is a court's business here. [It] is only when the legislation's justifying principle, critically valued, is so far from being commensurate with the individual interest as to be arbitrarily or pointlessly applied that the statute must give way. Only if this standard points against the statute can the individual claimant be said to have a constitutional right. * * *[10]

---

4. The status of the Harlan dissent in *Poe v. Ullman* is shown by the Court's adoption of its result in *Griswold* and by the Court's ac-knowledgment of its status and adoption of its reasoning in *Casey*. * * *

10. Our cases have used various terms to refer to fundamental liberty interests [and] at

[Justice] Harlan of course assumed that adjudication under the Due Process Clauses is like any other instance of judgment dependent on common-law method, being more or less persuasive according to the usual canons of critical discourse. [When] identifying and assessing the competing interests of liberty and authority, for example, the breadth of expression that a litigant or a judge selects in stating the competing principles will have much to do with the outcome and may be dispositive. As in any process of rational argumentation, we recognize that when a generally accepted principle is challenged, the broader the attack the less likely it is to succeed. The principle's defenders will, indeed, often try to characterize any challenge as just such a broadside, perhaps by couching the defense as if a broadside attack had occurred. So the Court in *Dred Scott* treated prohibition of slavery in the Territories as nothing less than a general assault on the concept of property.

Just as results in substantive due process cases are tied to the selections of statements of the competing interests, the acceptability of the results is a function of the good reasons for the selections made. It is here that the value of common-law method becomes apparent, for the usual thinking of the common law is suspicious of the all-or-nothing analysis that tends to produce legal petrification instead of an evolving boundary between the domains of old principles. Common-law method tends to pay respect instead to detail, seeking to understand old principles afresh by new examples and new counterexamples.

[So,] in *Poe,* Justice Harlan viewed it as essential to the plaintiffs' claimed right to use contraceptives that they sought to do so within the privacy of the marital bedroom. This detail in fact served two crucial and complementary functions, and provides a lesson for today. It rescued the individuals' claim from a breadth that would have threatened all state regulation of contraception or intimate relations; extramarital intimacy, no matter how privately practiced, was outside the scope of the right Justice Harlan would have recognized in that case. It was, moreover, this same restriction that allowed the interest to be valued as an aspect of a broader liberty to be free from all unreasonable intrusions into the privacy of the home and the family life within it, a liberty exemplified in constitutional provisions such as the Third and Fourth Amendments, in prior decisions of the Court involving unreasonable intrusions into the home and family life, and in the then-prevailing status of marriage as the sole lawful locus of intimate relations.[11] The individuals' interest was therefore at its peak in *Poe,* because it was supported by a principle that distinguished of its own force

---

times we have also called such an interest a "right" even before balancing it against the government's interest, see, e.g., *Roe v. Wade; Carey v. Population Services Int'l.* * * * Precision in terminology, however, favors reserving the label "right" for instances in which the individual's liberty interest actually trumps the government's countervailing interests; only then does the individual have anything legally enforceable as against the state's attempt at regulation.

11. Thus, as the *Poe* dissent illustrates, the task of determining whether the concrete right claimed by an individual in a particular case falls within the ambit of a more generalized protected liberty requires explicit analysis when what the individual wants to do could arguably be characterized as belonging to different strands of our legal tradition requiring

different degrees of constitutional scrutiny. See also Laurence H. Tribe & Michael C. Dorf, *Levels of Generality in the Definition of Rights,* 57 U.Chi.L.Rev. 1057, 1091 (1990) (abortion might conceivably be assimilated either to the tradition regarding women's reproductive freedom in general, which places a substantial burden of justification on the State, or to the tradition regarding protection of fetuses, as embodied in laws criminalizing feticide by someone other than the mother, which generally requires only rationality on the part of the State). Selecting among such competing characterizations demands reasoned judgment about which broader principle, as exemplified in the concrete privileges and prohibitions embodied in our legal tradition, best fits the particular claim asserted in a particular case.

between areas in which government traditionally had regulated (sexual relations outside of marriage) and those in which it had not (private marital intimacies), and thus was broad enough to cover the claim at hand without being so broad as to be shot-through by exceptions.

On the other side of the balance, the State's interest in *Poe* was not fairly characterized simply as preserving sexual morality, or doing so by regulating contraceptive devices. [It] was assumed that the State might legitimately enforce limits on the use of contraceptives through laws regulating divorce and annulment, or even through its tax policy, *ibid.*, but not necessarily be justified in criminalizing the same practice in the marital bedroom, which would entail the consequence of authorizing state enquiry into the intimate relations of a married couple who chose to close their door.

The same insistence on exactitude lies behind questions, in current terminology, about the proper level of generality at which to analyze claims and counterclaims, and the demand for fitness and proper tailoring of a restrictive statute is just another way of testing the legitimacy of the generality at which the government sets up its justification. We may therefore classify Justice Harlan's example of proper analysis in any of these ways: as applying concepts of normal critical reasoning, as pointing to the need to attend to the levels of generality at which countervailing interests are stated, or as examining the concrete application of principles for fitness with their own ostensible justifications. But whatever the categories in which we place the dissent's example, it stands in marked contrast to earlier cases whose reasoning was marked by comparatively less discrimination, and it points to the importance of evaluating the claims of the parties now before us with comparable detail. For here we are faced with an individual claim not to a right on the part of just anyone to help anyone else commit suicide under any circumstances, but to the right of a narrow class to help others also in a narrow class under a set of limited circumstances. And the claimants are met with the State's assertion, among others, that rights of such narrow scope cannot be recognized without jeopardy to individuals whom the State may concededly protect through its regulations.

Respondents claim that a patient facing imminent death, who anticipates physical suffering and indignity, and is capable of responsible and voluntary choice, should have a right to a physician's assistance in providing counsel and drugs to be administered by the patient to end life promptly. They accordingly claim that a physician must have the corresponding right to provide such aid, contrary to the provisions of [state law]. I do not understand the argument to rest on any assumption that rights either to suicide or to assistance in committing it are historically based on such. Respondents, rather, acknowledge the prohibition of each historically, but rely on the fact that to a substantial extent the State has repudiated that history. The result of this, respondents say, is to open the door to claims of such a patient to be accorded one of the options open to those with different, traditionally cognizable claims to autonomy in deciding how their bodies and minds should be treated.

[The] principal significance of [the history of suicide] in the State of Washington, according to respondents, lies in its repudiation of the old tradition to the extent of eliminating the criminal suicide prohibitions. Respondents do not argue that the State's decision goes further, to imply that the State has repudiated any legitimate claim to discourage suicide or to limit its encouragement. The reasons for the decriminalization, after all, may have had more to do with difficulties of law enforcement than with a shift in the value ascribed to life in various circumstances or in the perceived legitimacy of taking one's own. Thus it may indeed make sense for the State to take its hands off suicide as such, while continuing to prohibit the sort of assistance that would make its commission easier. Decriminalization does not, then, imply the existence of a constitutional liberty interest in suicide as such; it simply opens the door to the assertion of a cognizable liberty interest in bodily integrity and associated medical care that would otherwise have been inapposite so long as suicide, as well as assisting a suicide, was a criminal offense.

* * * Constitutional recognition of the right to bodily integrity underlies the assumed right, good against the State, to require physicians to terminate artificial life support, *Cruzan,* [and] the affirmative right to obtain medical intervention to cause abortion, see *Casey.* It is, indeed, in the abortion cases that the most telling recognitions of the importance of bodily integrity and the concomitant tradition of medical assistance have occurred. [The] analogies between the abortion cases and this one are several. Even though the State has a legitimate interest in discouraging abortion, the Court recognized a woman's right to a physician's counsel and care. Like the decision to commit suicide, the decision to abort potential life can be made irresponsibly and under the influence of others, and yet the Court has held in the abortion cases that physicians are fit assistants. Without physician assistance in abortion, the woman's right would have too often amounted to nothing more than a right to self-mutilation, and without a physician to assist in the suicide of the dying, the patient's right will often be confined to crude methods of causing death, most shocking and painful to the decedent's survivors.

There is, finally, one more reason for claiming that a physician's assistance here would fall within the accepted tradition of medical care in our society, and the abortion cases are only the most obvious illustration of the further point. While the Court has held that the performance of abortion procedures can be restricted to physicians, the Court's opinion in *Roe* recognized the doctors' role in yet another way. For, in the course of holding that the decision to perform an abortion called for a physician's assistance, the Court recognized that the good physician is not just a mechanic of the human body whose services have no bearing on a person's moral choices, but one who does more than treat symptoms, one who ministers to the patient. [This] idea of the physician as serving the whole person is a source of the high value traditionally placed on the medical relationship. Its value is surely as apparent here as in the abortion cases, for just as the decision about abortion is not directed to correcting some pathology, so the decision in which a dying patient seeks help is not so limited.

[Respondents] argue that the State has in fact already recognized enough evolving examples of this tradition of patient care to demonstrate the strength of their claim. Washington, like other States, authorizes physicians to withdraw life-sustaining medical treatment and artificially delivered food and water from patients who request it, even though such actions will hasten death. The State permits physicians to alleviate anxiety and discomfort when withdrawing artificial life-supporting devices by administering medication that will hasten death even further. And it generally permits physicians to administer medication to patients in terminal conditions when the primary intent is to alleviate pain, even when the medication is so powerful as to hasten death and the patient chooses to receive it with that understanding.

The argument supporting respondents' position thus progresses through three steps of increasing forcefulness. First, it emphasizes the decriminalization of suicide. Reliance on this fact is sanctioned under the standard that looks not only to the tradition retained, but to society's occasional choices to reject traditions of the legal past. See *Poe* (Harlan, J., dissenting). [The] second step in the argument is to emphasize that the State's own act of decriminalization gives a freedom of choice much like the individual's option in recognized instances of bodily autonomy. One of these, abortion, is a legal right to choose in spite of the interest a State may legitimately invoke in discouraging the practice, just as suicide is now subject to choice, despite a state interest in discouraging it. The third step is to emphasize that respondents claim a right to assistance not on the basis of some broad principle that would be subject to exceptions if that continuing interest of the State's in discouraging suicide were to be recognized at all. Respondents base their claim on the traditional right to medical care and counsel, subject to the limiting conditions of informed, responsible choice when death is imminent, conditions that support a strong analogy to rights of care in other situations in which medical counsel and assistance have been available as a matter of course. There can be no stronger claim to a physician's assistance than at the time when death is imminent, a moral judgment implied by the State's own recognition of the legitimacy of medical procedures necessarily hastening the moment of impending death.

In my judgment, the importance of the individual interest here, as within that class of "certain interests" demanding careful scrutiny of the State's contrary claim, see *Poe,* cannot be gainsaid. Whether that interest might in some circumstances, or at some time, be seen as "fundamental" to the degree entitled to prevail is not, however, a conclusion that I need draw here, for I am satisfied that the State's interests [are] sufficiently serious to defeat the present claim that its law is arbitrary or purposeless.

The State has put forward several interests to justify the Washington law as applied to physicians treating terminally ill patients, even those competent to make responsible choices: protecting life generally, discouraging suicide even if knowing and voluntary, and protecting terminally ill patients from involuntary suicide and euthanasia, both voluntary and nonvoluntary.

It is not necessary to discuss the exact strengths of the first two claims of justification in the present circumstances, for the third is dispositive for me. That third justification is different from the first two, for it addresses specific features of respondents' claim, and it opposes that claim not with a moral judgment contrary to respondents', but with a recognized state interest in the protection of nonresponsible individuals and those who do not stand in relation either to death or to their physicians as do the patients whom respondents describe. The State claims interests in protecting patients from mistakenly and involuntarily deciding to end their lives, and in guarding against both voluntary and involuntary euthanasia. [The] argument is that a progression would occur, obscuring the line between the ill and the dying, and between the responsible and the unduly influenced, until ultimately doctors and perhaps others would abuse a limited freedom to aid suicides by yielding to the impulse to end another's suffering under conditions going beyond the narrow limits the respondents propose. The State thus argues, essentially, that respondents' claim is not as narrow as it sounds, simply because no recognition of the interest they assert could be limited to vindicating those interests and affecting no others. The State says that the claim, in practical effect, would entail consequences that the State could, without doubt, legitimately act to prevent.

[The State argues] that dependence on the vigilance of physicians will not be enough. First, the lines proposed here (particularly the requirement of a knowing and voluntary decision by the patient) would be more difficult to draw than the lines that have limited other recently recognized due process rights. Limiting a state from prosecuting use of artificial contraceptives by married couples posed no practical threat to the State's capacity to regulate contraceptives in other ways that were assumed at the time of *Poe* to be legitimate; the trimester measurements of *Roe* and the viability determination of *Casey* were easy to make with a real degree of certainty. But the knowing and responsible mind is harder to assess.[16] Second, this difficulty could become the greater by combining with another fact within the realm of plausibility, that physicians simply would not be assiduous to preserve the line. They have compassion, and those who would be willing to assist in suicide at all might be the most susceptible to the wishes of a patient, whether the patient were technically quite responsible or not. Physicians, and their hospitals, have their own financial incentives, too, in this new age of managed care. Whether acting from compassion or under some other influence, a physician who would provide a drug for a patient to administer might well go the further step of administering the drug himself; so, the barrier between assisted suicide and euthanasia could become porous, and the line between voluntary and involuntary euthanasia as well.[17] The case for the slippery slope is fairly made out here, not because recognizing one due process right would leave a court with no principled basis to avoid recognizing another, but because there is a plausible case that the right claimed would not be readily containable by reference to facts about the mind that are matters of difficult judgment, or by gatekeepers who are subject to temptation, noble or not.

Respondents propose an answer to all this, the answer of state regulation with teeth. Legislation proposed in several States, for example, would authorize physician-assisted suicide but require two qualified physicians to confirm the patient's diagnosis, prognosis, and competence; and would mandate that the patient make repeated requests witnessed by at least two others over a specified time span; and would impose reporting requirements and criminal penalties for various acts of coercion.

But at least at this moment there are reasons for caution in predicting the effectiveness of the teeth proposed. Respondents' proposals, as it turns out, sound much like the guidelines now in place in the Netherlands, the only place where experience with physician-assisted suicide and euthanasia has yielded empirical evidence about how such regulations might affect actual practice. [There] is, however, a substantial dispute today about what the Dutch experience

---

16. While it is also more difficult to assess in cases involving limitations on life incidental to pain medication and the disconnection of artificial life support, there are reasons to justify a lesser concern with the punctilio of responsibility in these instances. The purpose of requesting and giving the medication is presumably not to cause death but to relieve the pain so that the State's interest in preserving life is not unequivocally implicated by the practice; and the importance of pain relief is so clear that there is less likelihood that relieving pain would run counter to what a responsible patient would choose, even with the consequences for life expectancy. As for ending artificial life support, the State again may see its interest in preserving life as weaker here than in the general case just because artificial life support preserves life when nature would

not; and, because such life support is a frequently offensive bodily intrusion, there is a lesser reason to fear that a decision to remove it would not be the choice of one fully responsible. Where, however, a physician writes a prescription to equip a patient to end life, the prescription is written to serve an affirmative intent to die (even though the physician need not and probably does not characteristically have an intent that the patient die but only that the patient be equipped to make the decision). The patient's responsibility and competence are therefore crucial when the physician is presented with the request.

17. Again, the same can be said about life support and shortening life to kill pain, but the calculus may be viewed as different in these instances, as noted just above.

shows. Some commentators marshall evidence that the Dutch guidelines have in practice failed to protect patients from involuntary euthanasia and have been violated with impunity. This evidence is contested. The day may come when we can say with some assurance which side is right, but for now it is the substantiality of the factual disagreement, and the alternatives for resolving it, that matter. They are, for me, dispositive of the due process claim at this time.

I take it that the basic concept of judicial review with its possible displacement of legislative judgment bars any finding that a legislature has acted arbitrarily when the following conditions are met: there is a serious factual controversy over the feasibility of recognizing the claimed right without at the same time making it impossible for the State to engage in an undoubtedly legitimate exercise of power; facts necessary to resolve the controversy are not readily ascertainable through the judicial process; but they are more readily subject to discovery through legislative factfinding and experimentation. It is assumed in this case, and must be, that a State's interest in protecting those unable to make responsible decisions and those who make no decisions at all entitles the State to bar aid to any but a knowing and responsible person intending suicide, and to prohibit euthanasia. How, and how far, a State should act in that interest are judgments for the State, but the legitimacy of its action to deny a physician the option to aid any but the knowing and responsible is beyond question.

The capacity of the State to protect the others if respondents were to prevail is, however, subject to some genuine question, underscored by the responsible disagreement over the basic facts of the Dutch experience. This factual controversy is not open to a judicial resolution with any substantial degree of assurance at this time. [While] an extensive literature on any subject can raise the hopes for judicial understanding, the literature on this subject is only nascent. Since there is little experience directly bearing on the issue, the most that can be said is that whichever way the Court might rule today, events could overtake its assumptions, as experimentation in some jurisdictions confirmed or discredited the concerns about progression from assisted suicide to euthanasia.

Legislatures, on the other hand, have superior opportunities to obtain the facts necessary for a judgment about the present controversy. [Moreover,] their mechanisms include the power to experiment, moving forward and pulling back as facts emerge within their own jurisdictions. * * *

I do not decide here what the significance might be of legislative foot-dragging in ascertaining the facts going to the State's argument that the right in question could not be confined as claimed. [Now,] it is enough to say that our examination of legislative reasonableness should consider the fact that the Legislature of the State of Washington is no more obviously at fault than this Court is in being uncertain about what would happen if respondents prevailed today. We therefore have a clear question about which institution, a legislature or a court, is relatively more competent to deal with an emerging issue as to which facts currently unknown could be dispositive. The answer has to be, for the reasons already stated, that the legislative process is to be preferred. There is a closely related further reason as well.

One must bear in mind that the nature of the right claimed, if recognized as one constitutionally required, would differ in no essential way from other constitutional rights guaranteed by enumeration or derived from some more definite textual source than "due process." An unenumerated right should not therefore be recognized, with the effect of displacing the legislative ordering of things, without the assurance that its recognition would prove as durable as the recognition of those other rights differently derived. To recognize a right of lesser promise would simply create a constitutional regime too uncertain to bring with it the expectation of finality that is one of this Court's central obligations in making constitutional decisions.

Legislatures, however, are not so constrained. The experimentation that should be out of the question in constitutional adjudication displacing legislative judgments is entirely proper, as well as highly desirable, when the legislative power addresses an emerging issue like assisted suicide. The Court should accordingly stay its hand to allow reasonable legislative consideration. While I do not decide for all time that respondents' claim should not be recognized, I acknowledge the legislative institutional competence as the better one to deal with that claim at this time.

JUSTICE GINSBURG, concurring in the judgments.

I concur in the Court's judgments in these cases substantially for the reasons stated by Justice O'Connor in her concurring opinion.

JUSTICE BREYER, concurring in the judgments.

I believe that Justice O'Connor's views, which I share, have greater legal significance than the Court's opinion suggests. I join her separate opinion, except insofar as it joins the majority. And I concur in the judgments. I shall briefly explain how I differ from the Court.

I agree with the Court in *Vacco v. Quill*, [infra] that the articulated state interests justify the distinction drawn between physician assisted suicide and withdrawal of life-support. I also agree [that] the critical question in both of the cases before us is whether "the 'liberty' specially protected by the Due Process Clause includes a right" of the sort that the respondents assert. *Washington v. Glucksberg.* I do not agree, however, with the Court's formulation of that claimed "liberty" interest. The Court describes it as a "right to commit suicide with another's assistance." But I would not reject the respondents' claim without considering a different formulation, for which our legal tradition may provide greater support. That formulation would use words roughly like a "right to die with dignity." But irrespective of the exact words used, at its core would lie personal control over the manner of death, professional medical assistance, and the avoidance of unnecessary and severe physical suffering—combined.

As Justice Souter points out, Justice Harlan's dissenting opinion in *Poe* offers some support for such a claim. In that opinion, Justice Harlan referred to the "liberty" that the Fourteenth Amendment protects as including "a freedom from all substantial arbitrary impositions and purposeless restraints" and also as recognizing that "*certain interests* require particularly careful scrutiny of the state needs asserted to justify their abridgment." The "certain interests" to which Justice Harlan referred may well be similar (perhaps identical) to the rights, liberties, or interests that the Court today, as in the past, regards as "fundamental."

Justice Harlan concluded that marital privacy was such a "special interest." He found in the Constitution a right of "privacy of the home"—with the home, the bedroom, and "intimate details of the marital relation" at its heart—by examining the protection that the law had earlier provided for related, but not identical, interests described by such words as "privacy," "home," and "family." The respondents here essentially ask us to do the same. They argue that one can find a "right to die with dignity" by examining the protection the law has provided for related, but not identical, interests relating to personal dignity, medical treatment, and freedom from state-inflicted pain.

I do not believe, however, that this Court need or now should decide whether or a not such a right is "fundamental." That is because, in my view, the avoidance of severe physical pain (connected with death) would have to comprise an essential part of any successful claim and because, as Justice O'Connor points out, the laws before us do not *force* a dying person to undergo that kind of pain. Rather, the laws of New York and of Washington do not prohibit doctors from providing patients with drugs sufficient to control pain despite the risk that those drugs themselves will kill. And under these circumstances the laws of New York and Washington would overcome any remaining significant interests and would be justified, regardless.

Medical technology, we are repeatedly told, makes the administration of pain-relieving drugs sufficient, except for a very few individuals for whom the ineffectiveness of pain control medicines can mean, not pain, but the need for sedation which can end in a coma. We are also told that there are many instances in which patients do not receive the palliative care that, in principle, is available, but that is so for institutional reasons or inadequacies or obstacles, which would seem possible to overcome, and which do *not* include *a prohibitive set of laws.*

This legal circumstance means that the state laws before us do not infringe directly upon the (assumed) central interest (what I have called the core of the interest in dying with dignity) as, by way of contrast, the state anticontraceptive laws at issue in *Poe* did interfere with the central interest there at stake—by bringing the State's police powers to bear upon the marital bedroom.

Were the legal circumstances different—for example, were state law to prevent the provision of palliative care, including the administration of drugs as needed to avoid pain at the end of life—then the law's impact upon serious and otherwise unavoidable physical pain (accompanying death) would be more directly at issue. And as Justice O'Connor suggests, the Court might have to revisit its conclusions in these cases.

VACCO v. QUILL

521 U.S. 793, 117 S.Ct. 2293, 138 L.Ed.2d 834 (1997).

CHIEF JUSTICE REHNQUIST delivered the opinion of the Court.

In New York, as in most States, it is a crime to aid another to commit or attempt suicide, but patients may refuse even lifesaving medical treatment. The question presented by this case is whether New York's prohibition on assisting suicide therefore violates the Equal Protection Clause of the Fourteenth Amendment. We hold that it does not.

[Respondent New York physicians] assert that although it would be "consistent with the standards of [their] medical practice[s]" to prescribe lethal medication for "mentally competent, terminally ill patients" who are suffering great pain and desire a doctor's help in taking their own lives, they are deterred from doing so by New York's ban on assisting suicide. Respondents, and three gravely ill patients who have since died, [maintain] that because New York permits a competent person to refuse life-sustaining medical treatment, and because the refusal of such treatment is "essentially the same thing" as physician-assisted suicide, New York's assisted-suicide ban violates the Equal Protection Clause.

The District Court disagreed, [but the] Court of Appeals for the Second Circuit reversed, [concluding that] "New York law does not treat equally all competent persons who are in the final stages of fatal illness and wish to hasten their deaths," because "those in the final stages of terminal illness who are on life-support systems are allowed to hasten their deaths by directing the removal of such systems; but those who are similarly situated, except for the previous attachment of life-sustaining equipment, are not allowed to hasten death by self-administering prescribed drugs." In the court's view, "[t]he ending of life by [the withdrawal of life-support systems] is *nothing more nor less than assisted suicide*" (emphasis added). The Court of Appeals then examined whether this supposed unequal treatment was rationally related to any legitimate state interests,[5] and concluded that [it was not].

[The] Equal Protection Clause [embodies] a general rule that States must treat like cases alike but may treat unlike cases accordingly. If a legislative classification or distinction "neither burdens a fundamental right nor targets a suspect class, we will uphold [it] so long as it bears a rational relation to some legitimate end." *Romer v. Evans* [p. 119 of this Supplement].

New York's statutes outlawing assisting suicide [neither] infringe fundamental rights nor involve suspect classifications. [These] laws are therefore entitled to a "strong presumption of validity."

On their faces, neither New York's ban on assisting suicide nor its statutes permitting patients to refuse medical treatment treat anyone differently than anyone else or draw any distinctions between persons. *Everyone,* regardless of physical condition, is entitled, if competent, to refuse unwanted lifesaving medical treatment; *no one* is permitted to assist a suicide. Generally speaking, laws that apply evenhandedly to all "unquestionably comply" with the Equal Protection Clause.

The Court of Appeals, however, concluded that some terminally ill people—those who are on life-support systems—are treated differently than those who are not, in that the former may "hasten death" by ending treatment, but the latter may not "hasten death" through physician-assisted suicide. This conclusion depends on the submission that ending or refusing lifesaving medical treatment "is nothing more nor less than assisted suicide." Unlike the Court of Appeals, we think the distinction between assisting suicide and withdrawing life-sustaining treatment, a distinction widely recognized and endorsed in the medical profession and in our legal traditions, is both important and logical; it is certainly rational.

The distinction comports with fundamental legal principles of causation and intent. First, when a patient refuses life-sustaining medical treatment, he dies from an underlying fatal disease or pathology; but if a patient ingests lethal medication prescribed by a physician, he is killed by that medication. * * *

Furthermore, a physician who withdraws, or honors a patient's refusal to begin, life-sustaining medical treatment purposefully intends, or may so intend, only to respect his patient's wishes and "to cease doing useless and futile or degrading things to the patient when [the patient] no longer stands to benefit from them." The same is true when a doctor provides aggressive palliative care; in some cases, painkilling drugs may hasten a patient's death, but the physician's purpose and intent is, or may be, only to ease his patient's pain. A doctor who assists a suicide, however, "must, necessarily and indubitably, intend primarily that the patient be made dead." Similarly, a patient who commits suicide with a

---

5. The court acknowledged that because New York's assisted-suicide statutes "do not impinge on any fundamental rights [or] involve suspect classifications," they were subject only to rational-basis judicial scrutiny.

doctor's aid necessarily has the specific intent to end his or her own life, while a patient who refuses or discontinues treatment might not.

[The] law has long used actors' intent or purpose to distinguish between two acts that may have the same result. * * * Put differently, the law distinguishes actions taken "because of" a given end from actions taken "in spite of" their unintended but foreseen consequences.

[Given] these general principles, it is not surprising that many courts, including New York courts, have carefully distinguished refusing life-sustaining treatment from suicide. * * * Similarly, the overwhelming majority of state legislatures have drawn a clear line between assisting suicide and withdrawing or permitting the refusal of unwanted lifesaving medical treatment by prohibiting the former and permitting the latter. And "nearly all states expressly disapprove of suicide and assisted suicide either in statutes dealing with durable powers of attorney in health-care situations, or in 'living will' statutes." Thus, even as the States move to protect and promote patients' dignity at the end of life, they remain opposed to physician-assisted suicide.

New York is a case in point. The State enacted its current assisted-suicide statutes in 1965.[10] Since then, New York has acted several times to protect patients' common-law right to refuse treatment [but] reaffirmed the line between "killing" and "letting die." * * * More recently, the New York State Task Force on Life and the Law studied assisted suicide and euthanasia and, in 1994, unanimously recommended against legalization.

[This] Court has also recognized, at least implicitly, the distinction between letting a patient die and making that patient die. In *Cruzan* our assumption of a right to refuse treatment was grounded not, as the Court of Appeals supposed, on the proposition that patients have a general and abstract "right to hasten death," but on well established, traditional rights to bodily integrity and freedom from unwanted touching. In fact, we observed that "the majority of States in this country have laws imposing criminal penalties on one who assists another to commit suicide." *Cruzan* therefore provides no support for the notion that refusing life-sustaining medical treatment is "nothing more nor less than suicide."

For all these reasons, we disagree with respondents' claim that the distinction between refusing lifesaving medical treatment and assisted suicide is "arbitrary" and "irrational."[11] [By] permitting everyone to refuse unwanted medical treatment while prohibiting anyone from assisting a suicide, New York law follows a longstanding and rational distinction.

New York's reasons for recognizing and acting on this distinction—including prohibiting intentional killing and preserving life; preventing suicide; maintaining physicians' role as their patients' healers; protecting vulnerable people from

10. It has always been a crime, either by statute or under the common law, to assist a suicide in New York. See Marzen, O'Dowd, Crone, & Balch, *Suicide: A Constitutional Right?*, 24 Duquesne L.Rev. 1, 205–210 (1985) (Appendix).

11. Respondents also argue that the State irrationally distinguishes between physician-assisted suicide and "terminal sedation," a process respondents characterize as "induc[ing] barbiturate coma and then starv[ing] the person to death." Petitioners insist, however, that " '[a]lthough proponents of physician-assisted suicide and euthanasia contend that terminal sedation is covert physician-assisted suicide or euthanasia, the concept of sedating pharmacotherapy is based on informed consent and the principle of double effect.' " Just as a State may prohibit assisting suicide while permitting patients to refuse unwanted lifesaving treatment, it may permit palliative care related to that refusal, which may have the foreseen but unintended "double effect" of hastening the patient's death.

indifference, prejudice, and psychological and financial pressure to end their lives; and avoiding a possible slide towards euthanasia—are discussed in greater detail in our opinion in *Glucksberg.* These valid and important public interests easily satisfy the constitutional requirement that a legislative classification bear a rational relation to some legitimate end.[13]   * * *

[The concurring opinions of Justices O'Connor, Stevens, Ginsburg and Breyer in *Glucksberg,* supra, also constitute their concurring opinions in *Vacco v. Quill.* The portion of Justice Steven's opinion addressing the equal protection issue is set forth below.]

JUSTICE STEVENS, concurring in the judgments. * * *

In New York, a doctor must respect a competent person's decision to refuse or to discontinue medical treatment even though death will thereby ensue, but the same doctor would be guilty of a felony if she provided her patient assistance in committing suicide. Today we hold that the Equal Protection Clause is not violated by the resulting disparate treatment of two classes of terminally ill people who may have the same interest in hastening death. I agree that the distinction between permitting death to ensue from an underlying fatal disease and causing it to occur by the administration of medication or other means provides a constitutionally sufficient basis for the State's classification. Unlike the Court, however, I am not persuaded that in all cases there will in fact be a significant difference between the intent of the physicians, the patients or the families in the two situations.

There may be little distinction between the intent of a terminally-ill patient who decides to remove her life-support and one who seeks the assistance of a doctor in ending her life; in both situations, the patient is seeking to hasten a certain, impending death. The doctor's intent might also be the same in prescribing lethal medication as it is in terminating life support. A doctor who fails to administer medical treatment to one who is dying from a disease could be doing so with an intent to harm or kill that patient. Conversely, a doctor who prescribes lethal medication does not necessarily intend the patient's death—rather that doctor may seek simply to ease the patient's suffering and to comply with her wishes. The illusory character of any differences in intent or causation is confirmed by the fact that the American Medical Association unequivocally endorses the practice of terminal sedation—the administration of sufficient dosages of pain-killing medication to terminally ill patients to protect them from excruciating pain even when it is clear that the time of death will be advanced. The purpose of terminal sedation is to ease the suffering of the patient and comply with her wishes, and the actual cause of death is the administration of heavy doses of lethal sedatives. This same intent and causation may exist when a doctor complies with a patient's request for lethal medication to hasten her death.[15]

---

13. Justice Stevens observes that our holding today "does not foreclose the possibility that some applications of the New York statute may impose an intolerable intrusion on the patient's freedom." This is true, but, as we observe in *Glucksberg,* a particular plaintiff hoping to show that New York's assisted-suicide ban was unconstitutional in his particular case would need to present different and considerably stronger arguments than those advanced by respondents here.

15. If a doctor prescribes lethal drugs to be self-administered by the patient, it not at all clear that the physician's intent is that the patient "be made dead." Many patients prescribed lethal medications never actually take them; they merely acquire some sense of control in the process of dying that the availability of those medications provides.

Thus, although the differences the majority notes in causation and intent between terminating life-support and assisting in suicide support the Court's rejection of the respondents' facial challenge, these distinctions may be inapplicable to particular terminally ill patients and their doctors. Our holding today in *Vacco v. Quill* that the Equal Protection Clause is not violated by New York's classification, just like our holding in *Washington v. Glucksberg* that the Washington statute is not invalid on its face, does not foreclose the possibility that some applications of the New York statute may impose an intolerable intrusion on the patient's freedom.

There remains room for vigorous debate about the outcome of particular cases that are not necessarily resolved by the opinions announced today. How such cases may be decided will depend on their specific facts. In my judgment, however, it is clear that the so-called "unqualified interest in the preservation of human life" is not itself sufficient to outweigh the interest in liberty that may justify the only possible means of preserving a dying patient's dignity and alleviating her intolerable suffering.

JUSTICE SOUTER, concurring in the judgment.

Even though I do not conclude that assisted suicide is a fundamental right entitled to recognition at this time, I accord the claims raised by the patients and physicians in this case and *Washington v. Glucksberg* a high degree of importance, requiring a commensurate justification. The reasons that lead me to conclude in *Glucksberg* that the prohibition on assisted suicide is not arbitrary under the due process standard also support the distinction between assistance to suicide, which is banned, and practices such as termination of artificial life support and death-hastening pain medication, which are permitted. * * *

Notes and Questions

1. *Preventing pain relief; the "double effect" principle.* Providing medication to terminally ill people knowing that it will have a "double effect"—reduce the patient's pain and hasten death—is widely accepted by the medical profession. Many physicians and bioethicists seem to believe that providing risky pain relief is always justifiable, regardless of how certain or probable the risk of death may be. Recently, however, two law professors have maintained that as a matter of criminal law the physician's motive or desire to relieve pain does not automatically or necessarily justify the administration of pain relief. Norman Cantor & George Thomas, *Pain Relief, Acceleration of Death, and Criminal Law*, 6 Kennedy Inst. of Ethics J. 107 (June, 1996). They argue that if, for example, the situation were such that no analgesic dosage could provide pain relief without also causing prompt death (or if under the circumstances it was almost certain that the required analgesic dosage would cause death) the physician who administered the analgesic would be criminally liable for the resulting death even though death was not intended. According to the authors, as defined by the Model Penal Code these deaths would be "knowing" homicides (acting with awareness that one's conduct is "practically certain" to bring about a particular result). Moreover, according to the authors, if it were *highly likely* that the administration of an analgesic would cause prompt death (for example a 75–90% chance), the physician who used the painkillers that caused the death would also be criminally liable (for having acted "recklessly").

Suppose, inspired by the Cantor–Thomas article, a state legislature criminalized the use of medication designed to relieve severe pain when it is highly likely (or more probable than not) that administration of such pain relief would cause death. In such an event, how many members of the Supreme Court would be inclined to "revisit" the questions raised by the physician-assisted suicide cases? See Robert A. Burt, *The Supreme Court Speaks—Not Assisted Suicide but a Constitutional Right to Palliative Care*, 337 New Eng. J. Med, 1234 (1997); Lawrence O. Gostin, *Deciding Life and Death in the Courtroom*, 278 JAMA 1523, 1527–28 (1997); Yale Kamisar, *On the Meaning and Impact of the Physician–Assisted Suicide Cases*, 82 Minn. L. Rev. 895, 904–09 (1998).

2. *Judicial "minimalism" and the 1997 physician-assisted suicide cases.* As he explains at considerable length in his book, *One Case at a Time: Judicial Minimalism on the Supreme Court* (1999), Professor Cass R. Sunstein is a strong proponent of judicial "minimalism." As a general matter, this approach leaves important questions unresolved by saying no more than necessary to justify the outcome of a case. (Judicial "maximalism," on the other hand, is the practice of deciding cases in a way that establishes broad rules for the future.)

Professor Sunstein maintains (p. 89) that because "it is extremely difficult to produce any verbal formula that is satisfying, consistent with current law, and adequate to resolve the issue of physician-assisted suicide, * * * the best and appropriately minimalist route is for the Court simply to assume that the right qualifies as fundamental and to proceed from there to the question of justification." According to Sunstein, although Rehnquist, C.J., rejected this approach, the five justices who wrote concurring opinions did not.[a] "In good minimalist fashion," these five justices "left open the question whether people facing pain and imminent death" may have a constitutional right to physician-assisted suicide and "[t]he Court was right not to decide that question" (p. 76).[b]

Professor Sunstein criticizes Rehnquist, C.J., for writing "the ambitious, emphatically nonminimalist opinion that he and Justice Scalia have been (unsuccessfully) urging on the Court in the abortion cases—an opinion that would limit the right of privacy, and indeed all fundamental rights under the due process clause, to those rights that are 'deeply rooted' in our long-standing traditions and practices" (Preface, p. xii).

But consider Jeffrey Rosen, *The Age of Mixed Results*, (essay review of Sunstein's book), The New Republic, June 28, 1999, pp. 43, 46: "[W]hy is Rehnquist's opinion 'emphatically nonminimalist'? The conventional tools of legal interpretation—text, history, tradition, constitutional structure, and judicial precedent—all fail to support the claim that there is a fundamental right to physician-assisted suicide, even to alleviate great pain when death is imminent. By recognizing the weakness of the argument for a judicially created right to die, and by removing the courts from the debate entirely, Rehnquist's approach would seem to preserve the largest space for democratic deliberation.

"Yet Sunstein prefers the far more elusive approach of Justice O'Connor, who stressed that the Court had not decided whether or not a competent person

---

a. Professor Sunstein is well aware that five justices signed the Chief Justice's opinion, but he observes that O'Connor, J., who signed the Chief Justice's opinion, "wrote one of her characteristic separate opinions, * * * caution[ing] that the Court had not decided whether a competent person experiencing great suffering had a constitutional right to control the circumstances of an imminent death. That issue remained to be decided on another day." (Preface, p. xii) "What this means," continues Sunstein, "is that a majority of five justices on the Court has signaled the possible existence of a right to physician-assisted suicide in compelling circumstances—and thus a five-justice majority has rejected the whole approach in Rehnquist's opinion (for a five-justice majority)." (Ibid.)

b. Sunstein adds, however, that when and if it is forced to decide that question, the Court should conclude that "the state has sufficient reason to override the individual interest even in such extreme cases" (p. 76).

experiencing great suffering might have a constitutional right to control the circumstances of imminent death. * * *

"Sunstein, like O'Connor, says that the Court should assume that the right to physician-assisted suicide is 'presumptively protected' in medically hopeless cases, but should also hold that the state's interests are sufficiently strong to override it. Why is this opaque holding more 'minimalist' than Rehnquist's far less intrusive alternative? Since neither Sunstein nor O'Connor explains the reasons that might persuade the Court to recognize a presumptive right to die under medically hopeless conditions, all this has the feel of a fiat, and it raises the specter that the Court might create other unenumerated rights in the future with similarly thin support in text, history, and precedent. Wasn't it precisely this threat of an untethered court inventing constitutional rights without coherent explanations that the minimalist project was designed to avoid?"

3. *The significance of the informally agreed-upon "right" to assisted suicide, especially in compelling cases.* A number of prominent commentators opposed to the legalization of physician-assisted suicide (e.g., John Arras, Ezekiel Emanuel and Mark Siegler) defend the flat prohibition partly on the ground that it is *not really* a flat ban—that the availability of informal practice and informally agreed-upon "rights," especially in the most compelling cases, *reduces the pressure* to legalize these practices formally. But which way does "the availability of informal practice" cut? See the discussion in Yale Kamisar, *Physician–Assisted Suicide: The Problems Presented by the Compelling, Heartwrenching Case*, 88 J.Crim.L. & Crim. 1121 (1998).

4. *What next?* Should the question of whether and how physician-assisted suicide (PAS) is to be legalized be left to state legislatures? Consider Charles H. Baron, *Pleading for Physician–Assisted Suicide in the Courts*, 19 W. New Eng. L.Rev. 371, 373, 389, 398–99 (1997) (written before the Supreme Court's PAS decisions):

"Both courts and legislatures have played important roles in the development of contemporary American law regarding the 'right to die,' but many of the most significant first steps were taken by the courts [discussing, inter alia, *In re Quinlan*, 70 N.J. 10, 355 A.2d 647 (1976); *Superintendent of Belchertown State School v. Saikewicz*, 373 Mass. 728, 370 N.E.2d 417 (1977); *In re Conroy*, 98 N.J. 321, 486 A.2d 1209 (1985); and *Brophy v. New England Sinai Hospital*, 398 Mass. 417, 497 N.E.2d 626 (1986)].

"[Until the 1990s] the law of the right to die in New Jersey was governed entirely by principles and procedures developed by New Jersey courts, out of decisions in cases that cried out for recognition of a right to die on the facts presented. At each step along the way, the New Jersey Supreme Court described itself as being forced to act, at least in part, in the face of the legislature's failure to do so—going so far as to establish, on its own authority, the legality of living wills and durable powers of attorney for health care. [Even] in states where comprehensive right to die legislation has been enacted, courts have been required to fashion common law as part of the comprehensive package of rules governing the right to die.

"[The] various state supreme courts that have bottomed the right to die on various provisions of their state constitutions and the federal constitutions [have] continually urged the state legislatures to develop comprehensive rules for dealing with the issues that were raised. Indeed, as time has passed, the state supreme courts have emphasized the constitutional aspects less and have used state common law increasingly—in part, presumably, to provide a greater scope of experimentation for state legislatures. The New Jersey Supreme Court, for example, beginning [in 1985], has relied primarily upon the common law principles of informed consent, and only secondarily upon the constitutional right to privacy.

"[The] fears that have kept state legislatures from leading the way in developing the right to die law in the past still seem to haunt the corridors of our legislative assemblies. Oregon has thus far been the only state to legalize [PAS] by legislation, and that law was enacted through a citizen initiative vote—not by the normal legislative process."

5. *After Glucksberg and Quill, how will PAS proponents fare in the state courts? Krischer v. McIver,* 697 So.2d 97 (Fla. 1997), indicates that they may meet heavy resistance. About six months *before* the U.S. Supreme Court's decisions in the PAS cases, a Florida trial court held that a terminally ill AIDS patient was entitled, under the Privacy Amendment of the Florida Constitution, to determine the time and manner of his death and that, in order to do so, he had the right to seek and obtain the assistance of his physician in committing suicide. However, a few weeks *after* the U.S. Supreme Court's PAS decisions, the Florida Supreme Court reversed the trial court (5–1).

Since Florida's Privacy Amendment establishes a right much broader in scope than that of the U.S. Constitution, the Florida Supreme Court could have distinguished *Glucksberg* and *Quill* quite easily. Instead, however, the Court quoted at length from Rehnquist C.J.'s opinion in *Glucksberg* and from the New York Task Force Report on assisted suicide and euthanasia, a report that recommended unanimously that New York's total ban against assisted suicide and euthanasia be maintained. (Rehnquist, C.J., had also relied heavily on the New York report.) After balking at arguments frequently made by PAS proponents, the Florida Supreme Court concluded: "By broadly construing the privacy amendment to include the right to assisted suicide, we would run the risk of arrogating to ourselves those powers to make social policy that as a constitutional matter belong only to the legislature."

6. *The second-degree murder conviction of Dr. Kevorkian.* In March of 1999, after having assisted, by his own count, in over 100 suicides, and after been acquitted of assisted suicide in several previous cases, Dr. Jack Kevorkian was convicted of second-degree murder (and sentenced to 10 to 25 years in prison) for administering a lethal injection to Lou Gehrig's disease patient Thomas Youk. *The New York Times* editorialized, March 27, 1999, p. A26: "Most advocates of physician-assisted suicide hold as a first principle that the patient must be the one in full control. The Oregon laws that have legalized assisted suicide, for example, honor that principle. Dr. Kevorkian's mercy killing violates it. Previous juries have let him off the hook for assisting in suicides. But this jury drew the line at direct killing."

Is this the message of the Kevorkian conviction? How significant was it that a videotape of Kevorkian injecting Youk with a lethal dose was shown on CBS's "60 Minutes" in a segment in which Kevorkian dared prosecutors to charge him? How significant was it that the trial judge ruled that the issue of whether Mr. Youk consented to his death was irrelevant and that the jury never heard Youk's wife or mother or brother tell how grateful they were that Kevorkian was available? How significant was it that in all the previous cases Dr. Kevorkian had been represented by Geoffrey Fieger, a prominent trial attorney, but in the Youk case he represented himself?

Many opponents of assisted suicide applauded Kevorkian's conviction and hoped that it signaled a change in public attitude. However, as pointed out in Charles H. Baron, *Assisted Dying*, Trial, July 1999, at 44, recent opinion polls in the United States indicate that this is not so: "[These polls] show a high and increasing level of support for legalization and regulation of physician-assisted suicide. A Field poll taken after [Kevorkian's] conviction shows that support in California has increased in the last two years from 70 percent to 75 percent (from 61 percent to 68 percent among Roman Catholics). An ABC News poll showed that 55 percent of the public disagreed with the jury's verdict [in the trial of Dr. Kevorkian for the death of Mr. Youk], and only 39 percent agreed."

7.   The Supreme Court's rulings in *Glucksberg* and *Quill* have generated a considerable amount of commentary. See, e.g., *Symposium: Physician–Assisted Suicide: Facing Death after* Glucksberg *and* Quill, 82 Minn. L. Rev. 885–1101 (1998) (contributions by Howard Brody, Robert Burt, Ezekiel Emanual, Yale Kamisar, Patricia King, Sylvia Law, Kathryn Tucker, Leslie Wolf and Susan Wolf); Lawrence Gostin, note 1 supra; Martha Minow, *Which Question? Which Lie? Reflections on the Physician–Assisted Suicide Case*, 1997 Sup. Ct. Rev. 1; David Orentlicher, *The Supreme Court and Physician–Assisted Suicide—Rejecting Assisted Suicide, but Embracing Euthanasia*, 337 New Eng. J. Med. 1236 (1997); Note, 111 Harv. L. Rev. 237 (1997); Robert A Sedler, *Abortion, Physician–Assisted Suicide and the Constitution*, 12 Notre Dame J. L., Ethics & Pub. Policy 529 (1998); Sunstein, note 2 supra.

THE RIGHT TO TRAVEL

CON LAW: P. 555, add after note 4

RTS & LIB: P. 461, add after note 4

5.   *The three different components of the right to travel.* In SAENZ v. ROE, discussed at greater length at p. 128 of this Supplement, in the course of holding that state welfare programs may not restrict new residents, for the first year they live in the state, to the welfare benefits they would have received in the state of their prior residence, a 7–2 majority, per STEVENS, J., observed: "The 'right to travel' discussed in our cases embraces at least three different components. It protects the right of a citizen of one State to enter and to leave another State, the right to be treated as a welcome visitor rather than an unfriendly alien when temporarily present in the second State, and, for those travelers who elect to become permanent residents, the right to be treated like other citizens of that State. * * *

"What is at issue in this case [is the] third aspect of the right to travel—the right of the newly arrived citizen to the same privilege and immunities enjoyed by other citizens of the same State. That right is protected not only by the new arrival's status as a state citizen, but also by her status as a citizen of the United States. That additional source of protection is plainly identified in the opening words of the Fourteenth Amendment: ' * * * No State shall make or enforce any law which shall abridge the privileges or immunities of citizens of the United States.' Despite fundamentally differing views concerning the coverage of the Privileges or Immunities Clause of the Fourteenth Amendment, most notably expressed in the majority and dissenting opinions in the *Slaughter-House Cases*, it has always been common ground that this Clause protects the third component of the right to travel."

PROCEDURAL DUE PROCESS IN NON–CRIMINAL CASES

DEPRIVATION OF "LIBERTY" AND "PROPERTY" INTERESTS

CON LAW: P. 595, add after note 6 (b)

RTS & LIB: P. 502, add after note 6 (b)

(c) COLLEGE SAVINGS BANK v. FLORIDA PREPAID POSTSECONDARY EDUCATION EXPENSE BOARD, __ U.S. __, 119 S.Ct. 2219, __ L.Ed.2d __ (1999): Petitioner markets and sells certificates of deposit designed to finance college costs. When respondent, a Florida state entity, began its own tuition prepayment program, petitioner filed suit, alleging that by its false and misleading advertising respondent had violated the Lanham Act and that the Trademark Remedy Clarification Act (TRCA) had subjected states to suits brought under the Lanham Act. Congress's abrogation of sovereign immunity in the TRCA was effective, argued petitioner, since it was enacted to enforce the Fourteenth Amendment's Due Process Clause. The Court, per SCALIA, J., disagreed: "[The] object of valid [legislation under § 5 of the fourteenth amendment] must be the carefully delimited remediation or prevention of constitutional violations. Petitioner claims [that] Congress enacted the TRCA to remedy and prevent state deprivations without due process of two species of 'property' rights: (1) a right to be free from a business competitor's false advertising about its own product, and (2) a more generalized right to be secure in one's business interests. Neither of these qualifies as a property right protected by the Due Process Clause.

"As to the first: The hallmark of a protected property interest is the right to exclude others. [The] Lanham Act may well contain provisions that protect constitutionally cognizable property interests—notably, its provisions dealing with infringement of trademarks, which are the 'property' of the new owner because he can exclude others from using them. [The] Lanham Act's false-advertising provisions, however, bear no relationship to any right to exclude; and Florida Prepaid's alleged misrepresentations concerning its own products intruded upon no interest over which petitioner had exclusive dominion. * * *

"Petitioner's second assertion of a property interest rests upon an argument [that] businesses are 'property' within the meaning of the Due Process Clause, and that Congress legislates under § 5 when it passes a law that prevents state interference with business (which false advertising does). The assets of a business (including its good will) unquestionably are property, and any state taking of those assets is unquestionably a 'deprivation' under the Fourteenth Amendment. But business in the sense of the activity of doing business, or the activity of making a profit, is not property in the ordinary sense—and it is only that, and not any business asset, which is impinged upon by a competitor's false advertising."

Stevens, Souter, Ginsburg and Breyer, JJ., dissented from the Court's opinion, but only Stevens, J., expressed disagreement with this part.

CON LAW: P. 597, end of note 7

RTS & LIB: P. 504, end of note 7

It is not easy to reconcile KANSAS v. HENDRICKS, 521 U.S. 346, 117 S.Ct. 2072, 138 L.Ed.2d 501 (1997) with *Foucha*. In 1994, the year Hendricks was scheduled to complete his 10–year prison term for taking "indecent liberties" with two 13–year old boys, Kansas enacted the Sexually Violent Predators Act (SVPA), establishing procedures for civilly committing persons who, because of a "mental abnormality" or a "personality disorder," are likely to commit "predatory acts of sexual violence." The legislature explained in the preamble to the new law that it did not consider the existing involuntary civil commitment statute adequate to deal with SVPs because such persons "do not have a mental disease or defect that renders them appropriate for involuntary commitment." The Act was invoked for the first time against Hendricks, just before he was scheduled to be released from prison.

The state did not deny that Supreme Court precedents seemed to require that a person subject to civil commitment be "mentally ill," but argued that the Court had not constitutionalized any particular definition of the term. Hendricks, continued the state, was diagnosed as having pedophilia—a condition the psychiatric profession classifies as a "mental disorder" and a condition that Hendricks admitted made him unable to control the urge to molest children.

The Court, per THOMAS, J. (who had dissented in *Foucha*), concluded that the Kansas statute satisfied the "mental Illness" requirement, pointing out that no case had ever required state legislatures to adopt any particular nomenclature in drafting civil commitment statutes. Breyer, J., joined by Stevens, Souter, and Ginsburg, JJ., dissented on other grounds,[a] but supported the majority on the substantive due process issue. Hendricks's abnormality, emphasized Breyer, J., "does not consist simply of a long course of antisocial behavior, but rather it includes a specific, serious and highly unusual inability to control his actions. [The] law traditionally has considered this kind of abnormality akin to insanity for purposes of confinement."

CON LAW: P. 598, at end of note 8 (a)
RTS & LIB: P. 505, at end of note 8 (a)

How, if at all, can *College Savings Bank*, p. 55 of this Supplement, be reconciled with *Zimmerman Brush*?

a. Because the SVPA did not provide Hendricks (or others like him) any treatment until after he completed his prison term and only inadequate treatment then the dissenters maintained that the Act was really "an effort to inflict further punishment" upon Hendricks in violation of the Ex Post Facto Clause. However the majority rejected the ex post facto claim because it considered the SVPA civil in nature and confinement under it not tantamount to "punishment."

FREEDOM OF EXPRESSION
AND ASSOCIATION

REPUTATION AND PRIVACY

EMOTIONAL DISTRESS

CON LAW: P. 690, after note 1

AMER CON: P. 700, after note 1

RTS & LIB: P. 597, after note 1

SCHENCK v. PRO–CHOICE NETWORK OF WESTERN NEW YORK, 519 U.S. 357, 117 S.Ct. 855, 137 L.Ed.2d 1 (1997), per REHNQUIST, C.J., maintained that an injunction ordering abortion protesters to cease and desist from "counseling" women entering abortion clinics, who indicate they do not wish to be counseled, could not be sustained in order to protect privacy: "As [a] general matter, we have indicated that in public debate our own citizens must tolerate insulting, and often outrageous, speech in order to provide adequate breathing space to the freedoms protected by the First Amendment." [a]

DISCLOSURE OF PRIVATE FACTS

CON LAW: p. 696, after note 2

AMER CON: p. 706, after note 2

RTS & LIB: P. 603, after note 2

3. *Media ride-alongs.* WILSON v. LAYNE, ___ U.S. ___, 119 S.Ct. 1692, ___ L.Ed.2d ___ (1999), per REHNQUIST, C.J., held that privacy considerations outweighed the interests served by having *Washington Post* reporters accompany police in executing an arrest warrant in the home: "Respondents argue that the presence of the *Washington Post* reporters in the Wilsons' home [served] a number of legitimate law enforcement purposes. They first assert that officers should be able to exercise reasonable discretion about when it would 'further their law enforcement mission to permit members of the news media to accompany them in executing a warrant.' But this claim ignores the importance of the right of residential privacy at the core of the Fourth Amendment. It may well be that media ride-alongs further the law enforcement objectives of the police in a general

---

a. This portion of the injunction was sustained on other grounds. Demonstrators had previously engaged in physical intimidation against women and their escorts. The lower court ordered demonstrators to stay 15 feet away from doorways, driveways, and driveway entrances except for two sidewalk counselors in order to accommodate free speech rights. The Court observed that the counselors, if ordered to desist, and other demonstrators could present their messages outside the 15– foot buffer zone and that their consignment to that area was a result of their own previous intimidation. Agreeing with the Court that the privacy ground had no merit and finding no other basis in the lower court's findings to support the cease and desist rule (once the counselors had already been admitted within the 15–foot zone), Scalia, J., joined by Kennedy and Thomas, JJ., dissenting would have upheld this portion of the injunction.

sense, but that is not the same as furthering the purposes of the search. Were such generalized 'law enforcement objectives' themselves sufficient to trump the Fourth Amendment, the protections guaranteed by that Amendment's text would be significantly watered down.

"Respondents next argue that the presence of third parties could serve the law enforcement purpose of publicizing the government's efforts to combat crime, and facilitate accurate reporting on law enforcement activities. There is certainly language in our opinions interpreting the First Amendment which points to the importance of 'the press' in informing the general public about the administration of criminal justice. *Cox Broadcasting.* [No] one could gainsay the truth of these observations, or the importance of the First Amendment in protecting press freedom from abridgement by the government. But the Fourth Amendment also protects a very important right, and in the present case it is in terms of that right that the media ride-alongs must be judged.

"Surely the possibility of good public relations for the police is simply not enough, standing alone, to justify the ride-along intrusion into a private home. And even the need for accurate reporting on police issues in general bears no direct relation to the constitutional justification for the police intrusion into a home in order to execute a felony arrest warrant.

"Finally, respondents argue that the presence of third parties could serve in some situations to minimize police abuses and protect suspects, and also to protect the safety of the officers. While it might be reasonable for police officers to themselves videotape home entries as part of a 'quality control' effort to ensure that the rights of homeowners are being respected, or even to preserve evidence, such a situation is significantly different from the media presence in this case. The *Washington Post* reporters in the Wilsons' home were working on a story for their own purposes. They were not present for the purpose of protecting the officers, much less the Wilsons. A private photographer was acting for private purposes, as evidenced in part by the fact that the newspaper and not the police retained the photographs. Thus, although the presence of third parties during the execution of a warrant may in some circumstances be constitutionally permissible, the presence of these third parties was not.

"The reasons advanced by respondents, taken in their entirety, fall short of justifying the presence of media inside a home. We hold that it is a violation of the Fourth Amendment for police to bring members of the media or other third parties into a home during the execution of a warrant when the presence of the third parties in the home was not in aid of the execution of the warrant."[a]

SHOULD NEW CATEGORIES BE CREATED?

HARM TO CHILDREN AND THE OVERBREADTH DOCTRINE

CON LAW: P. 737, add to fn. 26

AMER CON: P. 747, add to fn. 26

RTS & LIB: P. 644, add to note fn. 26

[Scalia, J., dissenting in *Chicago v. Morales*, ___ U.S. ___, 119 S.Ct. 1849, ___ L.Ed.2d ___ (1999), argues that in order to avoid advisory opinions, federal courts should limit themselves to as applied attacks, but that if they insist on considering

---

a. Stevens, J., concurring in part and dissenting in part, agreed that media ride-alongs violated the fourth amendment, but dissented on a different issue.

facial attacks, they should insist that a statute be unconstitutional in all its applications before declaring it unconstitutional. Are either of these positions acceptable?]

IS SOME PROTECTED SPEECH LESS EQUAL THAN OTHER PROTECTED SPEECH?

COMMERCIAL SPEECH

CON LAW: P. 822, substitute for Central Hudson, Posadas, and notes thereafter

AMER CON: P. 832, after note 5

RTS & LIB: P. 729, substitute for Central Hudson, Posadas, and notes thereafter

44 LIQUORMART, INC. v. RHODE ISLAND

517 U.S. 484, 116 S.Ct. 1495, 134 L.Ed.2d 711 (1996).

JUSTICE STEVENS announced the judgment of the Court and delivered the opinion of the Court with respect to Parts I, II, VII,[a] and VIII,[b] an opinion with respect to Parts III and V, in which JUSTICE KENNEDY, JUSTICE SOUTER, and JUSTICE GINSBURG join, an opinion with respect to Part VI, in which JUSTICE KENNEDY, JUSTICE THOMAS, and JUSTICE GINSBURG join, and an opinion with respect to Part IV, in which JUSTICE KENNEDY and JUSTICE GINSBURG join. * * *

I

In 1956, the Rhode Island Legislature enacted two separate prohibitions against advertising the retail price of alcoholic beverages. The first applies to vendors licensed in Rhode Island as well as to out-of-state manufacturers, wholesalers, and shippers. It prohibits them from "advertising in any manner whatsoever" the price of any alcoholic beverage offered for sale in the State; the only exception is for price tags or signs displayed with the merchandise within licensed premises and not visible from the street. The second statute applies to the Rhode Island news media. It contains a categorical prohibition against the publication or broadcast of any advertisements—even those referring to sales in other States—that "make reference to the price of any alcoholic beverages." * * *

III

Advertising has been a part of our culture throughout our history. Even in colonial days, the public relied on "commercial speech" for vital information about the market. Early newspapers displayed advertisements for goods and services on their front pages, and town criers called out prices in public squares. Indeed, commercial messages played such a central role in public life prior to the Founding that Benjamin Franklin authored his early defense of a free press in support of his decision to print, of all things, an advertisement for voyages to Barbados.

In accord with the role that commercial messages have long played, the law has developed to ensure that advertising provides consumers with accurate

---

a. Scalia, Kennedy, Souter, Thomas, and Ginsburg, JJ., joined parts I, II, and VII of the Stevens, J., opinion. Section VII concluded that the twenty-first amendment does not qualify the first. The same conclusion was reached in O'Connor, J.'s concurring opinion joined by Rehnquist, C.J., Souter and Breyer, JJ.

b. Scalia, Kennedy, Souter, and Ginsburg, JJ., joined part VIII of the Stevens, J.'s opinion.

information about the availability of goods and services. In the early years, the common law, and later, statutes, served the consumers' interest in the receipt of accurate information in the commercial market by prohibiting fraudulent and misleading advertising. It was not until the 1970's, however, that this Court held that the First Amendment protected the dissemination of truthful and nonmisleading commercial messages about lawful products and services. See generally Alex Kozinski & Stuart Banner, *The Anti–History and Pre–History of Commercial Speech*, 71 Texas L.Rev. 747 (1993). * * *

[O]ur early cases uniformly struck down several broadly based bans on truthful, nonmisleading commercial speech, each of which served ends unrelated to consumer protection.[8] Indeed, one of those cases [*Linmark*] expressly likened the rationale that *Virginia Pharmacy Bd.* employed to the one that Justice Brandeis adopted in his concurrence in *Whitney v. California*[:] "the remedy to be applied is more speech, not enforced silence. Only an emergency can justify repression." * * *

At the same time, our early cases recognized that the State may regulate some types of commercial advertising more freely than other forms of protected speech. * * *

In *Central Hudson Gas & Elec. Corp. v. Public Serv. Comm'n of N.Y.*, 447 U.S. 557, 100 S.Ct. 2343, 65 L.Ed.2d 341 (1980), we took stock of our developing commercial speech jurisprudence. In that case, we considered a regulation "completely" banning all promotional advertising by electric utilities. Our decision acknowledged the special features of commercial speech but identified the serious First Amendment concerns that attend blanket advertising prohibitions that do not protect consumers from commercial harms.[c]

Five Members of the Court recognized that the state interest in the conservation of energy was substantial, and that there was "an immediate connection between advertising and demand for electricity." Nevertheless, they concluded that the regulation was invalid because the Commission had failed to make a showing that a more limited speech regulation would not have adequately served the State's interest.[9]

In reaching its conclusion, the majority explained that although the special nature of commercial speech may require less than strict review of its regulation, special concerns arise from "regulations that entirely suppress commercial speech in order to pursue a nonspeech-related policy." *Id.* n. 9. In those circumstances,

8. See *Bates* (ban on lawyer advertising); *Carey* (ban on contraceptive advertising); *Linmark* (ban on "For Sale" signs); *Virginia Bd. of Pharmacy* (ban on prescription drug prices); *Bigelow* (ban on abortion advertising). Although *Linmark* involved a prohibition against a particular means of advertising the sale of one's home, we treated the restriction as if it were a complete ban because it did not leave open "satisfactory" alternative channels of communication.

c. *Central Hudson* referred to commercial speech as "expression related solely to the economic interests of the speaker and its audience." Was the speech in *Central Hudson* solely in the economic interests of the speaker and its audience? Is the *Central Hudson* locution broader or narrower than the category of promoting a commercial transaction? Reconsider this question in connection with the Greenmoss case, CON LAW, p. 832; AMER CON, p. 832; RTS & LIB, p. 739.

9. In other words, the regulation failed the fourth step in the four-part inquiry that the majority announced in its opinion. It wrote: "In commercial speech cases, then, a four-part analysis has developed. At the outset, we must determine whether the expression is protected by the First Amendment. For commercial speech to come within that provision, it at least must concern lawful activity and not be misleading. Next, we ask whether the asserted governmental interest is substantial. If both inquiries yield positive answers, we must determine whether the regulation directly advances the governmental interest asserted, and whether it is not more extensive than is necessary to serve that interest."

"a ban on speech could screen from public view the underlying governmental policy." As a result, the Court concluded that "special care" should attend the review of such blanket bans, and it pointedly remarked that "in recent years this Court has not approved a blanket ban on commercial speech unless the speech itself was flawed in some way, either because it was deceptive or related to unlawful activity."[10]

IV

[W]hen a State entirely prohibits the dissemination of truthful, nonmisleading commercial messages for reasons unrelated to the preservation of a fair bargaining process, there is far less reason to depart from the rigorous review that the First Amendment generally demands. * * *

The special dangers that attend complete bans on truthful, nonmisleading commercial speech cannot be explained away by appeals to the "commonsense distinctions" that exist between commercial and noncommercial speech. Regulations that suppress the truth are no less troubling because they target objectively verifiable information, nor are they less effective because they aim at durable messages. As a result, neither the "greater objectivity" nor the "greater hardiness" of truthful, nonmisleading commercial speech justifies reviewing its complete suppression with added deference. * * *

Precisely because bans against truthful, nonmisleading commercial speech rarely seek to protect consumers from either deception or overreaching, they usually rest solely on the offensive assumption that the public will respond "irrationally" to the truth. The First Amendment directs us to be especially skeptical of regulations that seek to keep people in the dark for what the government perceives to be their own good.

V

[Although] the record suggests that the price advertising ban may have some impact on the purchasing patterns of temperate drinkers of modest means, the State has presented no evidence to suggest that its speech prohibition will significantly reduce market-wide consumption. Indeed, the District Court's considered and uncontradicted finding on this point is directly to the contrary. Moreover, the evidence suggests that the abusive drinker will probably not be deterred by a marginal price increase, and that the true alcoholic may simply reduce his purchases of other necessities. * * *

As is evident, any conclusion that elimination of the ban would significantly increase alcohol consumption would require us to engage in the sort of "speculation or conjecture" that is an unacceptable means of demonstrating that a restriction on commercial speech directly advances the State's asserted interest. Such speculation certainly does not suffice when the State takes aim at accurate commercial information for paternalistic ends.

The State also cannot satisfy the requirement that its restriction on speech be no more extensive than necessary. It is perfectly obvious that alternative forms of regulation that would not involve any restriction on speech would be more likely to achieve the State's goal of promoting temperance. As the State's own expert conceded, higher prices can be maintained either by direct regulation or by

---

10. The Justices concurring in the judgment adopted a somewhat broader view. They expressed "doubt whether suppression of information concerning the availability and price of a legally offered product is ever a permissible way for the State to 'dampen' the demand for or use of the product." Indeed, Justice Blackmun believed that even "though 'commercial' speech is involved, such a regulation strikes at the heart of the First Amendment."

increased taxation. Per capita purchases could be limited as is the case with prescription drugs. Even educational campaigns focused on the problems of excessive, or even moderate, drinking might prove to be more effective.

As a result, even under the less than strict standard that generally applies in commercial speech cases, the State has failed to establish a "reasonable fit" between its abridgment of speech and its temperance goal. *Board of Trustees v. Fox*, 492 U.S. 469, 109 S.Ct. 3028, 106 L.Ed.2d 388 (1989);[d] see also *Rubin v. Coors Brewing Co.*, 514 U.S. 476, 115 S.Ct. 1585, 131 L.Ed.2d 532 (1995)(explaining that defects in a federal ban on alcohol advertising are "further highlighted by the availability of alternatives that would prove less intrusive to the First Amendment's protections for commercial speech").[e] It necessarily follows that the price advertising ban cannot survive the more stringent constitutional review that *Central Hudson* itself concluded was appropriate for the complete suppression of truthful, nonmisleading commercial speech.

VI

The State responds by arguing that it merely exercised appropriate "legislative judgment" in determining that a price advertising ban would best promote temperance. Relying on the *Central Hudson* analysis set forth in *Posadas de Puerto Rico Associates v. Tourism Co. of P. R.*, 478 U.S. 328, 106 S.Ct. 2968, 92 L.Ed.2d 266 (1986), and *United States v. Edge Broadcasting Co.*, 509 U.S. 418, 113 S.Ct. 2696, 125 L.Ed.2d 345 (1993), Rhode Island first argues that, because expert opinions as to the effectiveness of the price advertising ban "go both ways," the Court of Appeals correctly concluded that the ban constituted a "reasonable choice" by the legislature. The State next contends that precedent requires us to give particular deference to that legislative choice because the State could, if it chose, ban the sale of alcoholic beverages outright. See *Posadas*. Finally, the State argues that deference is appropriate because alcoholic beverages are so-called "vice" products. We consider each of these contentions in turn.

The State's first argument fails to justify the speech prohibition at issue. Our commercial speech cases recognize some room for the exercise of legislative judgment. See *Metromedia*. However, Rhode Island errs in concluding that *Edge* and *Posadas* establish the degree of deference that its decision to impose a price advertising ban warrants.

d. *Fox*, per Scalia, J., joined by Rehnquist, C.J., White, Stevens, O'Connor, and Kennedy, JJ., in the course of considering a provision that operated to bar commercial organizations from making sales demonstrations in students' dormitory rooms, held that the *Central Hudson* test did not require government to foreclose the possibility of all less restrictive alternatives. The university sought to promote an educational rather than a commercial atmosphere and to prevent commercial exploitation. Scalia, J., characterized these interests as substantial, but stated that it was enough if the fit between means and ends were "reasonable." It did not need to be "perfect." Like time, place, and manner regulations, however, the relationship between means and ends had to be "narrowly tailored to achieve the desired objective." Under that standard, as interpreted (see *Ward*, CON LAW, p. 894; AMER CON, p.

894; RTS & LIB, p. 801), government may not " 'burden substantially more speech than is necessary to further the government's legitimate interest,' " but need not foreclose "all conceivable alternatives." Scalia, J., argued that to have a more demanding test in commercial speech than that used for time, place, and manner regulations would be inappropriate because time, place, and manner regulations can apply to political speech.

e. *Rubin* held that a federal provision prohibiting the display of alcoholic content on beer labels violated the first amendment. The Court argued among other things that the overall federal scheme was irrational in that it prohibited alcoholic beverage advertising from mentioning alcoholic content in many circumstances and required disclosures of alcoholic content in the labeling of wines in some circumstances.

In *Edge*, we upheld a federal statute that permitted only those broadcasters located in States that had legalized lotteries to air lottery advertising. The statute was designed to regulate advertising about an activity that had been deemed illegal in the jurisdiction in which the broadcaster was located. Here, by contrast, the commercial speech ban targets information about entirely lawful behavior.[f]

Posadas is more directly relevant. There, a five-Member majority held that, under the *Central Hudson* test, it was "up to the legislature" to choose to reduce gambling by suppressing in-state casino advertising rather than engaging in educational speech. Rhode Island argues that this logic demonstrates the constitutionality of its own decision to ban price advertising in lieu of raising taxes or employing some other less speech-restrictive means of promoting temperance.

The reasoning in *Posadas* does support the State's argument, but, on reflection, we are now persuaded that *Posadas* erroneously performed the First Amendment analysis. The casino advertising ban was designed to keep truthful, nonmisleading speech from members of the public for fear that they would be more likely to gamble if they received it. * * *

Because the 5-to-4 decision in *Posadas* marked such a sharp break from our prior precedent, and because it concerned a constitutional question about which this Court is the final arbiter, we decline to give force to its highly deferential approach.

Instead, in keeping with our prior holdings, we conclude that a state legislature does not have the broad discretion to suppress truthful, nonmisleading information for paternalistic purposes that the *Posadas* majority was willing to tolerate. * * *

We also cannot accept the State's second contention, which is premised entirely on the "greater-includes-the-lesser" reasoning endorsed toward the end of the majority's opinion in *Posadas*. * * * The majority concluded that it would "surely be a strange constitutional doctrine which would concede to the legislature the authority to totally ban a product or activity, but deny to the legislature the authority to forbid the stimulation of demand for the product or activity through advertising on behalf of those who would profit from such increased demand." * * *

Although we do not dispute the proposition that greater powers include lesser ones, we fail to see how that syllogism requires the conclusion that the State's power to regulate commercial activity is "greater" than its power to ban truthful, nonmisleading commercial speech. Contrary to the assumption made in *Posadas*, we think it quite clear that banning speech may sometimes prove far more intrusive than banning conduct. As a venerable proverb teaches, it may prove more injurious to prevent people from teaching others how to fish than to prevent fish from being sold.[19] Similarly, a local ordinance banning bicycle lessons may

---

f. *Edge* upheld federal legislation prohibiting the broadcast of lottery advertising if the broadcaster were located in a state that does not permit lotteries even in circumstances where 92% of the broadcaster's audience resided in a state that permitted lotteries and where the advertisement was for the lottery in the state where it was legal.

Greater New Orleans Broadcasting v. United States, ___ U.S. ___, 119 S.Ct. 1923, ___ L.Ed.2d. ___ (1999), held that the congressional ban on the broadcasting of lottery information could not constitutionally be applied to advertisements of casino gambling when the broadcaster was located in a state where such gambling was legal. In addition, as in *Rubin,* fn. e, the Court objected to the lack of rationale for many of the exceptions to the legislation.

19. "Give a man a fish, and you feed him for a day. Teach a man to fish, and you feed him for a lifetime." *The International Thesaurus of Quotations* 646 (compiled by R. Tripp 1970).

curtail freedom far more than one that prohibits bicycle riding within city limits. In short, we reject the assumption that words are necessarily less vital to freedom than actions, or that logic somehow proves that the power to prohibit an activity is necessarily "greater" than the power to suppress speech about it.

As a matter of First Amendment doctrine, the *Posadas* syllogism is even less defensible. The text of the First Amendment makes clear that the Constitution presumes that attempts to regulate speech are more dangerous than attempts to regulate conduct.

[J]ust as it is perfectly clear that Rhode Island could not ban all obscene liquor ads except those that advocated temperance, we think it equally clear that its power to ban the sale of liquor entirely does not include a power to censor all advertisements that contain accurate and nonmisleading information about the price of the product. As the entire Court apparently now agrees, the statements in the *Posadas* opinion on which Rhode Island relies are no longer persuasive.

Finally, we find unpersuasive the State's contention that, under *Posadas* and *Edge*, the price advertising ban should be upheld because it targets commercial speech that pertains to a "vice" activity.

[T]he scope of any "vice" exception to the protection afforded by the First Amendment would be difficult, if not impossible, to define. Almost any product that poses some threat to public health or public morals might reasonably be characterized by a state legislature as relating to "vice activity". Such characterization, however, is anomalous when applied to products such as alcoholic beverages, lottery tickets, or playing cards, that may be lawfully purchased on the open market. The recognition of such an exception would also have the unfortunate consequence of either allowing state legislatures to justify censorship by the simple expedient of placing the "vice" label on selected lawful activities, or requiring the federal courts to establish a federal common law of vice. * * *

VIII

Because Rhode Island has failed to carry its heavy burden of justifying its complete ban on price advertising, we conclude that R.I. Gen. Laws §§ 3–8–7 and 3–8–8.1, as well as Regulation 32 of the Rhode Island Liquor Control Administration, abridge speech in violation of the First Amendment as made applicable to the States by the Due Process Clause of the Fourteenth Amendment. * * *

JUSTICE SCALIA, concurring in part and concurring in the judgment.

I share Justice Thomas's discomfort with the *Central Hudson* test, which seems to me to have nothing more than policy intuition to support it. I also share Justice Stevens' aversion towards paternalistic governmental policies that prevent men and women from hearing facts that might not be good for them. On the other hand, it would also be paternalism for us to prevent the people of the States from enacting laws that we consider paternalistic, unless we have good reason to believe that the Constitution itself forbids them. I will take my guidance as to what the Constitution forbids, with regard to a text as indeterminate as the First Amendment's preservation of "the freedom of speech," and where the core offense of suppressing particular political ideas is not at issue, from the long accepted practices of the American people.

The briefs and arguments of the parties in the present case provide no illumination on that point; understandably so, since both sides accepted *Central Hudson*. The amicus brief on behalf of the American Advertising Federation et al. did examine various expressions of view at the time the First Amendment was adopted; they are consistent with First Amendment protection for commercial speech, but certainly not dispositive. I consider more relevant the state legislative practices prevalent at the time the First Amendment was adopted, since almost all of the States had free-speech constitutional guarantees of their own, whose meaning was not likely to have been different from the federal constitutional provision derived from them. Perhaps more relevant still are the state legislative practices at the time the Fourteenth Amendment was adopted, since it is most improbable that that adoption was meant to overturn any existing national consensus regarding free speech. Indeed, it is rare that any nationwide practice would develop contrary to a proper understanding of the First Amendment itself— for which reason I think also relevant any national consensus that had formed regarding state regulation of advertising after the Fourteenth Amendment, and before this Court's entry into the field. The parties and their amici provide no evidence on these points.

Since I do not believe we have before us the wherewithal to declare *Central Hudson* wrong—or at least the wherewithal to say what ought to replace it—I must resolve this case in accord with our existing jurisprudence, which [would] prohibit the challenged regulation. * * * [A]ccordingly [I] join Parts I, II, VII, and VIII of Justice Stevens' opinion.

Justice Thomas, concurring in Parts I, II, VI, and VII, and concurring in the judgment.

In cases such as this, in which the government's asserted interest is to keep legal users of a product or service ignorant in order to manipulate their choices in the marketplace, the balancing test adopted in *Central Hudson* should not be applied, in my view. Rather, such an "interest" is per se illegitimate and can no more justify regulation of "commercial" speech than it can justify regulation of "noncommercial" speech. * * *

Although the Court took a sudden turn away from *Virginia Pharmacy Bd.* in *Central Hudson*, it has never explained why manipulating the choices of consumers by keeping them ignorant is more legitimate when the ignorance is maintained through suppression of "commercial" speech than when the same ignorance is maintained through suppression of "noncommercial" speech. * * *

Justice O'Connor, with whom The Chief Justice, Justice Souter, and Justice Breyer join, concurring in the judgment. * * *

I agree with the Court that Rhode Island's price-advertising ban is invalid. I would resolve this case more narrowly, however, by applying our established *Central Hudson* test to determine whether this commercial-speech regulation survives First Amendment scrutiny. * * *

The fit between Rhode Island's method and [its goal of reducing consumption] is not reasonable. If the target is simply higher prices generally to discourage consumption, the regulation imposes too great, and unnecessary, a prohibition on speech in order to achieve it. The State has other methods at its disposal— methods that would more directly accomplish this stated goal without intruding on sellers' ability to provide truthful, nonmisleading information to customers. * * * A tax, for example, is not normally very difficult to administer and would have a far more certain and direct effect on prices, without any restriction on speech. The principal opinion suggests further alternatives, such as limiting per capita purchases or conducting an educational campaign about the dangers of alcohol consumption. The ready availability of such alternatives—at least some of which would far more effectively achieve Rhode Island's only professed goal, at comparatively small additional administrative cost—demonstrates that the fit between ends and means is not narrowly tailored. Too, this regulation prevents sellers of alcohol from communicating price information anywhere but at the point of purchase. No channels exist at all to permit them to publicize the price of their products.

Respondents point for support to *Posadas*. The closer look that we have required since *Posadas* comports better with the purpose of the analysis set out in *Central Hudson*, by requiring the State to show that the speech restriction directly advances its interest and is narrowly tailored. Under such a closer look, Rhode Island's price-advertising ban clearly fails to pass muster.

Because Rhode Island's regulation fails even the less stringent standard set out in *Central Hudson*, nothing here requires adoption of a new analysis for the evaluation of commercial speech regulation. [Because] we need go no further, I would not here undertake the question whether the test we have employed since *Central Hudson* should be displaced. * * *

CONCEIVING AND RECONCEIVING THE STRUCTURE OF FIRST AMENDMENT DOCTRINE: HATE SPEECH REVISITED—AGAIN

CON LAW: P. 850, add to note 3

AMER CON: P. 849, add to note 3

RTS & LIB: P. 757, add to note 3

See also *Davis v. Monroe County Board of Educ.*, ___ U.S. ___, 119 S.Ct. 1661, ___ L.Ed.2d ___ (1999) (Kennedy, J., dissenting).

FAIR ADMINISTRATION OF JUSTICE AND THE FIRST AMENDMENT AS SWORD

JUSTICE AND THE FIRST AMENDMENT AS SWORD

CON LAW: P. 890, add to note 2

AMER CON: P. 880, add to note 2

RTS & LIB: P. 797, add to note 2

For the conclusion that the police may generally not invite members of the media to accompany them in executing an arrest warrant in the home without violating the fourth amendment, see *Wilson v. Layne*, ___ U.S. ___, 119 S.Ct. 1692, ___ L.Ed.2d ___ (1999).

GOVERNMENT PROPERTY AND THE PUBLIC FORUM

FOUNDATION CASES

MANDATORY ACCESS

CON LAW: P. 894, add to note 3

AMER CON: P. 883, add to note 3

RTS & LIB: P. 801, add to note 3

CHICAGO v. MORALES, ___ U.S. ___, 119 S.Ct. 1849, ___ L.Ed.2d. ___ (1999), per STEVENS, J., joined by Souter and Ginsburg, JJ., in dictum contended that an ordinance ordering street gang members and associates loitering in a public place to disperse upon an officer's order did not violate the first amendment although it was void for vagueness under the due process clause: "Because the term 'loiter' is defined as remaining in one place 'with no apparent purpose,' it is [clear] that it does not prohibit any form of conduct that is apparently intended to convey a message. By its terms, the ordinance is inapplicable to assemblies that are designed to demonstrate a group's support of, or opposition to, a particular point of view. Its impact on the social contact between gang members and others does not impair the First Amendment 'right of association' that our cases have recognized."[b]

GOVERNMENT SUPPORT OF SPEECH

SUBSIDIES AND TAX EXPENDITURES

CON LAW: P. 921, after note 4

AMER CON: P. 906, after note 4

RTS & LIB: P. 828, after note 4

In 1989 the National Endowment for the Arts ("NEA") supported two artists whose work sparked controversy: Robert Mapplethorpe's exhibit, *The Perfect Moment*, included homoerotic photographs; Andres Serrano's photograph, *Piss Christ*, showed a crucifix immersed in urine. In reaction, Congress reduced appropriations in 1990 by the amount that had been granted to the two recipients and took a number of steps leading up to the passage of Title 20 U.S.C. § 954(d) which provided that, "No payment shall be made under this section except upon application therefor which is submitted to the National Endowment for the Arts in accordance with regulations issued and procedures established by the Chairperson. In establishing such regulations and procedures, the Chairperson shall ensure that (1) artistic excellence and artistic merit are the criteria by which applications are judged, taking into consideration general standards of decency and respect for the diverse beliefs and values of the American public; and (2) applications are consistent with the purposes of this section. Such regulations and procedures shall clearly indicate that obscenity is without artistic merit, is not protected speech, and shall not be funded."

The National Council on the Arts which advises the NEA Chairperson resolved to implement the provision by ensuring that the panels conducting initial

---

b. Breyer, Kennedy, and O'Connor, JJ., in separate concurring opinions agreed with Stevens, J.'s vagueness conclusion, but did not address the first amendment question. Scalia, J., and Thomas, J., joined by Rehnquist, C.J. and Scalia, J., dissented on the vagueness issue, but agreed with the conclusion that no first amendment right was at stake.

reviews of grant applications represent geographic, ethnic, and aesthetic diversity, and the Chairperson agreed. Several artists, whose grant applications had been approved before the passage of § 954(d), but reconsidered and denied afterwards, brought suit, challenging § 954(d)(1) on its face. The district court and the court of appeals declared § 954(d)(1) unconstitutional.

NATIONAL ENDOWMENT FOR THE ARTS v. FINLEY, 524 U.S. 569, 118 S.Ct. 2168, 141 L.Ed.2d 500 (1998), per O'CONNOR, J., joined by Rehnquist, C.J., and Stevens, Kennedy, and Breyer, JJ.,[a] upheld § 954(d)(1) maintaining that it did not impermissibly discriminate on the basis of point of view and was not unconstitutionally vague: "Respondents argue that the provision is a paradigmatic example of viewpoint discrimination because it rejects any artistic speech that either fails to respect mainstream values or offends standards of decency. The premise of respondents' claim is that § 954(d)(1) constrains the agency's ability to fund certain categories of artistic expression. The NEA, however, reads the provision as merely hortatory, and contends that it stops well short of an absolute restriction. Section 954(d)(1) adds 'considerations' to the grant-making process; it does not preclude awards to projects that might be deemed 'indecent' or 'disrespectful,' nor place conditions on grants, or even specify that those factors must be given any particular weight in reviewing an application. Indeed, the agency asserts that it has adequately implemented § 954(d)(1) merely by ensuring the representation of various backgrounds and points of view on the advisory panels that analyze grant applications. We do not decide whether the NEA's view—that the formulation of diverse advisory panels is sufficient to comply with Congress' command—is in fact a reasonable reading of the statute. It is clear, however, that the text of § 954(d)(1) imposes no categorical requirement. The advisory language stands in sharp contrast to congressional efforts to prohibit the funding of certain classes of speech. When Congress has in fact intended to affirmatively constrain the NEA's grant-making authority, it has done so in no uncertain terms. See § 954(d)(2) ('[O]bscenity is without artistic merit, is not protected speech, and shall not be funded').

"Furthermore, like the plain language of § 954(d), the political context surrounding the adoption of the 'decency and respect' clause is inconsistent with respondents' assertion that the provision compels the NEA to deny funding on the basis of viewpoint discriminatory criteria. The legislation was a bipartisan proposal introduced as a counterweight to amendments aimed at eliminating the NEA's funding or substantially constraining its grant-making authority. [B]efore the vote on § 954(d)(1), one of its sponsors stated: 'If we have done one important thing in this amendment, it is this. We have maintained the integrity of freedom of expression in the United States.'

"That § 954(d)(1) admonishes the NEA merely to take 'decency and respect' into consideration, and that the legislation was aimed at reforming procedures rather than precluding speech, undercut respondents' argument that the provision inevitably will be utilized as a tool for invidious viewpoint discrimination.

"Respondents' claim that the provision is facially unconstitutional may be reduced to the argument that the criteria in § 954(d)(1) are sufficiently subjective that the agency could utilize them to engage in viewpoint discrimination. Given the varied interpretations of the criteria and the vague exhortation to 'take them

a. Ginsburg, J., also joined O'Connor, J.'s opinion except for the paragraph accompanying footnote b infra.

into consideration,' it seems unlikely that this provision will introduce any greater element of selectivity than the determination of 'artistic excellence' itself. * * *

"Any content-based considerations that may be taken into account in the grant-making process are a consequence of the nature of arts funding. The NEA has limited resources and it must deny the majority of the grant applications that it receives, including many that propose 'artistically excellent' projects. The agency may decide to fund particular projects for a wide variety of reasons, 'such as the technical proficiency of the artist, the creativity of the work, the anticipated public interest in or appreciation of the work, the work's contemporary relevance, its educational value, its suitability for or appeal to special audiences (such as children or the disabled), its service to a rural or isolated community, or even simply that the work could increase public knowledge of an art form.'

"Respondent's reliance on our decision in *Rosenberger v. Rector and Visitors of Univ. of Va.*, 515 U.S. 819, 115 S.Ct. 2510, 132 L.Ed.2d 700 (1995), is therefore misplaced. In *Rosenberger*, a public university declined to authorize disbursements from its Student Activities Fund to finance the printing of a Christian student newspaper. We held that by subsidizing the Student Activities Fund, the University had created a limited public forum, from which it impermissibly excluded all publications with religious editorial viewpoints. Although the scarcity of NEA funding does not distinguish this case from *Rosenberger*, the competitive process according to which the grants are allocated does. In the context of arts funding, in contrast to many other subsidies, the Government does not indiscriminately 'encourage a diversity of views from private speakers.' The NEA's mandate is to make aesthetic judgments, and the inherently content-based 'excellence' threshold for NEA support sets it apart from the subsidy at issue in *Rosenberger*—which was available to all student organizations that were 'related to the educational purpose of the University' —and from comparably objective decisions on allocating public benefits, such as access to a school auditorium or a municipal theater, see *Lamb's Chapel v. Center Moriches Union Free School Dist.*, 508 U.S. 384, 386, 113 S.Ct. 2141, 124 L.Ed.2d 352 (1993); *Southeastern Promotions, Ltd. v. Conrad*, 420 U.S. 546, 555, 95 S.Ct. 1239, 43 L.Ed.2d 448 (1975), or the second class mailing privileges available to 'all newspapers and other periodical publications,' see *Hannegan v. Esquire, Inc.*, 327 U.S. 146, 148, n. 1, 66 S.Ct. 456, 90 L.Ed. 586 (1946).

"Respondents do not allege discrimination in any particular funding decision. * * * Thus, we have no occasion here to address an as-applied challenge in a situation where the denial of a grant may be shown to be the product of invidious viewpoint discrimination. If the NEA were to leverage its power to award subsidies on the basis of subjective criteria into a penalty on disfavored viewpoints, then we would confront a different case. We have stated that, even in the provision of subsidies, the Government may not 'ai[m] at the suppression of dangerous ideas,'and if a subsidy were 'manipulated' to have a 'coercive effect,' then relief could be appropriate. * * * Unless and until § 954(d)(1) is applied in a manner that raises concern about the suppression of disfavored viewpoints, however, we uphold the constitutionality of the provision.

"Finally, although the First Amendment certainly has application in the subsidy context, we note that the Government may allocate competitive funding according to criteria that would be impermissible were direct regulation of speech or a criminal penalty at stake. So long as legislation does not infringe on other constitutionally protected rights, Congress has wide latitude to set spending priorities. See *Regan v. Taxation with Representation of Wash.*, 461 U.S. 540, 549,

103 S.Ct. 1997, 76 L.Ed.2d 129 (1983). In the 1990 Amendments that incorporated § 954(d)(1), Congress modified the declaration of purpose in the NEA's enabling act to provide that arts funding should 'contribute to public support and confidence in the use of taxpayer funds,' and that '[p]ublic funds [must] ultimately serve public purposes the Congress defines.' § 951(5). And as we held in *Rust*, Congress may 'selectively fund a program to encourage certain activities it believes to be in the public interest, without at the same time funding an alternative program which seeks to deal with the problem in another way.' In doing so, 'the Government has not discriminated on the basis of viewpoint; it has merely chosen to fund one activity to the exclusion of the other.'[b]

"The lower courts also erred in invalidating § 954(d)(1) as unconstitutionally vague. * * * The terms of the provision are undeniably opaque, and if they appeared in a criminal statute or regulatory scheme, they could raise substantial vagueness concerns. It is unlikely, however, that speakers will be compelled to steer too far clear of any 'forbidden area' in the context of grants of this nature. But when the Government is acting as patron rather than as sovereign, the consequences of imprecision are not constitutionally severe.

"In the context of selective subsidies, it is not always feasible for Congress to legislate with clarity. Indeed, if this statute is unconstitutionally vague, then so too are all government programs awarding scholarships and grants on the basis of subjective criteria such as 'excellence.' To accept respondents' vagueness argument would be to call into question the constitutionality of these valuable government programs and countless others like them.

"Section 954(d)(1) merely adds some imprecise considerations to an already subjective selection process. It does not, on its face, impermissibly infringe on First or Fifth Amendment rights."

Scalia, J., joined by Thomas, J., concurred in the judgment: " 'The operation was a success, but the patient died.' What such a procedure is to medicine, the Court's opinion in this case is to law. It sustains the constitutionality of 20 U.S.C. § 954(d)(1) by gutting it. The most avid congressional opponents of the provision could not have asked for more. I write separately because, unlike the Court, I think that § 954(d)(1) must be evaluated as written, rather than as distorted by the agency it was meant to control. By its terms, it establishes content-and viewpoint-based criteria upon which grant applications are to be evaluated. And that is perfectly constitutional.

"[The statute means what it says. Under the statute, the] application reviewers must take into account 'general standards of decency' and 'respect for the diverse beliefs and values of the American public' when evaluating artistic excellence and merit. One can regard this as either suggesting that decency and respect are elements of what Congress regards as artistic excellence and merit, or as suggesting that decency and respect are factors to be taken into account in addition to artistic excellence and merit. But either way, it is entirely, 100% clear that decency and respect are to be taken into account in evaluating applications.

"This is so apparent that I am at a loss to understand what the Court has in mind (other than the gutting of the statute) when it speculates that the statute is merely 'advisory.' General standards of decency and respect for Americans' beliefs and values *must* (for the statute says that the Chairperson 'shall ensure' this

b. Ginsburg, J., joined O'Connor, J.'s opinion with the exception of the paragraph accompanying this footnote.

result) be taken into account [in] evaluating all applications. This does not mean that those factors must always be dispositive, but it *does* mean that they must always be considered. The method of compliance proposed by the National Endowment for the Arts (NEA)—selecting diverse review panels of artists and nonartists that reflect a wide range of geographic and cultural perspectives—is so obviously inadequate that it insults the intelligence. A diverse panel membership increases the odds that, *if and when* the panel takes the factors into account, it will reach an accurate assessment of what they demand. But it in no way increases the odds that the panel will take the factors into consideration—much less *ensures* that the panel will do so, which is the Chairperson's duty under the statute. Moreover, the NEA's fanciful reading of § 954(d)(1) would make it wholly superfluous. Section 959(c) already requires the Chairperson to 'issue regulations and establish procedures [to] ensure that all panels are composed, to the extent practicable, of individuals reflecting * * * diverse artistic and cultural points of view.'

"I agree with the Court that § 954(d)(1) 'imposes no categorical requirement' in the sense that it does not require the denial of all applications that violate general standards of decency or exhibit disrespect for the diverse beliefs and values of Americans. Compare § 954(d)(2) ('[O]bscenity * * * shall not be funded'). But the factors need not be conclusive to be discriminatory. To the extent a particular applicant exhibits disrespect for the diverse beliefs and values of the American public or fails to comport with general standards of decency, the likelihood that he will receive a grant diminishes. In other words, the presence of the 'tak[e] into consideration' clause 'cannot be regarded as mere surplusage; it means something.' And the 'something' is that the decisionmaker, all else being equal, will favor applications that display decency and respect, and disfavor applications that do not.

"This unquestionably constitutes viewpoint discrimination.[1] That conclusion is not altered by the fact that the statute does not 'compe[l]' the denial of funding any more than a provision imposing a five-point handicap on all black applicants for civil service jobs is saved from being race discrimination by the fact that it does not compel the rejection of black applicants. If viewpoint discrimination in this context is unconstitutional (a point I shall address anon), the law is invalid unless there are some situations in which the decency and respect factors *do not constitute viewpoint discrimination*. And there is none. [T]he conclusion of viewpoint discrimination is not affected by the fact that what constitutes 'decency' or 'the diverse beliefs and values of the American people' is difficult to pin down—any more than a civil-service preference in favor of those who display 'Republican-party values' would be rendered nondiscriminatory by the fact that there is plenty of room for argument as to what Republican-party values might be . . .

"The 'political context surrounding the adoption of the "decency and respect" clause,' [does] not change its meaning or affect its constitutionality. All that is proved by the various statements [from] the floor debates is (1) that the provision was not meant categorically to exclude any particular viewpoint (which I have conceded, and which is plain from the text), and (2) that the language was not meant to do anything that is unconstitutional. That in no way propels the Court's leap to the countertextual conclusion that the provision was merely 'aimed at reforming procedures,' and cannot be 'utilized as a tool for invidious viewpoint

---

1. [O]ne might argue that the decency and respect factors constitute content discrimination rather than viewpoint discrimination, which would render them easier to uphold. Since I believe this statute must be upheld in either event, I pass over this conundrum and assume the worst.

discrimination.' It is evident in the legislative history that § 954(d)(1) was prompted by, and directed at, the public funding of such offensive productions as Serrano's 'Piss Christ,' the portrayal of a crucifix immersed in urine, and Mapplethorpe's show of lurid homoerotic photographs. Thus, even if one strays beyond the plain text it is perfectly clear that the statute was meant to disfavor—that is, to discriminate against—such productions. Not to ban their funding absolutely, to be sure (though as I shall discuss, that also would not have been unconstitutional); but to make their funding more difficult.

"More fundamentally, of course, all this legislative history has no valid claim upon our attention at all. It is a virtual certainty that very few of the Members of Congress who voted for this language both (1) knew of, and (2) agreed with, the various statements that the Court has culled from * * * the floor debate (probably conducted on an almost empty floor). And it is wholly irrelevant that the statute was a 'bipartisan proposal introduced as a counterweight' to an alternative proposal that would directly restrict funding on the basis of viewpoint. We do not judge statutes as if we are surveying the scene of an accident; each one is reviewed, not on the basis of how much worse it could have been, but on the basis of what it says. It matters not whether this enactment was the product of the most partisan alignment in history or whether, upon its passage, the Members all linked arms and sang, 'The more we get together, the happier we'll be.' It is 'not consonant with our scheme of government for a court to inquire into the motives of legislators.' The law at issue in this case is to be found in the text of § 954(d)(1), which passed both Houses and was signed by the President. And that law unquestionably disfavors—discriminates against—indecency and disrespect for the diverse beliefs and values of the American people. * * *

"With the enactment of § 954(d)(1), Congress did not *abridge* the speech of those who disdain the beliefs and values of the American public, nor did it *abridge* indecent speech. Those who wish to create indecent and disrespectful art are as unconstrained now as they were before the enactment of this statute. *Avant-garde artistes* such as respondents remain entirely free to *epater les bourgeois*; they are merely deprived of the additional satisfaction of having the bourgeoisie taxed to pay for it. * * *

"As we noted in *Rust*, when Congress chose to establish the National Endowment for Democracy it was not constitutionally required to fund programs encouraging competing philosophies of government—an example of funding discrimination that cuts much closer than this one to the core of political speech which is the primary concern of the First Amendment. It takes a particularly high degree of chutzpah for the NEA to contradict this proposition, since the agency itself discriminates—and is required by law to discriminate—in favor of artistic (as opposed to scientific, or political, or theological) expression. Not all the common folk, or even all great minds, for that matter, think that is a good idea. In 1800, when John Marshall told John Adams that a recent immigration of Frenchmen would include talented artists, "Adams denounced all Frenchmen, but most especially 'schoolmasters, painters, poets, & C.' He warned Marshall that the fine arts were like germs that infected healthy constitutions." J. Ellis, *After the Revolution: Profiles of Early American Culture* 36 (1979). Surely the NEA itself is nothing less than an institutionalized discrimination against that point of view. Nonetheless it is constitutional, as is the congressional determination to favor decency and respect for beliefs and values over the opposite.[3]

3. I suppose it would be unconstitutional for the government to give money to an organization devoted to the promotion of candidates nominated by the Republican party—but it

"The nub of the difference between me and the Court is that I regard the distinction between 'abridging' speech and funding it as a fundamental divide, on this side of which the First Amendment is inapplicable. The Court, by contrast, seems to believe that the First Amendment, despite its words, has some ineffable effect upon funding, imposing constraints of an indeterminate nature which it announces (without troubling to enunciate any particular test) are not violated by the statute here—or, more accurately, are not violated by the quite different, emasculated statute that it imagines."

SOUTER, J., dissented: "The decency and respect proviso mandates viewpoint-based decisions in the disbursement of government subsidies, and the Government has wholly failed to explain why the statute should be afforded an exemption from the fundamental rule of the First Amendment that viewpoint discrimination in the exercise of public authority over expressive activity is unconstitutional. * * *[2]

"[An argument] for avoiding unconstitutionality that the Court appears to regard with some favor is the Government's argument that the NEA may comply with § 954(d) merely by populating the advisory panels that analyze grant applications with members of diverse backgrounds. Would that it were so easy; this asserted implementation of the law fails *even* to 'reflec[t] a plausible construction of the plain language of the statute.' *Rust v. Sullivan*, 500 U.S. 173, 184, 111 S.Ct. 1759, 114 L.Ed.2d 233 (1991).

"The Government notes that § 954(d) actually provides that '[i]n establishing * * * regulations and procedures, the Chairperson [of the NEA] shall ensure that (1) artistic excellence and artistic merit are the criteria by which applications are judged, taking into consideration general standards of decency and respect for the diverse beliefs and values of the American public.' According to the Government, this language requires decency and respect to be considered not in judging applications, but in making regulations. If, then, the Chairperson takes decency and respect into consideration through regulations ensuring diverse panels, the statute is satisfied. But it would take a great act of will to find any plausibility in this reading. The reference to considering decency and respect occurs in the subparagraph speaking to the 'criteria by which applications are judged,' not in the preamble directing the Chairperson to adopt regulations; it is in judging applications that decency and respect are most obviously to be considered. * * *

"[Another] try at avoiding constitutional problems is the Court's disclaimer of any constitutional issue here because '[s]ection 954(d)(1) adds "considerations" to the grant-making process; it does not preclude awards to projects that might be deemed "indecent" or "disrespectful," nor place conditions on grants, or even specify that those factors must be given any particular weight in reviewing an application.' * * *

"That is not a fair reading. Just as the statute cannot be read as anything but viewpoint based, or as requiring nothing more than diverse review panels, it cannot be read as tolerating awards to spread indecency or disrespect, so long as the review panel, the National Counsel on the Arts, and the Chairperson have

would be just as unconstitutional for the government itself to promote candidates nominated by the Republican party, and I do not think that that unconstitutionality has anything to do with the First Amendment.

2. [Congress] has no obligation to support artistic enterprises that many people detest.

The First Amendment speaks up only when Congress decides to participate in the Nation's artistic life by legal regulation, as it does through a subsidy scheme like the NEA. If Congress does choose to spend public funds in this manner, it may not discriminate by viewpoint in deciding who gets the money.

given some thought to the offending qualities and decided to underwrite them anyway. That, after all, is presumably just what prompted the congressional outrage in the first place, and there was nothing naive about the Representative who said he voted for the bill because it does 'not tolerate wasting Federal funds for sexually explicit photographs [or] sacrilegious works.'

"But even if I found the Court's view of 'consideration' plausible, that would make no difference at all on the question of constitutionality. What if the statute required a panel to apply criteria 'taking into consideration the centrality of Christianity to the American cultural experience,' or 'taking into consideration whether the artist is a communist,' or 'taking into consideration the political message conveyed by the art,' or even 'taking into consideration the superiority of the white race'? Would the Court hold these considerations facially constitutional, merely because the statute had no requirement to give them any particular, much less controlling, weight? I assume not.

"A second basic strand in the Court's treatment of today's question and the heart of Justice Scalia's in effect assumes that whether or not the statute mandates viewpoint discrimination, there is no constitutional issue here because government art subsidies fall within a zone of activity free from First Amendment restraints. The Government calls attention to the roles of government-as-speaker [in] which the government is of course entitled to engage in viewpoint discrimination: if the Food and Drug Administration launches an advertising campaign on the subject of smoking, it may condemn the habit without also having to show a cowboy taking a puff on the opposite page; and if the Secretary of Defense wishes to buy a portrait to decorate the Pentagon, he is free to prefer George Washington over George the Third.

"The Government freely admits, however, that it neither speaks through the expression subsidized by the NEA,[6] nor buys anything for itself with its NEA grants. On the contrary, believing that '[t]he arts * * * reflect the high place accorded by the American people to the nation's rich cultural heritage,' § 951(6), and that '[i]t is vital to a democracy * * * to provide financial assistance to its artists and the organizations that support their work,' § 951(10), the Government acts as a patron, financially underwriting the production of art by private artists and impresarios for independent consumption. Accordingly, the Government would have us liberate government-as-patron from First Amendment strictures not by placing it squarely within the categories of government-as-buyer or government-as-speaker, but by recognizing a new category by analogy to those accepted ones. The analogy is, however, a very poor fit, and this patronage falls embarrassingly on the wrong side of the line between government-as-buyer or-speaker and government-as-regulator-of-private-speech.

"[Rosenberger] controls here. The NEA, like the student activities fund in Rosenberger, is a subsidy scheme created to encourage expression of a diversity of views from private speakers. Congress brought the NEA into being to help all Americans 'achieve a better understanding of the past, a better analysis of the present, and a better view of the future.' § 951(3). The NEA's purpose is to 'support new ideas' and 'to help create and sustain [a] climate encouraging freedom of thought, imagination, and inquiry.' §§ 951(10),(7). Given this congressional choice to sustain freedom of expression, Rosenberger teaches that the First

6. Here, the "communicative element inherent in the very act of funding itself," Rosenberger (Souter, J., dissenting), is an endorsement of the importance of the arts collectively, not an endorsement of the individual message espoused in a given work of art.

Amendment forbids decisions based on viewpoint popularity. So long as Congress chooses to subsidize expressive endeavors at large, it has no business requiring the NEA to turn down funding applications of artists and exhibitors who devote their 'freedom of thought, imagination, and inquiry' to defying our tastes, our beliefs, or our values. It may not use the NEA's purse to 'suppres[s] dangerous ideas.' *Regan v. Taxation with Representation.*

"The Court says otherwise, claiming to distinguish *Rosenberger* on the ground that the student activities funds in that case were generally available to most applicants, whereas NEA funds are disbursed selectively and competitively to a choice few. But the Court in *Rosenberger* anticipated and specifically rejected just this distinction when it held in no uncertain terms that '[t]he government cannot justify viewpoint discrimination among private speakers on the economic fact of scarcity.'[8] Scarce money demands choices, of course, but choices 'on some acceptable [viewpoint] neutral principle,' like artistic excellence and artistic merit;[9] 'nothing in our decision[s] indicate[s] that scarcity would give the State the right to exercise viewpoint discrimination that is otherwise impermissible.'[[10]]."

BROADCAST REGULATION AND ACCESS TO THE MASS MEDIA

ACCESS TO THE MASS MEDIA

CON LAW: P. 953, after Turner

AMER CON: P. 939, after Turner

RTS & LIB: P. 861, after Turner

After remand, TURNER BROADCASTING SYSTEM, INC. v. FCC, 520 U.S. 180, 117 S.Ct. 1174, 137 L.Ed.2d 369 (1997), per KENNEDY, J., joined by Rehnquist, C.J., Stevens, and Souter, JJ., upheld the must-carry provisions. Applying the *O'Brien* test, he emphasized the importance of deferring to Congress so long as it had "drawn reasonable inferences based upon substantial evidence." He found that the legislation was narrowly tailored to preserve the benefits of local broadcast television, to promote widespread dissemination of information from a multiplicity of sources, and to promote fair competition.

BREYER, J., concurring, joined Kennedy, J.'s opinion except for his discussion

---

8. The Court's attempt to avoid *Rosenberger* by describing NEA funding in terms of competition, not scarcity, will not work. Competition implies scarcity, without which there is no exclusive prize to compete for; the Court's 'competition' is merely a surrogate for 'scarcity.'

9. While criteria of 'artistic excellence and artistic merit' may raise intractable issues about the identification of artistic worth, and could no doubt be used covertly to filter out unwanted ideas, there is nothing inherently viewpoint discriminatory about such merit-based criteria. [Decency] and respect, on the other hand, are inherently and facially viewpoint based, and serve no legitimate and permissible end. The Court's assertion that the mere fact that grants must be awarded according to artistic merit precludes 'absolute neu-

trality' on the part of the NEA is therefore misdirected. It is not to the point that the government necessarily makes choices among competing applications, or even that its judgments about artistic quality may be branded as subjective to some greater or lesser degree; the question here is whether the government may apply patently viewpoint-based criteria in making those choices.

10. [Leaving] aside the proper application of forum analysis to the NEA and its projects, I cannot agree that the holding of *Rosenberger* turned on characterizing its metaphorical forum as public in some degree. Like this case, *Rosenberger* involved viewpoint discrimination, and we have made it clear that such discrimination is impermissible in all forums, even non-public [ones].

and conclusion regarding the fair competition rationale.[a]

O'CONNOR, J., joined by Scalia, Thomas, and Ginsburg, JJ., dissenting, argued again that strict scrutiny should apply, agreed that deference was owed to Congress "in its predictive judgments and its evaluation of complex economic questions," but maintained that even under intermediate scrutiny, the Court had an independent duty to examine with care the Congressional interests, the findings, and the fit between the goals and consequences. She criticized the Court for being too deferential even on the assumption that the legislation was content neutral.

On O'Connor, J.'s analysis, the record did not support either the conclusion that cable posed a significant threat to local broadcast markets or that the act was narrowly tailored to deal with anti-competitive conduct.

———

ARKANSAS EDUCATIONAL TELEVISION COMMISSION v. FORBES, 523 U.S. 666, 118 S.Ct. 1633, 140 L.Ed.2d 875 (1998), per KENNEDY, J., concluded that a candidate debate sponsored by a state-owned public television broadcaster was a nonpublic forum subject to constitutional restraints, but that the broadcaster's decision to exclude the candidate was reasonable: "A state-owned public television broadcaster [Arkansas Educational Television Commission 'AETC'] sponsored a candidate debate from which it excluded an independent congressional candidate [Ralph Forbes] with little popular support. The issue before us is whether, by reason of its state ownership, the station had a constitutional obligation to allow every candidate access to the debate. We conclude that, unlike most other public television programs, the candidate debate was subject to constitutional constraints applicable to nonpublic fora under our forum precedents. Even so, the broadcaster's decision to exclude the candidate was a reasonable, viewpoint-neutral exercise of journalistic discretion. * * *

"Although public broadcasting as a general matter does not lend itself to scrutiny under the forum doctrine, candidate debates present the narrow exception to the rule. For two reasons, a candidate debate like the one at issue here is different from other programming. First, unlike AETC's other broadcasts, the debate was by design a forum for political speech by the candidates. Consistent with the long tradition of candidate debates, the implicit representation of the broadcaster was that the views expressed were those of the candidates, not its own. The very purpose of the debate was to allow the candidates to express their views with minimal intrusion by the broadcaster. In this respect the debate differed even from a political talk show, whose host can express partisan views and then limit the discussion to those ideas.

"Second, in our tradition, candidate debates are of exceptional significance in the electoral process. [Deliberation] on the positions and qualifications of candidates is integral to our system of government, and electoral speech may have its most profound and widespread impact when it is disseminated through televised debates. * * *

"Under our precedents, the AETC debate was not a designated public forum. [T]he government creates a designated public forum when it makes its property generally available to a certain class of speakers, as the university made its facilities generally available to student groups in *Widmar*. On the other hand, the

a. Stevens, J., also filed a concurring opinion.

government does not create a designated public forum when it does no more than reserve eligibility for access to the forum to a particular class of speakers, whose members must then, as individuals, 'obtain permission,' to use it. For instance, the Federal Government did not create a designated public forum in Cornelius when it reserved eligibility for participation in the CFC drive to charitable agencies, and then made individual, non-ministerial judgments as to which of the eligible agencies would participate.

"The [distinction] between general and selective access furthers First Amendment interests. By recognizing the distinction, we encourage the government to open its property to some expressive activity in cases where, if faced with an all-or-nothing choice, it might not open the property at all.[a] That this distinction turns on governmental intent does not render it unprotective of speech. Rather, it reflects the reality that, with the exception of traditional public fora, the government retains the choice of whether to designate its property as a forum for specified classes of speakers.

"Here, the debate did not have an open-microphone format. [AETC] did not make its debate generally available to candidates for Arkansas' Third Congressional District seat. Instead, just as the Federal Government in *Cornelius* reserved eligibility for participation in the CFC program to certain classes of voluntary agencies, AETC reserved eligibility for participation in the debate to candidates for the Third Congressional District seat (as opposed to some other seat). At that point, just as the Government in *Cornelius* made agency-by-agency determinations as to which of the eligible agencies would participate in the CFC, AETC made candidate-by-candidate determinations as to which of the eligible candidates would participate in the debate. 'Such selective access, unsupported by evidence of a purposeful designation for public use, does not create a public forum.' Thus the debate was a nonpublic forum.

"The debate's status as a nonpublic forum, however, did not give AETC unfettered power to exclude any candidate it wished. [To] be consistent with the First Amendment, the exclusion of a speaker from a nonpublic forum must not be based on the speaker's viewpoint and must otherwise be reasonable in light of the purpose of the property. *Cornelius.* * * *

"There is no substance to Forbes' suggestion that he was excluded because his views were unpopular or out of the mainstream. * * * Nor did AETC exclude Forbes in an attempted manipulation of the political process. The evidence provided powerful support for the jury's express finding that AETC's exclusion of Forbes was not the result of 'political pressure from anyone inside or outside [AETC].' There is no serious argument that AETC did not act in good faith in this case. AETC excluded Forbes because the voters lacked interest in his candidacy,

a. In a later section, the Court stated: "In each of the 1988, 1992, and 1996 Presidential elections, for example, no fewer than 22 candidates appeared on the ballot in at least one State. In the 1996 congressional elections, it was common for 6 to 11 candidates to qualify for the ballot for a particular seat. In the 1993 New Jersey gubernatorial election, to illustrate further, sample ballot mailings included the written statements of 19 candidates. On logistical grounds alone, a public television editor might, with reason, decide that the inclusion of all ballot-qualified candidates would 'actually undermine the educational value and quality of debates.'

"Were it faced with the prospect of cacophony, on the one hand, and First Amendment liability, on the other, a public television broadcaster might choose not to air candidates' views at [all]. These concerns are more than speculative. As a direct result of the Court of Appeals' decision in this case, the Nebraska Educational Television Network canceled a scheduled debate between candidates in Nebraska's 1996 United States Senate race. A First Amendment jurisprudence yielding these results does not promote speech but represses it."

not because AETC itself did. The broadcaster's decision to exclude Forbes was a reasonable, viewpoint-neutral exercise of journalistic discretion consistent with the First Amendment."

STEVENS, J., joined by Souter and Ginsburg, JJ., dissented: "The official action that led to the exclusion of respondent Forbes from a debate with the two major-party candidates for election to one of Arkansas' four seats in Congress does not adhere to well-settled constitutional principles. The ad hoc decision of the staff of [AETC] raises precisely the concerns addressed by 'the many decisions of this Court over the last 30 years, holding that a law subjecting the exercise of First Amendment freedoms to the prior restraint of a license, without narrow, objective, and definite standards to guide the licensing authority, is unconstitutional.' *Shuttlesworth v. Birmingham.*

"Given the fact that the Republican winner in the Third Congressional District race in 1992 received only 50.22% of the vote and the Democrat received 47.20%, it would have been necessary for Forbes, who had made a strong showing in recent Republican primaries, to divert only a handful of votes from the Republican candidate to cause his defeat. Thus, even though the AETC staff may have correctly concluded that Forbes was 'not a serious candidate,' their decision to exclude him from the debate may have determined the outcome of the election in the Third District.

"If a comparable decision were made today by a privately owned network, it would be subject to scrutiny under the Federal Election Campaign Act unless the network used 'pre-established objective criteria to determine which candidates may participate in [the] debate.' 11 CFR § 110.13(c) (1997). No such criteria governed AETC's refusal to permit Forbes to participate in the debate. Indeed, whether that refusal was based on a judgment about 'newsworthiness'—as AETC has argued in this Court—or a judgment about 'political viability'—as it argued in the Court of Appeals—the facts in the record presumably would have provided an adequate basis either for a decision to include Forbes in the Third District debate or a decision to exclude him * * *.

"The apparent flexibility of AETC's purported standard suggests the extent to which the staff had nearly limitless discretion to exclude Forbes from the debate based on ad hoc justifications. Thus, the Court of Appeals correctly concluded that the staff's appraisal of 'political viability' was 'so subjective, so arguable, so susceptible of variation in individual opinion, as to provide no secure basis for the exercise of governmental power consistent with the First Amendment.' * * *

"The reasons that support the need for narrow, objective, and definite standards to guide licensing decisions apply directly to the wholly subjective access decisions made by the staff of AETC.[18] The importance of avoiding arbitrary or viewpoint-based exclusions from political debates militates strongly in favor of requiring the controlling state agency to use (and adhere to) pre-established, objective criteria to determine who among qualified candidates may participate. A constitutional duty to use objective standards—i.e., 'neutral principles'—for determining whether and when to adjust a debate format would impose only a modest

---

18. Ironically, it is the standardless character of the decision to exclude Forbes that provides the basis for the Court's conclusion that the debates were a nonpublic forum rather than a limited public forum. [T]he Court explains that "[a] designated public forum is not created when the government allows selective access for individual speakers rather than general access for a class of speakers." If, as AETC claims, it did invite either the entire class of 'viable' candidates, or the entire class of 'newsworthy' candidates, under the Court's reasoning, it created a designated public forum.

requirement that would fall far short of a duty to grant every multiple-party request. Such standards would also have the benefit of providing the public with some assurance that state-owned broadcasters cannot select debate participants on arbitrary grounds."

BROADCASTING AND CONTENT REGULATION: INDECENT SPEECH

CON LAW: P. 963, after note 3

AMER CON: P. 948, after note 3

RTS & LIB: P. 870, after note 3

Cable operators are required under federal law to reserve channels for commercial lease ("leased access channels") and are routinely required by their franchise agreements with municipalities to reserve channels for public, educational, and governmental access ("public access channels" or "pegs"). For some years federal law prevented cable operators from employing any editorial control over the content of leased access or public access channels. The Cable Television Consumer Protection and Competition of 1992, however, permitted cable operators to prohibit the broadcast of material that the cable operator "reasonably believes describes or depicts sexual or excretory activities or organs in a patently offensive manner" on leased access channels (47 U.S.C.§ 10(a)) and public access channels (47 U.S.C.§ 10(c)). In addition, if the cable operator did not prohibit such material from being broadcast on leased access channels, the Act required the cable operator to provide a separate channel for the material, to scramble or otherwise block its presentation, and to permit its viewing only upon written request (47 U.S.C.§ 10(b))(the "block and segregate requirements"). After the adoption of § 10(b), Congress passed block and segregate requirements for channels primarily dedicated to sexual programming and required cable operators to honor a subscriber's request to block any undesired programs.

DENVER AREA EDUCATIONAL TELECOMMUNICATIONS CONSOR-TIUM, INC. v. FCC, 518 U.S. 727, 116 S.Ct. 2374, 135 L.Ed.2d 888 (1996) upheld the constitutionality of § 10(a), but invalidated §§ 10 (b) and (c). BREYER, J., joined by Stevens, O'Connor, Kennedy, and Souter, JJ., held that the segregate and block requirements (§ 10(b)) were invalid: "We agree with the Government that protection of children is a 'compelling interest.' But we do not agree that the 'segregate and block' requirements properly accommodate the speech restrictions they impose and the legitimate objective they seek to attain. Nor need we here determine whether, or the extent to which, *Pacifica* does, or does not, impose some lesser standard of review where indecent speech is at issue, compare (opinion of Stevens, J.)(indecent materials enjoy lesser First Amendment protection), with (Powell, J., concurring in part and concurring in judgment)(refusing to accept a lesser standard for nonobscene, indecent material). That is because once one examines this governmental restriction, it becomes apparent that, not only is it not a 'least restrictive alternative,' and is not 'narrowly tailored' to meet its legitimate objective, it also seems considerably 'more extensive than necessary.' That is to say, it fails to satisfy this Court's formulations of the First Amendment's 'strictest,' as well as its somewhat less 'strict,' requirements. * * *

"The record does not explain why, under the new Act, blocking alone—without written access-requests—adequately protects children from exposure to regular sex-dedicated channels, but cannot adequately protect those children from programming on similarly sex-dedicated channels that are leased. It does not explain why a simple subscriber blocking request system, perhaps a phone-call based system, would adequately protect children from 'patently offensive' material broadcast on ordinary non-sex- dedicated channels (i.e., almost all channels) but a far more restrictive segregate/block/written-access system is needed to protect children from similar broadcasts on what (in the absence of the segregation requirement) would be non-sex-dedicated channels that are leased. Nor is there any indication Congress thought the new ordinary channel protections less than adequate."

In a portion of his opinion joined by Stevens, O'Connor, and Souter, JJ., Breyer, J., concluded that § 10(a) was valid, but, in a portion of his opinion joined by Stevens and Souter, JJ., he concluded that § 10(c) was invalid. As to § 10(a), BREYER, J., observed: "Justices Kennedy and Thomas would have us decide this case simply by transferring and applying literally categorical standards this Court has developed in other contexts. For Justice Kennedy, leased access channels are like a common carrier, cablecast is a protected medium, strict scrutiny applies, § 10(a) fails this test, and, therefore, § 10(a) is invalid. For Justice Thomas, the case is simple because the cable operator who owns the system over which access channels are broadcast, like a bookstore owner with respect to what it displays on the shelves, has a predominant First Amendment interest. Both categorical approaches suffer from the same flaws: they import law developed in very different contexts into a new and changing environment, and they lack the flexibility necessary to allow government to respond to very serious practical problems without sacrificing the free exchange of ideas the First Amendment is designed to protect. * * *

"Over the years, this Court has restated and refined [basic] First Amendment principles, adopting them more particularly to the balance of competing interests and the special circumstances of each field of application. [This] tradition teaches that the First Amendment embodies an overarching commitment to protect speech from Government regulation through close judicial scrutiny, thereby enforcing the Constitution's constraints, but without imposing judicial formulae so rigid that they become a straightjacket that disables Government from responding to serious problems. This Court, in different contexts, has consistently held that the Government may directly regulate speech to address extraordinary problems, where its regulations are appropriately tailored to resolve those problems without imposing an unnecessarily great restriction on speech. Justices Kennedy and Thomas would have us further declare which, among the many applications of the general approach that this Court has developed over the years, we are applying here. But no definitive choice among competing analogies (broadcast, common carrier, bookstore) allows us to declare a rigid single standard, good for now and for all future media and purposes. That is not to say that we reject all the more specific formulations of the standard—they appropriately cover the vast majority of cases involving Government regulation of speech. Rather, aware as we are of the changes taking place in the law, the technology, and the industrial structure, related to telecommunications, we believe it unwise and unnecessary definitively to pick one analogy or one specific set of words now.

"[W]e can decide this case more narrowly, by closely scrutinizing § 10(a) to assure that it properly addresses an extremely important problem, without imposing, in light of the relevant interests, an unnecessarily great restriction on speech. The importance of the interest at stake here—protecting children from exposure to patently offensive depictions of sex; the accommodation of the interests of programmers in maintaining access channels and of cable operators in editing the contents of their channels; the similarity of the problem and its solution to those

at issue in *Pacifica*, and the flexibility inherent in an approach that permits private cable operators to make editorial decisions, lead us to conclude that § 10(a) is a sufficiently tailored response to an extraordinarily important problem.
* * *

"[W]e part company with Justice Kennedy on two issues. First, Justice Kennedy's focus on categorical analysis forces him to disregard the cable system operators' interests. We, on the other hand, recognize that in the context of cable broadcast that involves an access requirement (here, its partial removal), and unlike in most cases where we have explicitly required 'narrow tailoring,' the expressive interests of cable operators do play a legitimate role. Cf. *Turner*. While we cannot agree with Justice Thomas that everything turns on the rights of the cable owner, we also cannot agree with Justice Kennedy that we must ignore the expressive interests of cable operators altogether. Second, Justice Kennedy's application of a very strict 'narrow tailoring' test depends upon an analogy with a category ('the public forum cases'), which has been distilled over time from the similarities of many cases. Rather than seeking an analogy to a category of cases, however, we have looked to the cases themselves. And, [we find] that *Pacifica* provides the closest analogy. * * *

"The Court's distinction in *Turner*, [between] cable and broadcast television, relied on the inapplicability of the spectrum scarcity problem to cable. While that distinction was relevant in *Turner* to the justification for structural regulations at issue there (the 'must carry' rules), it has little to do with a case that involves the effects of television viewing on children. Those effects are the result of how parents and children view television programming, and how pervasive and intrusive that programming is. In that respect, cable and broadcast television differ little, if at all.

"[I]f one wishes to view the permissive provisions before us through a 'public forum' lens, one should view those provisions as limiting the otherwise totally open nature of the forum that leased access channels provide for communication of other than patently offensive sexual material—taking account of the fact that the limitation was imposed in light of experience gained from maintaining a totally open 'forum.' One must still ask whether the First Amendment forbids the limitation. But unless a label alone were to make a critical First Amendment difference (and we think here it does not), the features of this case that we have already discussed—the government's interest in protecting children, the 'permissive' aspect of the statute, and the nature of the medium—sufficiently justify the 'limitation' on the availability of this forum."

BREYER, J., argued that the balance was different in § 10(c): "[C]able operators have traditionally agreed to reserve channel capacity for public, governmental, and educational channels as part of the consideration they give municipalities that award them cable franchises. [Thus] these are channels over which cable operators have not historically exercised editorial control. Unlike § 10(a) therefore, s 10(c) does not restore to cable operators editorial rights that they once had, and the countervailing First Amendment interest is nonexistent, or at least much diminished.

"[A] second difference is the institutional background that has developed as a result of the historical difference. When a 'leased channel' is made available by the operator to a private lessee, the lessee has total control of programming during the leased time slot. Public access channels, on the other hand, are normally subject to complex supervisory systems of various sorts, often with both public and private elements. [G]iven present supervisory mechanisms, the need for this particular provision, aimed directly at public access channels, is not obvious."

STEVENS, J., concurring, agreed with Breyer, J., that it was unwise to characterize leased channels as public fora: "When the Federal Government opens cable channels that would otherwise be left entirely in private hands, it deserves more deference than a rigid application of the public forum doctrine would allow. At this early stage in the regulation of this developing industry, Congress should not be put to an all or nothing-at-all choice in deciding whether to open certain cable channels to programmers who would otherwise lack the resources to participate in the marketplace of ideas."

With respect to § 10(c), Stevens, J., stated: "What is of critical importance to me, however, is that if left to their own devices, those authorities may choose to carry some programming that the Federal Government has decided to restrict. As I read § 10(c), the federal statute would disable local governments from making that choice. It would inject federally authorized private censors into forums from which they might otherwise be excluded, and it would therefore limit local forums that might otherwise be open to all constitutionally protected speech."[3]

SOUTER, J., concurred: "All of the relevant characteristics of cable are presently in a state of technological and regulatory flux. Recent and far-reaching legislation not only affects the technical feasibility of parental control over children's access to undesirable material but portends fundamental changes in the competitive structure of the industry and, therefore, the ability of individual entities to act as bottlenecks to the free flow of information. As cable and telephone companies begin their competition for control over the single wire that will carry both their services, we can hardly settle rules for review of regulation on the assumption that cable will remain a separable and useful category of First Amendment scrutiny. And as broadcast, cable, and the cyber-technology of the Internet and the World Wide Web approach the day of using a common receiver, we can hardly assume that standards for judging the regulation of one of them will not have immense, but now unknown and unknowable, effects on the others. * * *

"The upshot of appreciating the fluidity of the subject that Congress must regulate is simply to accept the fact that not every nuance of our old standards will necessarily do for the new technology, and that a proper choice among existing doctrinal categories is not obvious. Rather than definitively settling the issue now, Justice Breyer wisely reasons by direct analogy rather than by rule, concluding that the speech and the restriction at issue in this case may usefully be measured against the ones at issue in *Pacifica*. If that means it will take some time before reaching a final method of review for cases like this one, there may be consolation in recalling that 16 years passed, from *Roth* to *Miller*, before the modern obscenity rule jelled; that it took over 40 years, from *Hague v. CIO* to *Perry*, for the public forum category to settle out; and that a round half-century passed before the clear and present danger of *Schenck* evolved into the modern incitement rule of *Brandenburg*.

3. Although in 1984 Congress essentially barred cable operators from exercising editorial control over PEG channels, see 47 U.S.C. § 531(e), Section 10(c) does not merely restore the status quo ante. Section 10(c) authorizes private operators to exercise editorial discretion over "indecent" programming even if the franchising authority objects. Under the pre–1984 practice, local franchising authorities were free to exclude operators from exercising any such control on PEG channels.

"I cannot guess how much time will go by until the technologies of communication before us today have matured and their relationships become known. But until a category of indecency can be defined both with reference to the new technology and with a prospect of durability, the job of the courts will be just what Justice Breyer does today: recognizing established First Amendment interests through a close analysis that constrains the Congress, without wholly incapacitating it in all matters of the significance apparent here, maintaining the high value of open communication, measuring the costs of regulation by exact attention to fact, and compiling a pedigree of experience with the changing subject. These are familiar judicial responsibilities in times when we know too little to risk the finality of precision, and attention to them will probably take us through the communications revolution. Maybe the judicial obligation to shoulder these responsibilities can itself be captured by a much older rule, familiar to every doctor of medicine: 'First, do no harm.' "

O'CONNOR, J., concurring in part and dissenting in part, agreed with Breyer, J.'s assessment that § 10(a) was valid and § 10(b) invalid. She argued, however, that Breyer, J.'s distinctions regarding § 10(c) were insufficiently weighty: "The interest in protecting children remains the same, whether on a leased access channel or a public access channel, and allowing the cable operator the option of prohibiting the transmission of indecent speech seems a constitutionally permissible means of addressing that interest. Nor is the fact that public access programming may be subject to supervisory systems in addition to the cable operator sufficient in my mind to render § 10(c) so ill-tailored to its goal as to be unconstitutional."

KENNEDY, J., joined by Ginsburg, J., concurring in part and dissenting in part, agreed that § 10(b) and (c) were invalid, but faulted the plurality opinion for its upholding of § 10(a): "The plurality opinion, insofar as it upholds § 10(a) [is] adrift. The opinion treats concepts such as public forum, broadcaster, and common carrier as mere labels rather than as categories with settled legal significance; it applies no standard, and by this omission loses sight of existing First Amendment doctrine. When confronted with a threat to free speech in the context of an emerging technology, we ought to have the discipline to analyze the case by reference to existing elaborations of constant First Amendment principles. This is the essence of the case-by-case approach to ensuring protection of speech under the First Amendment, even in novel settings. * * *

"The plurality begins its flight from standards with a number of assertions nobody disputes. I agree, of course, that it would be unwise 'to declare a rigid single standard, good for now and for all future media and purposes.' I do think it necessary, however, to decide what standard applies to discrimination against indecent programming on cable access channels in the present state of the industry. We owe at least that much to public and leased access programmers whose speech is put at risk nationwide by these laws. * * *

"The plurality claims its resistance to standards is in keeping with our case law, where we have shown a willingness to be flexible in confronting novel First Amendment problems. [W]e have developed specialized or more or less stringent standards when certain contexts demanded them; we did not avoid the use of standards altogether. Indeed, the creation of standards and adherence to them, even when it means affording protection to speech unpopular or distasteful, is the central achievement of our First Amendment jurisprudence. Standards are the means by which we state in advance how to test a law's validity, rather than letting the height of the bar be determined by the apparent exigencies of the day.

They also provide notice and fair warning to those who must predict how the courts will respond to attempts to suppress their speech. Yet formulations like strict scrutiny, used in a number of constitutional settings to ensure that the inequities of the moment are subordinated to commitments made for the long run mean little if they can be watered down whenever they seem too strong. They mean still less if they can be ignored altogether when considering a case not on all fours with what we have seen before.

"The plurality seems distracted by the many changes in technology and competition in the cable industry. The laws challenged here, however, do not retool the structure of the cable industry or (with the exception of § 10(b)) involve intricate technologies. The straightforward issue here is whether the Government can deprive certain speakers, on the basis of the content of their speech, of protections afforded all others. There is no reason to discard our existing First Amendment jurisprudence in answering this question.

"While it protests against standards, the plurality does seem to favor one formulation of the question in this case: namely, whether the Act 'properly addresses an extremely important problem, without imposing, in light of the relevant interests, an unnecessarily great restriction on speech.' [This] description of the question accomplishes little, save to clutter our First Amendment case law by adding an untested rule with an uncertain relationship to the others we use to evaluate laws restricting speech. * * *

"Justice Souter recommends to the Court the precept ' "First, do no harm." ' The question, though, is whether the harm is in sustaining the law or striking it down. If the plurality is concerned about technology's direction, it ought to begin by allowing speech, not suppressing it. We have before us an urgent claim for relief against content-based discrimination, not a dry run.

"The constitutionality under *Turner Broadcasting* of requiring a cable operator to set aside leased access channels is not before us. For purposes of this case, we should treat the cable operator's rights in these channels as extinguished, and address the issue these petitioners present: namely, whether the Government can discriminate on the basis of content in affording protection to certain programmers. I cannot agree with Justice Thomas that the cable operator's rights inform this analysis.

"Laws requiring cable operators to provide leased access are the practical equivalent of making them common carriers, analogous in this respect to telephone companies: They are obliged to provide a conduit for the speech of others. [Laws] removing common-carriage protection from a single form of speech based on its content should be reviewed under the same standard as content-based restrictions on speech in a public forum. Making a cable operator a common carrier does not create a public forum in the sense of taking property from private control and dedicating it to public use; rather, regulations of a common carrier dictate the manner in which private control is exercised. A common-carriage mandate, nonetheless, serves the same function as a public forum. It ensures open, nondiscriminatory access to the means of communication.

"*Pacifica* did not purport, however, to apply a special standard for indecent broadcasting. Emphasizing the narrowness of its holding, the Court in *Pacifica* conducted a context-specific analysis of the FCC's restriction on indecent programming during daytime hours. It relied on the general rule that 'broadcasting * * * has received the most limited First Amendment protection.' We already have rejected the application of this lower broadcast standard of review to infringements on the liberties of cable operators, even though they control an important communications medium. *Turner.* * * *

"[Indecency] often is inseparable from the ideas and viewpoints conveyed, or separable only with loss of truth or expressive power. Under our traditional First Amendment jurisprudence, factors perhaps justifying some restriction on indecent cable programming may all be taken into account without derogating this category of protected speech as marginal.

"Congress does have, however, a compelling interest in protecting children from indecent speech. So long as society gives proper respect to parental choices, it may, under an appropriate standard, intervene to spare children exposure to material not suitable for minors. This interest is substantial enough to justify some regulation of indecent speech even under, I will assume, the [strict scrutiny standard].

"Sections 10(a) and (c) nonetheless are not narrowly tailored to protect children from indecent programs on access channels. First, to the extent some operators may allow indecent programming, children in localities those operators serve will be left unprotected. Partial service of a compelling interest is not narrow tailoring. Put another way, the interest in protecting children from indecency only at the caprice of the cable operator is not compelling. Perhaps Congress drafted the law this way to avoid the clear constitutional difficulties of banning indecent speech from access channels, but the First Amendment does not permit this sort of ill fit between a law restricting speech and the interest it is said to serve.

"Second, to the extent cable operators prohibit indecent programming on access channels, not only children but adults will be deprived of it."

THOMAS, J., joined by Rehnquist, C.J., and Scalia, J., concurring in part and dissenting in part, argued that §§ 10(a),(b), and (c) validly protected the constitutional rights of cable operators: "It is one thing to compel an operator to carry leased and public access speech, in apparent violation of *Tornillo*, but it is another thing altogether to say that the First Amendment forbids Congress to give back part of the operators' editorial discretion, which all recognize as fundamentally protected, in favor of a broader access right. It is no answer to say that leased and public access are content neutral and that §§ 10(a) and (c) are not, for that does not change the fundamental fact, which petitioners never address, that it is the operators' journalistic freedom that is infringed, whether the challenged restrictions be content neutral or content based.

"Because the access provisions are part of a scheme that restricts the free speech rights of cable operators, and expands the speaking opportunities of access programmers, who have no underlying constitutional right to speak through the cable medium, I do not believe that access programmers can challenge the scheme, or a particular part of it, as an abridgment of their 'freedom of speech.' Outside the public forum doctrine, government intervention that grants access programmers an opportunity to speak that they would not otherwise enjoy—and which does not directly limit programmers' underlying speech rights—cannot be an abridgement of the same programmers' First Amendment rights, even if the new speaking opportunity is content-based.

"The permissive nature of §§ 10(a) and (c) is important in this regard. If Congress had forbidden cable operators to carry indecent programming on leased and public access channels, that law would have burdened the programmer's right, recognized in *Turner* to compete for space on an operator's system. The Court would undoubtedly strictly scrutinize such a law. * * *

"Petitioners argue that public access channels are public fora in which they have First Amendment rights to speak and that § 10(c) is invalid because it imposes content-based burdens on those rights. * * *

"Cable systems are not public property. Cable systems are privately owned and privately managed, and petitioners point to no case in which we have held that government may designate private property as a public forum.

"Pursuant to federal and state law, franchising authorities require cable operators to create public access channels, but nothing in the record suggests that local franchising authorities take any formal easement or other property interest in those channels that would permit the government to designate that property as a public forum.

"Public access channels are not public fora, and, therefore, petitioners' attempt to redistribute cable speech rights in their favor must fail. For this reason, and the other reasons articulated earlier, I would sustain both § 10(a) and § 10(c).

"Unlike §§ 10(a) and (c), § 10(b) clearly implicates petitioners' free speech rights. Though § 10(b) by no means bans indecent speech, it clearly places content-based restrictions on the transmission of private speech by requiring cable operators to block and segregate indecent programming that the operator has agreed to carry. Consequently, § 10(b) must be subjected to strict scrutiny and can be upheld only if it furthers a compelling governmental interest by the least restrictive means available.

"The Court strikes down § 10(b) by pointing to alternatives, such as reverse-blocking [that] it says are less restrictive than segregation and blocking. Though these methods attempt to place in parents' hands the ability to permit their children to watch as little, or as much, indecent programming as the parents think proper, they do not effectively support parents' authority to direct the moral upbringing of their children. The FCC recognized that leased-access programming comes 'from a wide variety of independent sources, with no single editor controlling [its] selection and presentation.' Thus, indecent programming on leased access channels is 'especially likely to be shown randomly or intermittently between non-indecent programs.' Rather than being able to simply block out certain channels at certain times, a subscriber [must] carefully monitor all leased-access programming. [The Court's alternative is] largely ineffective."

Two provisions of the Communications Decency Act ("CDA") seek to protect minors from material on the Internet. 47 U.S.C. § 223(a) prohibits the knowing transmission of indecent messages to any recipient under 18 years of age. 47 U.S.C. § 223(d) prohibits the knowing sending or displaying of patently offensive messages in a manner that is available to a person under 18 years of age. Patently offensive is defined as any "image or other communication that in context, depicts or describes, in terms patently offensive as measured by contemporary community standards, sexual or excretory activities or organs * * * ."

RENO v. AMERICAN CIVIL LIBERTIES UNION, 521 U.S. 844, 117 S.Ct. 2329, 138 L.Ed.2d 874 (1997), per Stevens, J., held that both provisions were too vague and overbroad to withstand first amendment scrutiny.[a] After providing a lengthy description of the Internet focussing on e-mail, automatic mailing list services, newsgroups, chatrooms, and the WORLD Wide Web, Stevens, J., distinguished prior cases: "In four important respects, the statute upheld in *Ginsberg* was narrower than the CDA. First, we noted in *Ginsberg* that 'the prohibition against sales to minors does not bar parents who so desire from purchasing the magazines for their children.' Under the CDA, by contrast, neither the parents' consent—nor even their participation—in the communication would avoid the application of the statute.[32] Second, the New York statute applied only to commercial transactions, whereas the CDA contains no such limitation. Third, the New York statute cabined its definition of material that is harmful to minors with the requirement that it be 'utterly without redeeming social importance for minors.' The CDA fails to provide us with any definition of the term 'indecent' as used in § 223(a)(1) and, importantly, omits any requirement that the 'patently offensive' material covered by § 223(d) lack serious literary, artistic, political, or scientific value. Fourth, the New York statute defined a minor as a person under the age of 17, whereas the CDA, in applying to all those under 18 years, includes an additional year of those nearest majority. * * *"

"[S]ome of our cases have recognized special justifications for regulation of the broadcast media that are not applicable to other speakers. In these cases, the Court relied on the history of extensive government regulation of the broadcast medium, see, e.g., *Red Lion;* the scarcity of available frequencies at its inception, see, e.g., *Turner Broadcasting System, Inc. v. FCC;* and its 'invasive' nature, see *Sable Communications of Cal., Inc. v. FCC.*

"Those factors are not present in cyberspace. Neither before nor after the enactment of the CDA have the vast democratic fora of the Internet been subject to the type of government supervision and regulation that has attended the broadcast industry. Moreover, the Internet is not as 'invasive' as radio or television. The District Court specifically found that '[c]ommunications over the Internet do not "invade" an individual's home or appear on one's computer screen unbidden. Users seldom encounter content "by accident."' It also found that '[a]lmost all sexually explicit images are preceded by warnings as to the content,' and cited testimony that '"odds are slim" that a user would come across a sexually explicit sight by accident.' * * *

"Finally, unlike the conditions that prevailed when Congress first authorized regulation of the broadcast spectrum, the Internet can hardly be considered a 'scarce' expressive commodity. It provides relatively unlimited, low-cost capacity for communication of all kinds. The Government estimates that '[a]s many as 40 million people use the Internet today, and that figure is expected to grow to 200 million by 1999.' This dynamic, multifaceted category of communication includes not only traditional print and news services, but also audio, video, and still images, as well as interactive, real-time dialogue. Through the use of chat rooms, any person with a phone line can become a town crier with a voice that resonates farther than it could from any soapbox. Through the use of Web pages, mail exploders, and newsgroups, the same individual can become a pamphleteer. As

---

a. The CDA also prohibited obscenity on the Internet. That portion of the statute was not challenged, and the Court specifically noted that it had not struck down that part of the statute.

32. Given the likelihood that many E-mail transmissions from an adult to a minor are conversations between family members, it is therefore incorrect for the dissent to suggest that the provisions of the CDA, even in this narrow area, "are no different from the law we sustained in *Ginsberg.*"

the District Court found, 'the content on the Internet is as diverse as human thought.' We agree with its conclusion that our cases provide no basis for qualifying the level of First Amendment scrutiny that should be applied to this medium.

"Regardless of whether the CDA is so vague that it violates the Fifth Amendment, the many ambiguities concerning the scope of its coverage render it problematic for purposes of the First Amendment. For instance, each of the two parts of the CDA uses a different linguistic form. The first uses the word 'indecent,' 47 U.S.C.A. § 223(a), while the second speaks of material that 'in context, depicts or describes, in terms patently offensive as measured by contemporary community standards, sexual or excretory activities or organs,' § 223(d). Given the absence of a definition of either term,[35] this difference in language will provoke uncertainty among speakers about how the two standards relate to each other and just what they mean.[37] Could a speaker confidently assume that a serious discussion about birth control practices, homosexuality, the First Amendment issues raised by the Appendix to our *Pacifica* opinion, or the consequences of prison rape would not violate the CDA? This uncertainty undermines the likelihood that the CDA has been carefully tailored to the congressional goal of protecting minors from potentially harmful materials.

"The vagueness of the CDA is a matter of special concern for two reasons. First, the CDA is a content-based regulation of speech. [Second,] the CDA is a criminal statute. In addition to the opprobrium and stigma of a criminal conviction, the CDA threatens violators with penalties including up to two years in prison for each act of violation. The severity of criminal sanctions may well cause speakers to remain silent rather than communicate even arguably unlawful words, ideas, and images. As a practical matter, this increased deterrent effect, coupled with the 'risk of discriminatory enforcement' of vague regulations, poses greater First Amendment concerns than those implicated by the civil regulation reviewed in *Denver Area Ed. Telecommunications Consortium, Inc. v. FCC.* * * *

"Because the CDA's 'patently offensive' standard (and, we assume arguendo, its synonymous 'indecent' standard) is one part of the three-prong *Miller* test, the Government reasons, it cannot be unconstitutionally vague. [The] Government's assertion is incorrect as a matter of fact. The second prong of the *Miller* test— the purportedly analogous standard—contains a critical requirement that is omitted from the CDA: that the proscribed material be 'specifically defined by the applicable state law.' This requirement reduces the vagueness inherent in the open-ended term 'patently offensive' as used in the CDA. Moreover, the *Miller* definition is limited to 'sexual conduct,' whereas the CDA extends also to include (1) 'excretory activities' as well as (2) 'organs' of both a sexual and excretory nature.

"The Government's reasoning is also flawed. Just because a definition including three limitations is not vague, it does not follow that one of those limitations, standing by itself, is not vague. Each of *Miller's* additional two prongs—(1) that, taken as a whole, the material appeal to the 'prurient' interest,

---

35. "Indecent" does not benefit from any textual embellishment at all. "Patently offensive" is qualified only to the extent that it involves "sexual or excretory activities or organs" taken "in context" and "measured by contemporary community standards."

37. The statute does not indicate whether the "patently offensive" and "indecent" deter-minations should be made with respect to minors or the population as a whole. The Government asserts that the appropriate standard is "what is suitable material for minors." But the Conferees expressly rejected amendments that would have imposed such a "harmful to minors" standard.

and (2) that it 'lac[k] serious literary, artistic, political, or scientific value'—critically limits the uncertain sweep of the obscenity definition. The second requirement is particularly important because, unlike the 'patently offensive' and 'prurient interest' criteria, it is not judged by contemporary community standards. This 'societal value' requirement, absent in the CDA, allows appellate courts to impose some limitations and regularity on the definition by setting, as a matter of law, a national floor for socially redeeming value. The Government's contention that courts will be able to give such legal limitations to the CDA's standards is belied by Miller's own rationale for having juries determine whether material is 'patently offensive' according to community standards: that such questions are essentially ones of fact.

"In contrast to *Miller* and our other previous cases, the CDA thus presents a greater threat of censoring speech that, in fact, falls outside the statute's scope. Given the vague contours of the coverage of the statute, it unquestionably silences some speakers whose messages would be entitled to constitutional protection. That danger provides further reason for insisting that the statute not be overly broad. The CDA's burden on protected speech cannot be justified if it could be avoided by a more carefully drafted statute. * * *

"It is true that we have repeatedly recognized the governmental interest in protecting children from harmful materials. But that interest does not justify an unnecessarily broad suppression of speech addressed to adults. [In] arguing that the CDA does not so diminish adult communication, the Government relies on the incorrect factual premise that prohibiting a transmission whenever it is known that one of its recipients is a minor would not interfere with adult-to-adult communication. The findings of the District Court make clear that this premise is untenable. Given the size of the potential audience for most messages, in the absence of a viable age verification process, the sender must be charged with knowing that one or more minors will likely view it. Knowledge that, for instance, one or more members of a 100–person chat group will be [a] minor—and therefore that it would be a crime to send the group an indecent message—would surely burden communication among adults.[42]

"The District Court found that at the time of trial existing technology did not include any effective method for a sender to prevent minors from obtaining access to its communications on the Internet without also denying access to adults. The Court found no effective way to determine the age of a user who is accessing material through e-mail, mail exploders, newsgroups, or chat rooms. As a practical matter, the Court also found that it would be prohibitively expensive for noncommercial—as well as some commercial—speakers who have Web sites to verify that their users are adults. These limitations must inevitably curtail a significant amount of adult communication on the Internet. By contrast, the District Court found that '[d]espite its limitations, currently available user-based software suggests that a reasonably effective method by which parents can prevent their children from accessing sexually explicit and other material which parents may believe is inappropriate for their children will soon be widely available.'

"The breadth of the CDA's coverage is wholly unprecedented. Unlike the regulations upheld in *Ginsberg* and *Pacifica,* the scope of the CDA is not limited to commercial speech or commercial entities. Its open-ended prohibitions embrace

---

42. The Government agrees that these provisions are applicable whenever "a sender transmits a message to more than one recipi-

ent, knowing that at least one of the specific persons receiving the message is a minor."

all nonprofit entities and individuals posting indecent messages or displaying them on their own computers in the presence of minors. The general, undefined terms 'indecent' and 'patently offensive' cover large amounts of nonpornographic material with serious educational or other value. Moreover, the 'community standards' criterion as applied to the Internet means that any communication available to a nation-wide audience will be judged by the standards of the community most likely to be offended by the message. The regulated subject matter includes any of the seven 'dirty words' used in the *Pacifica* monologue, the use of which the Government's expert acknowledged could constitute a felony. It may also extend to discussions about prison rape or safe sexual practices, artistic images that include nude subjects, and arguably the card catalogue of the Carnegie Library.

"For the purposes of our decision, we need neither accept nor reject the Government's submission that the First Amendment does not forbid a blanket prohibition on all 'indecent' and 'patently offensive' messages communicated to a 17–year old—no matter how much value the message may contain and regardless of parental approval. It is at least clear that the strength of the Government's interest in protecting minors is not equally strong throughout the coverage of this broad statute. Under the CDA, a parent allowing her 17–year–old to use the family computer to obtain information on the Internet that she, in her parental judgment, deems appropriate could face a lengthy prison term. Similarly, a parent who sent his 17–year–old college freshman information on birth control via e-mail could be incarcerated even though neither he, his child, nor anyone in their home community, found the material 'indecent' or 'patently offensive,' if the college town's community thought otherwise."

"The breadth of this content-based restriction of speech imposes an especially heavy burden on the Government to explain why a less restrictive provision would not be as effective as the CDA. It has not done so. The arguments in this Court have referred to possible alternatives such as requiring that indecent material be 'tagged' in a way that facilitates parental control of material coming into their homes, making exceptions for messages with artistic or educational value, providing some tolerance for parental choice, and regulating some portions of the Internet—such as commercial web sites—differently than others, such as chat rooms. Particularly in the light of the absence of any detailed findings by the Congress, or even hearings addressing the special problems of the CDA, we are persuaded that the CDA is not narrowly tailored if that requirement has any meaning at all."

O'CONNOR, J., joined by Rehnquist, C.J., concurred in the judgment in part and dissented in part: "Given the present state of cyberspace, I agree with the Court that the 'display' provision cannot pass muster. Until gateway technology is available throughout cyberspace, and it is not in 1997, a speaker cannot be reasonably assured that the speech he displays will reach only adults because it is impossible to confine speech to an 'adult zone.' Thus, the only way for a speaker to avoid liability under the CDA is to refrain completely from using indecent speech. But this forced silence impinges on the First Amendment right of adults to make and obtain this speech and, for all intents and purposes, 'reduce[s] the adult population [on the Internet] to reading only what is fit for children.'

"The 'indecency transmission' and 'specific person' provisions present a closer issue, for they are not unconstitutional in all of their applications. [T]he 'indecency transmission' provision makes it a crime to transmit knowingly an indecent message to a person the sender knows is under 18 years of age. The 'specific person' provision proscribes the same conduct, although it does not as explicitly require the sender to know that the intended recipient of his indecent message is a minor. Appellant urges the Court to construe the provision to impose such a knowledge requirement, and I would do so.

"So construed, both provisions are constitutional as applied to a conversation involving only an adult and one or more minors—e.g., when an adult speaker sends an e-mail knowing the addressee is a minor, or when an adult and minor converse by themselves or with other minors in a chat room. In this context, these provisions are no different from the law we sustained in *Ginsberg*. Restricting what the adult may say to the minors in no way restricts the adult's ability to communicate with other adults. He is not prevented from speaking indecently to other adults in a chat room (because there are no other adults participating in the conversation) and he remains free to send indecent e-mails to other adults. The relevant universe contains only one adult, and the adult in that universe has the power to refrain from using indecent speech and consequently to keep all such speech within the room in an "adult" zone.

"The analogy to *Ginsberg* breaks down, however, when more than one adult is a party to the conversation. If a minor enters a chat room otherwise occupied by adults, the CDA effectively requires the adults in the room to stop using indecent speech. If they did not, they could be prosecuted under the 'indecency transmission' and 'specific person' provisions for any indecent statements they make to the group, since they would be transmitting an indecent message to specific persons, one of whom is a minor. The CDA is therefore akin to a law that makes it a crime for a bookstore owner to sell pornographic magazines to anyone once a minor enters his store. Even assuming such a law might be constitutional in the physical world as a reasonable alternative to excluding minors completely from the store, the absence of any means of excluding minors from chat rooms in cyberspace restricts the rights of adults to engage in indecent speech in those rooms. The 'indecency transmission' and 'specific person' provisions share this defect. * * *

"Whether the CDA substantially interferes with the First Amendment rights of minors, and thereby runs afoul of the second characteristic of valid zoning laws, presents a closer question. [The] Court neither 'accept[s] nor reject[s]' the argument that the CDA is facially overbroad because it substantially interferes with the First Amendment rights of minors. I would reject it. [In] my view, the universe of speech constitutionally protected as to minors but banned by the CDA—i.e., the universe of material that is 'patently offensive,' but which nonetheless has some redeeming value for minors or does not appeal to their prurient interest—is a very small one. Appellees cite no examples of speech falling within this universe and do not attempt to explain why that universe is substantial 'in relation to the statute's plainly legitimate sweep.' That the CDA might deny minors the right to obtain material that has some 'value' is largely beside the point. While discussions about prison rape or nude art, may have some redeeming education value for adults, they do not necessarily have any such value for minors, and under *Ginsberg,* minors only have a First Amendment right to obtain patently offensive material that has 'redeeming social importance for minors.' There is also no evidence in the record to support the contention that 'many [e]-mail transmissions from an adult to a minor are conversations between family members,' and no support for the legal proposition that such speech is absolutely immune from regulation. Accordingly, in my view, the CDA does not burden a substantial amount of minors' constitutionally protected speech.

"Thus, the constitutionality of the CDA as a zoning law hinges on the extent to which it substantially interferes with the First Amendment rights of adults. Because the rights of adults are infringed only by the 'display' provision and by the 'indecency transmission' and 'specific person' provisions as applied to communications involving more than one adult, I would invalidate the CDA only to that extent.   Insofar as the 'indecency transmission' and 'specific person' provisions prohibit the use of indecent speech in communications between an adult and one or more minors, however, they can and should be sustained.   The Court reaches a contrary conclusion, and from that holding that I respectfully dissent." [b]

THE RIGHT NOT TO SPEAK, THE RIGHT TO ASSOCIATE, AND THE RIGHT NOT TO ASSOCIATE

THE RIGHT NOT TO BE ASSOCIATED WITH PARTICULAR IDEAS

CON LAW: P. 970, add to note 6

AMER CON: P. 955, add to note 6

RTS & LIB: P. 877, add to note 6

Buckley v. American Constitutional Law Foundation, ___ U.S. ___, 119 S.Ct. 636, 142 L.Ed.2d 599 (1999), per Ginsburg, J., held unconstitutional a Colorado statute requiring that circulators of initiatives wear identification badges bearing their names and that sponsors of the initiative report the names and addresses of all paid circulators. By contrast, the Court was satisfied that the requirement of the filing of an affidavit containing the name and address of the circulator of petitions was consistent with the first amendment.

FREEDOM OF ASSOCIATION AND EMPLOYMENT

CON LAW: P. 974, addition to fn. b

AMER CON: P. 959, addition to fn. b

RTS & LIB: P. 881, addition to fn. b

Should *Elrod* and *Branti* be extended to independent contractors? See *O'Hare Truck Service v. City of Northlake,* 518 U.S. 712, 116 S.Ct. 2353, 135 L.Ed.2d 874 (1996).

CON LAW: P. 978, addition to fn. 5

AMER CON: P. 963, addition to fn. 5

RTS & LIB: P. 885, addition to fn. 5

[Should *Pickering* be extended to independent contractors? See *Board of County Commissioners v. Umbehr,* 518 U.S. 668, 116 S.Ct. 2342, 135 L.Ed.2d 843 (1996)].

CON LAW: P. 987, after note 4

AMER CON: P. 972, after note 4

RTS & LIB: P. 894, after note 4

5. *Beyond employment: the scope of Abood.* The Agricultural Marketing Agreement Act of 1937 enables committees of producers appointed by the Secre-

b. Stevens, J., argued that Congress had not provided guidance as to where lines should be drawn if the statute were otherwise to be struck down. Lacking guidance, he declined to find that the statute was readily subject to a narrowing construction.

tary of Agriculture to issue certain marketing orders without violating the antitrust laws provided that two thirds of the producers who market at least two thirds of the volume of a product approve. The purpose of such orders is to establish and maintain orderly marketing conditions and fair prices for agricultural commodities. Such orders, which are restricted to the smallest practicable production area, range from price fixing, joint research projects, standardized packaging, and joint advertising. Expenses of administering an order are paid from funds collected pursuant to the marketing order.

Some producers of California nectarines, plums, and peaches brought a proceeding challenging marketing orders requiring them to pay for generic advertising. They invoked a first amendment right not to be compelled to subsidize the speech of others.

GLICKMAN v. WILEMAN BROTHERS & ELLIOT, INC., 521 U.S. 457, 117 S.Ct. 2130, 138 L.Ed.2d 585 (1997), per STEVENS, J., held that the compelled funding of generic advertising did not violate the first amendment: "The legal question that we address is whether being compelled to fund this advertising raises a First Amendment issue for us to resolve, or rather is simply a question of economic policy for Congress and the Executive to resolve.

"Three characteristics of the regulatory scheme at issue distinguish it from laws that we have found to abridge the freedom of speech protected by the First Amendment. First, the marketing orders impose no restraint on the freedom of any producer to communicate any message to any audience. Second, they do not compel any person to engage in any actual or symbolic speech. Third, they do not compel the producers to endorse or to finance any political or ideological views. Indeed, since all of the respondents are engaged in the business of marketing California nectarines, plums, and peaches, it is fair to presume that they agree with the central message of the speech that is generated by the generic program.[a] Thus, none of our First Amendment jurisprudence provides any support for the suggestion that the promotional regulations should be scrutinized under a different standard than that applicable to the other anticompetitive features of the marketing orders. * * *

"Respondents argue that the assessments for generic advertising impinge on their First Amendment rights because they reduce the amount of money that producers have available to conduct their own advertising. This is equally true, however, of assessments to cover employee benefits, inspection fees, or any other activity that is authorized by a marketing order. * * *

"None of the advertising in this record promotes any particular message other than encouraging consumers to buy California tree fruit. Neither the fact that respondents may prefer to foster that message independently in order to promote and distinguish their own products, nor the fact that they think more or less money should be spent fostering it, makes this case comparable to those in which an objection rested on political or ideological disagreement with the content of the message. The mere fact that objectors believe their money is not being well spent 'does not mean [that] they have a First Amendment complaint.' * * *

"As with other features of the marketing orders, individual producers may not share the views or the interests of others in the same market. But decisions that are made by the majority, if acceptable for other regulatory programs, should

---

a. The producers objected to the content of some of the advertisements. Stevens, J., stated that these concerns might call into question portions of the program, but had no bearing on the entire program. He also stated that these concerns were more properly addressed to the Secretary.

be equally so for promotional advertising. Perhaps more money may be at stake when a generic advertising program is adopted than for other features of the cooperative endeavor, but that fact does not transform this question of business judgment into a constitutional issue. In sum, what we are reviewing is a species of economic regulation that should enjoy the same strong presumption of validity that we accord to other policy judgments made by Congress. The mere fact that one or more producers 'do not wish to foster' generic advertising of their product is not a sufficient reason for overriding the judgment of the majority of market participants, bureaucrats, and legislators who have concluded that such programs are beneficial."

SOUTER, J., joined by Rehnquist, C.J., and Scalia, J., and Thomas, J., in part, dissented: "The Court's first mistaken conclusion lies in treating *Abood* as permitting any enforced subsidy for speech that is germane to permissible economic regulation, in the sense that it relates to the subject matter of the regulation and tends to further its objectives. But *Abood* and its subsequent line of cases is not nearly so permissive as the Court makes out. In *Abood,* we recognized that even in matters directly related to collective bargaining, compulsory funding of union activities has an impact on employees' First Amendment interests, since the employees might disagree with positions taken by the union on issues such as the inclusion of abortion in a medical benefit plan, or negotiating no-strike agreements, or even the desirability of unionism in general. To be sure, we concluded that any interference with such interests was 'constitutionally justified by the legislative assessment of the important contribution of the union shop to the system of labor relations established by Congress.' But this was simply a way of saying that the government's objective of guaranteeing the opportunity for a union shop, the importance and legitimacy of which were already settled, could not be attained without the incidental infringements of the interests in unfettered speech and association that petitioners there claimed.
* * *

"Decisions postdating *Abood* have made clear, however, that its limited sanction for laws affecting First Amendment interests may not be expanded to cover every imposition that is in some way 'germane' to a regulatory program in the sense of relating sympathetically to it. Rather, to survive scrutiny under *Abood*, a mandatory fee must not only be germane to some otherwise legitimate regulatory scheme; it must also be justified by vital policy interests of the government and not add significantly to the burdening of free speech inherent in achieving those interests. *Lehnert v. Ferris Faculty Assn.*

"Thus, in *Lehnert* eight Justices concluded that a teachers' union could not constitutionally charge objecting employees for a public relations campaign meant to raise the esteem for teachers in the public mind and so increase the public's willingness to pay for public education. 'Expression of this kind extends beyond the negotiation and grievance-resolution contexts and imposes a substantially greater burden upon First Amendment rights than do [collective-bargaining functions].' The advertising campaigns here suffer from the same defect as the public relations effort to stimulate demand for the teachers' product: a local union can negotiate a particular contract for the benefit of a shop's whole labor force without globally espousing the virtues of teachers, and (in the absence of further explanation) produce markets can be directly regulated in the interest of stability and growth without espousing the virtues of fruit. They were, indeed, for a quarter century, and still are under the many agricultural marketing orders that authorize no advertising schemes. In each instance, the challenged burden on dissenters' First Amendment rights is substantially greater than anything inherent in regulation of the commercial transactions. Thus, the *Abood* line does not permit this program merely because it is germane to the marketing orders.

"The Court's second misemployment of *Abood* and its successors is its reliance on them for the proposition that when government neither forbids speech nor attributes it to an objector, it may compel subsidization for any objectionable message that is not political or ideological. * * * While it is perfectly true that cases like *Abood* and *Keller* did involve political or ideological speech, and the Court made reference to that character in explaining the gravity of the First Amendment interests at stake, nothing in those cases suggests that government has free rein to compel funding of nonpolitical speech (which might include art, for example, as well as commercial advertising). * * * The fact that no prior case of this Court has applied this principle to commercial and nonideological speech simply reflects the fortuity that this is the first commercial-speech subsidy case to come before us.

"An apparent third ground for the Court's conclusion that the First Amendment is not implicated here is its assumption that respondents do not disagree with the advertisements they object to subsidizing.[b] * * *

"What counts [here] is not whether respondents fail to disagree with the generalized message of the generic ads that California fruit is good, but that they do indeed deny that the general message is as valuable and worthy of their support as more particular claims about the merits of their own brands. One need not 'disagree' with an abstractionist when buying a canvas from a representational painter; one merely wishes to support a different act of expression.

"The Secretary of Agriculture has a further argument for minimizing or eliminating scrutiny of this subsidization mandate, which deserves some mention even though the Court does not adopt it. The Secretary calls for lesser scrutiny of forced payments for truthful advertising and promotion than for restrictions on commercial speech, on the ground that the effect of compelled funding is to increase the sum of information to the consuming public. This argument rests, however, on the assumption that regulation of commercial speech is justified solely or largely on preservation of public access to truthful information, an assumption we have already seen to be inaccurate. Truth is indeed a justifiable objective of commercial speech protection, but so is nonmisleading persuasion directed to the advertiser's own choice of what to promote."[c]

THOMAS, J., joined by Scalia, J., dissenting observed: "What we are now left with, if we are to take the majority opinion at face value, is one of two disturbing consequences: Either (1) paying for advertising is not speech at all, while such activities as draft card burning, flag burning, armband wearing, public sleeping, and nude dancing are, or (2) compelling payment for third party communication does not implicate speech, and thus the Government would be free to force payment for a whole variety of expressive conduct that it could not restrict. In either case, surely we have lost our way."

b. Souter, J., pointed out that the producers did object to some of the advertisements and whether these objections seemed "trivial to the Court, they in fact relate directly to a vendor's recognized First Amendment interest in touting his wares as he sees fit so long as he does not mislead."

c. Souter, J., proceeded to argue that the government's order did not meet the *Central Hudson* test. Thomas, J., did not join this section of the opinion because he maintained, as he had in *Liquormart*, that more stringent standards should apply to commercial speech.

POLITICAL ASSOCIATION AND POLITICAL PARTIES

CON LAW: P. 1011, after note 2
AMER CON: P. 996, after note 2
RTS & LIB: P. 918, after note 2

Minnesota's "antifusion" laws prohibit political candidates from appearing on the ballot as candidates for more than one party. Twin Cities Area New Party ("New Party") named a candidate for state representative, Andy Dawkins, who also was a candidate of the Minnesota–Democratic–Farmer–Labor Party ("DFL"). Dawkins signed an affidavit for the New Party, but local election officials refused to accept it since his affidavit of candidacy for DFL had already been filed.[a] The New Party brought suit maintaining that the antifusion laws violated the party's rights of association.

TIMMONS v. TWIN CITIES AREA NEW PARTY, 520 U.S. 351, 117 S.Ct. 1364, 137 L.Ed.2d 589 (1997), per REHNQUIST, C.J., upheld the antifusion laws: "The First Amendment protects the right of citizens to associate and to form political parties for the advancement of common political goals and ideas. * * * [On] the other hand, it is also clear that States may, and inevitably must, enact reasonable regulations of parties, elections, and ballots to reduce election- and campaign-related disorder. * * * When deciding whether a state election law violates First and Fourteenth Amendment associational rights, we weigh the ' "character and magnitude" ' of the burden the State's rule imposes on those rights against the interests the State contends justify that burden, and consider the extent to which the State's concerns make the burden necessary. Regulations imposing severe burdens on plaintiffs' rights must be narrowly tailored and advance a compelling state interest. Lesser burdens, however, trigger less exacting review, and a State's ' "important regulatory interests" ' will usually be enough to justify ' "reasonable, nondiscriminatory restrictions." ' No bright line separates permissible election-related regulation from unconstitutional infringements on First Amendment freedoms.

"The New Party's claim that it has a right to select its own candidate is uncontroversial, so far as it goes. That is, the New Party, and not someone else, has the right to select the New Party's 'standard bearer.' It does not follow, though, that a party is absolutely entitled to have its nominee appear on the ballot as that party's candidate. A particular candidate might be ineligible for office, unwilling to serve, or, as here, another party's candidate. That a particular individual may not appear on the ballot as a particular party's candidate does not severely burden that party's association rights.

"The New Party relies on *Eu v. San Francisco County Democratic Central Comm.,* 489 U.S. 214, 109 S.Ct. 1013, 103 L.Ed.2d 271 (1989) and *Tashjian v. Republican Party of Conn.,* 479 U.S. 208, 107 S.Ct. 544, 93 L.Ed.2d 514 (1986). In *Eu,* we struck down California election provisions that prohibited political parties from endorsing candidates in party primaries and regulated parties' internal affairs and structure. And in *Tashjian,* we held that Connecticut's closed-primary statute, which required voters in a party primary to be registered party members, interfered with a party's associational rights by limiting 'the group of registered voters whom the Party may invite to participate in the basic function of selecting the Party's candidates.' But while *Tashjian* and *Eu* involved regulation of political parties' internal affairs and core associational activities, Minnesota's fusion ban does not. The ban, which applies to major and minor parties alike, simply precludes one party's candidate from appearing on the ballot, as that

a. The DFL did not object.

party's candidate, if already nominated by another party. Respondent is free to try to convince Representative Dawkins to be the New Party's, not the DFL's, candidate. * * *

"The New Party contends that the fusion ban burdens its 'right ... to communicate its choice of nominees on the ballot on terms equal to those offered other parties, and the right of the party's supporters and other voters to receive that information,' and insists that communication on the ballot of a party's candidate choice is a 'critical source of information for the great majority of voters [who] rely upon party "labels" as a voting guide.'

"It is true that Minnesota's fusion ban prevents the New Party from using the ballot to communicate to the public that it supports a particular candidate who is already another party's candidate. In addition, the ban shuts off one possible avenue a party might use to send a message to its preferred *candidate* because, with fusion, a candidate who wins an election on the basis of two parties' votes will likely know more—if the parties' votes are counted separately—about the particular wishes and ideals of his constituency. We are unpersuaded, however, by the Party's contention that it has a right to use the ballot itself to send a particularized message, to its candidate and to the voters, about the nature of its support for the candidate. Ballots serve primarily to elect candidates, not as fora for political expression. Like all parties in Minnesota, the New Party is able to use the ballot to communicate information about itself and its candidate to the voters, so long as that candidate is not already someone else's candidate. * * *

"In sum, Minnesota's laws do not restrict the ability of the New Party and its members to endorse, support, or vote for anyone they like. The laws do not directly limit the Party's access to the ballot. They are silent on parties' internal structure, governance, and policy-making. Instead, these provisions reduce the universe of potential candidates who may appear on the ballot as the Party's nominee only by ruling out those few individuals who both have already agreed to be another party's candidate and also, if forced to choose, themselves prefer that other party. They also limit, slightly, the Party's ability to send a message to the voters and to its preferred candidates. We conclude that the burdens Minnesota imposes on the Party's First and Fourteenth Amendment associational rights—though not trivial—are not severe.

"[Therefore,] the State's asserted regulatory interests need only be 'sufficiently weighty to justify the limitation' imposed on the Party's rights. Nor do we require elaborate, empirical verification of the weightiness of the State's asserted justifications. * * *

"Minnesota argues here that its fusion ban is justified by its interests in avoiding voter confusion, promoting candidate competition (by reserving limited ballot space for opposing candidates), preventing electoral distortions and ballot manipulations, and discouraging party splintering and 'unrestrained factionalism.' States certainly have an interest in protecting the integrity, fairness, and efficiency of their ballots and election processes as means for electing public officials. Petitioners contend that a candidate or party could easily exploit fusion as a way of associating his or its name with popular slogans and catch phrases. For example, members of a major party could decide that a powerful way of 'sending a message' via the ballot would be for various factions of that party to nominate the major party's candidate as the candidate for the newly-formed 'No New Taxes,' 'Conserve Our Environment,' and 'Stop Crime Now' parties. In response, an opposing major party would likely instruct its factions to nominate that party's candidate as the 'Fiscal Responsibility,' 'Healthy Planet,' and 'Safe Streets' parties' candidate.

"Whether or not the putative 'fusion' candidates' names appeared on one or four ballot lines, such maneuvering would undermine the ballot's purpose by transforming it from a means of choosing candidates to a billboard for political advertising. The New Party responds to this concern, ironically enough, by insisting that the State could avoid such manipulation by adopting more demanding ballot-access standards rather than prohibiting multiple-party nomination. However, [because] the burdens the fusion ban imposes on the Party's associational rights are not severe, the State need not narrowly tailor the means it chooses to promote ballot integrity. The Constitution does not require that Minnesota compromise the policy choices embodied in its ballot-access requirements to accommodate the New Party's fusion strategy.

"Relatedly, petitioners urge that permitting fusion would undercut Minnesota's ballot-access regime by allowing minor parties to capitalize on the popularity of another party's candidate, rather than on their own appeal to the voters, in order to secure access to the ballot. That is, voters who might not sign a minor party's nominating petition based on the party's own views and candidates might do so if they viewed the minor party as just another way of nominating the same person nominated by one of the major parties. * * * The State surely has a valid interest in making sure that minor and third parties who are granted access to the ballot are bona fide and actually supported, on their own merits, by those who have provided the statutorily required petition or ballot support.

"States also have a strong interest in the stability of their political systems.[10] This interest does not permit a State to completely insulate the two-party system from minor parties' or independent candidates' competition and influence, nor is it a paternalistic license for States to protect political parties from the consequences of their own internal disagreements. That said, the States' interest permits them to enact reasonable election regulations that may, in practice, favor the traditional two-party system, and that temper the destabilizing effects of party-splintering and excessive factionalism. The Constitution permits the Minnesota Legislature to decide that political stability is best served through a healthy two-party system. And while an interest in securing the perceived benefits of a stable two-party system will not justify unreasonably exclusionary restrictions, States need not remove all of the many hurdles third parties face in the American political arena today.

"In *Storer v. Brown*, 415 U.S. 724, 94 S.Ct. 1274, 39 L.Ed.2d 714 (1974), we upheld a California statute that denied ballot positions to independent candidates who had voted in the immediately preceding primary elections or had a registered party affiliation at any time during the year before the same primary elections.[11]

---

10. The dissents state that we may not consider "what appears to be the true basis for [our] holding—the interest in preserving the two-party system," because Minnesota did not defend this interest in its briefs and "expressly rejected" it at oral argument. In fact, at oral argument, the State contended that it has an interest in the stability of its political system and that, even if certain election-related regulations, such as those requiring single-member districts, tend to work to the advantage of the traditional two-party system, the "States do have a permissible choice [there], as long as

they don't go so far as to close the door to minor part[ies]." We agree.

11. A similar provision applied to party candidates, and imposed a "flat disqualification upon any candidate seeking to run in a party primary if he has been 'registered as affiliated with a political party other than that political party the nomination of which he seeks within 12 months immediately prior to the filing of the declaration.'" Another provision stated that "no person may file nomination papers for a party nomination and an independent nomination for the same office...."

After surveying the relevant caselaw, we 'ha[d] no hesitation in sustaining' the party-disaffiliation provisions. We recognized that the provisions were part of a 'general state policy aimed at maintaining the integrity of [the] ballot,' and noted that the provision did not discriminate against independent candidates. We concluded that while a 'State need not take the course California [has], California apparently believes with the Founding Fathers that splintered parties and unrestrained factionalism may do significant damage to the fabric of government. It appears obvious to us that the one-year disaffiliation provision furthers the State's interest in the stability of its political system.' [12]

"Our decision in *Burdick v. Takushi*, 504 U.S. 428, 112 S.Ct. 2059, 119 L.Ed.2d 245 (1992) is also relevant. There, we upheld Hawaii's ban on write-in voting against a claim that the ban unreasonably infringed on citizens' First and Fourteenth Amendment rights. In so holding, we rejected the petitioner's argument that the ban 'deprive[d] him of the opportunity to cast a meaningful ballot,' emphasizing that the function of elections is to elect candidates and that 'we have repeatedly upheld reasonable, politically neutral regulations that have the effect of channeling expressive activit[ies] at the polls.'

"Minnesota's fusion ban is far less burdensome than the disaffiliation rule upheld in *Storer,* and is justified by similarly weighty state interests. By reading *Storer* as dealing only with 'sore-loser candidates,' the dissent, in our view, fails to appreciate the case's teaching. Under the California disaffiliation statute at issue in *Storer, any* person affiliated with a party at any time during the year leading up to the primary election was absolutely precluded from appearing on the ballot as an independent or as the candidate of another party. Minnesota's fusion ban is not nearly so restrictive; the challenged provisions say nothing about the previous party affiliation of would-be candidates but only require that, in order to appear on the ballot, a candidate not be the nominee of more than one party. California's disaffiliation rule limited the field of candidates by thousands; Minnesota's precludes only a handful who freely choose to be so limited. It is also worth noting that while California's disaffiliation statute absolutely banned many candidacies, Minnesota's fusion ban only prohibits a candidate from being named twice.

"We conclude that the burdens Minnesota's fusion ban imposes on the New Party's associational rights are justified by 'correspondingly weighty' valid state interests in ballot integrity and political stability.[13] In deciding that Minnesota's fusion ban does not unconstitutionally burden the New Party's First and Fourteenth Amendment rights, we express no views on the New Party's policy-based arguments concerning the wisdom of fusion. It may well be that, as support for new political parties increase, these arguments will carry the day in some States' legislatures. But the Constitution does not require Minnesota, and the approximately 40 other States that do not permit fusion, to allow it."

STEVENS, J., joined in part by Ginsburg and Souter, JJ., dissented: "The Court's conclusion that the Minnesota statute prohibiting multiple-party candidacies is constitutional rests on three dubious premises: (1) that the statute imposes

12. The dissent insists that New York's experience with fusion politics undermines Minnesota's contention that its fusion ban promotes political stability. California's experiment with cross-filing, on the other hand, provides some justification for Minnesota's concerns. In 1946, for example, Earl Warren was the nominee of both major parties, and was therefore able to run unopposed in California's general election. It appears to be widely accepted that California's cross-filing system stifled electoral competition and undermined the role of distinctive political parties.

13. The dissent rejects the argument that Minnesota's fusion ban serves its alleged paternalistic interest in "avoiding voter confusion." Although this supposed interest was discussed below, and in the parties' briefs before this Court, it plays no part in our analysis today.

only a minor burden on the Party's right to choose and to support the candidate of its choice; (2) that the statute significantly serves the State's asserted interests in avoiding ballot manipulation and factionalism; and (3) that, in any event, the interest in preserving the two-party system justifies the imposition of the burden at issue in this case. I disagree with each of these premises. * * *

"The members of a recognized political party unquestionably have a constitutional right to select their nominees for public office and to communicate the identity of their nominees to the voting public. Both the right to choose and the right to advise voters of that choice are entitled to the highest respect.

"The Minnesota statutes place a significant burden on both of those rights. The Court's recital of burdens that the statute does not inflict on the Party does nothing to minimize the severity of the burdens that it does impose. The fact that the Party may nominate its second choice surely does not diminish the significance of a restriction that denies it the right to have the name of its first choice appear on the ballot. Nor does the point that it may use some of its limited resources to publicize the fact that its first choice is the nominee of some other party provide an adequate substitute for the message that is conveyed to every person who actually votes when a party's nominees appear on the ballot.[1] [T]he right to be on the election ballot is precisely what separates a political party from any other interest group.

"The majority rejects as unimportant the limits that the fusion ban may impose on the Party's ability to express its political views, relying on our decision in *Burdick v. Takushi,* in which we noted that 'the purpose of casting, counting, and recording votes is to elect public officials, not to serve as a general forum for political expression.' But in *Burdick* we concluded simply that an individual voter's interest in expressing his disapproval of the single candidate running for office in a particular election did not require the State to finance and provide a mechanism for tabulating write-in votes. Our conclusion that the ballot is not principally a forum for the individual expression of political sentiment through the casting of a vote does not justify the conclusion that the ballot serves no expressive purpose for the parties who place candidates on the ballot. Indeed, the long-recognized right to choose a ' "standard bearer who best represents the party's ideologies and preferences," ' *Eu,* is inescapably an expressive right. 'To the extent that party labels provide a shorthand designation of the views of party candidates on matters of public concern, the identification of candidates with particular parties plays a role in the process by which voters inform themselves for the exercise of the franchise.' *Tashjian v. Republican Party of Conn.*

"In this case, and presumably in most cases, the burden of a statute of this kind is imposed upon the members of a minor party, but its potential impact is much broader. Popular candidates like Andy Dawkins sometimes receive nationwide recognition. Fiorello LaGuardia, Earl Warren, Ronald Reagan, and Franklin

---

1. The burden on the Party's right to nominate its first-choice candidate, by limiting the Party's ability to convey through its nominee what the Party represents, risks impinging on another core element of any political party's associational rights—the right to "broaden the base of public participation in and support for its activities." A fusion ban burdens the right of a minor party to broaden its base of support because of the political reality that the dominance of the major parties frequently makes a vote for a minor party or independent candidate a "wasted" vote. When minor parties can nominate a candidate also nominated by a major party, they are able to present their members with an opportunity to cast a vote for a candidate who will actually be elected. Although this aspect of a party's effort to broaden support is distinct from the ability to nominate the candidate who best represents the party's views, it is important to note that the party's right to broaden the base of its support is burdened in both ways by the fusion ban.

D. Roosevelt, are names that come readily to mind as candidates whose reputations and political careers were enhanced because they appeared on election ballots as fusion candidates. A statute that denied a political party the right to nominate any of those individuals for high office simply because he had already been nominated by another party would, in my opinion, place an intolerable burden on political expression and association.

"[E]ven accepting the majority's view that the burdens imposed by the law are not weighty, the State's asserted interests must at least bear some plausible relationship to the burdens it places on political parties. Although the Court today suggests that the State does not have to support its asserted justifications for the fusion ban with evidence that they have any empirical validity, we have previously required more than a bare assertion that some particular state interest is served by a burdensome election requirement.

"While the State describes some imaginative theoretical sources of voter confusion that could result from fusion candidacies, in my judgment the argument that the burden on First Amendment interests is justified by this concern is meritless and severely underestimates the intelligence of the typical voter. We have noted more than once that ' "[a] State's claim that it is enhancing the ability of its citizenry to make wise decisions by restricting the flow of information to them must be viewed with some skepticism." ' *Eu*; *Tashjian*.

"The State's concern about ballot manipulation, readily accepted by the majority, is similarly farfetched. The possibility that members of the major parties will begin to create dozens of minor parties with detailed, issue-oriented titles for the sole purpose of nominating candidates under those titles is entirely hypothetical.[3] The majority dismisses out-of-hand the Party's argument that the risk of this type of ballot manipulation and crowding is more easily averted by maintaining reasonably stringent requirements for the creation of minor parties. In fact, though, the Party's point merely illustrates the idea that a State can place some kinds—but not every kind—of limitation on the abilities of small parties to thrive. If the State wants to make it more difficult for any group to achieve the legal status of being a political party, it can do so within reason and still not run up against the First Amendment. 'The State has the undoubted right to require candidates to make a preliminary showing of substantial support in order to qualify for a place on the ballot, because it is both wasteful and confusing to encumber the ballot with the names of frivolous candidates.' *Anderson*, 460 U.S., at 788–789, n. 9, 103 S.Ct., at 1570, n. 9. See also *Jenness v. Fortson*, 403 U.S. 431, 442, 91 S.Ct. 1970, 1976, 29 L.Ed.2d 554 (1971). But once the State has established a standard for achieving party status, forbidding an acknowledged party from putting on the ballot its chosen candidate clearly frustrates core associational rights.[5]

---

3. [T]he parade of horribles that the majority appears to believe might visit Minnesota should fusion candidacies be allowed is fantastical, given the evidence from New York's experience with fusion. Thus, the evidence that actually is available diminishes, rather than strengthens, Minnesota's claims. The majority asserts that California's cross-filing system, in place during the first half of this century, provides a compelling counter-example. But cross-filing, which "allowed candidates to file in the primary of any or all parties without specifying party affiliation." D. Mazmanian, *Third Parties in Presidential Elections* 132–133

(1974) is simply not the same as fusion politics, and the problems suffered in California do not provide empirical support for Minnesota's position.

5. A second "ballot manipulation" argument accepted by the majority is that minor parties will attempt to "capitalize on the popularity of another party's candidate, rather than on their own appeal to the voters, in order to secure access to the ballot." What the majority appears unwilling to accept is that *Andy Dawkins was the New Party's chosen candidate.* The Party was not trying to capitalize

"The State argues that the fusion ban promotes political stability by preventing intra-party factionalism and party raiding. States do certainly have an interest in maintaining a stable political system. But the State has not convincingly articulated how the fusion ban will prevent the factionalism it fears. Unlike the law at issue in *Storer v. Brown,* for example, this law would not prevent sore-loser candidates from defecting with a disaffected segment of a major party and running as an opposition candidate for a newly formed minor party. Nor does this law, like those aimed at requiring parties to show a modicum of support in order to secure a place on the election ballot, prevent the formation of numerous small parties. Indeed, the activity banned by Minnesota's law is the formation of coalitions, not the division and dissension of ' "splintered parties and unrestrained factionalism" ' * * *

"[The interest in preserving the two-party system is not] sufficient to justify the fusion ban.[b] In most States, perhaps in all, there are two and only two major political parties. It is not surprising, therefore, that most States have enacted election laws that impose burdens on the development and growth of third parties. The law at issue in this case is undeniably such a law. The fact that the law was both intended to disadvantage minor parties and has had that effect is a matter that should weigh against, rather than in favor of, its constitutionality.

"Our jurisprudence in this area reflects a certain tension: on the one hand, we have been clear that political stability is an important state interest and that incidental burdens on the formation of minor parties are reasonable to protect that interest, see *Storer;* on the other, we have struck down state elections laws specifically because they give 'the two old, established parties a decided advantage over any new parties struggling for existence,' *Williams v. Rhodes,* 393 U.S. 23, 89 S.Ct. 5, 21 L.Ed.2d 24 (1968).[7] * * * [c]

"Nothing in the Constitution prohibits the States from maintaining single-member districts with winner-take-all voting arrangements. And these elements of an election system do make it significantly more difficult for third parties to thrive. But these laws are different in two respects from the fusion bans at issue here. First, the method by which they hamper third-party development is not one that impinges on the associational rights of those third parties; minor parties remain free to nominate candidates of their choice, and to rally support for those candidates. The small parties' relatively limited likelihood of ultimate success on election day does not deprive them of the right to try. Second, the establishment of single-member districts correlates directly with the States' interests in political stability. Systems of proportional representation, for example, may tend toward

on his status as someone else's candidate, but to identify him as their own choice.

b. Stevens, J., maintained that the majority should not have considered the interest in maintaining the two-party system because it was not argued in the briefs and was rejected by the state at oral arguments. Ginsburg and Souter, JJ., did not join the section of Stevens, J.'s opinion about the two-party system.

7. In *Anderson v. Celebrezze,* 460 U.S. 780, 103 S.Ct. 1564, 75 L.Ed.2d 547 (1983) the State argued that its interest in political stability justified the early filing deadline for presidential candidates at issue in the case. We recognized that the "asserted interest in political stability amounts to a desire to protect

existing political parties from competition," and rejected that interest.

c. *Williams* dealt with ballot access requirements making it virtually impossible for new political parties, even ones with hundreds of thousands of members, to gain access to the ballot. In Presidential elections, for example, Ohio had required new parties to submit petitions totaling 15% of the number of ballots cast in the prior gubernatorial election. (Most states require less than 1% of the ballots cast). The result was to confine the ballot to the two major parties. The Court struck down the statute on equal protection grounds: "There is, of course, no reason why two parties should retain a permanent monopoly on the right to have people vote for or against them."

factionalism and fragile coalitions that diminish legislative effectiveness. In the context of fusion candidacies, the risks to political stability are extremely attenuated.[8] Of course, the reason minor parties so ardently support fusion politics is because it allows the parties to build up a greater base of support, as potential minor party members realize that a vote for the smaller party candidate is not necessarily a "wasted" vote. Eventually, a minor party might gather sufficient strength that—were its members so inclined—it could successfully run a candidate not endorsed by any major party, and legislative coalition-building will be made more difficult by the presence of third party legislators. But the risks to political stability in that scenario are speculative at best. * * *

"The strength of the two-party system—and of each of its major components—is the product of the power of the ideas, the traditions, the candidates, and the voters that constitute the parties. It demeans the strength of the two-party system to assume that the major parties need to rely on laws that discriminate against independent voters and minor parties in order to preserve their positions of power.[12] Indeed, it is a central theme of our jurisprudence that the entire electorate, which necessarily includes the members of the major parties, will benefit from robust competition in ideas and governmental policies that ' "is at the core of our electoral process and of the First Amendment freedoms." ' " * * *

SOUTER, J., dissenting, was willing to "judge the challenged statutes only on the interests the State has raised in their defense and would hold them unconstitutional. I am, however, unwilling to go the further distance of considering and rejecting the majority's 'preservation of the two-party system' rationale. For while Minnesota has made no such argument before us, I cannot discount the possibility of a forceful one. There is considerable consensus that party loyalty among American voters has declined significantly in the past four decades and that the overall influence of the parties in the political process has decreased considerably. [I]t may not be unreasonable to infer that the two-party system is in some jeopardy.

"Surely the majority is right that States 'have a strong interest in the stability of their political systems,' that is, in preserving a political system capable of governing effectively. If it could be shown that the disappearance of the two-party system would undermine that interest, and that permitting fusion candidacies poses a substantial threat to the two-party scheme, there might well be a sufficient predicate for recognizing the constitutionality of the state action presented by this case. Right now, however, no State has attempted even to make this argument, and I would therefore leave its consideration for another day.

The Virginia Republican Party required those who wished to become delegates to the 1994 state nominating convention for United States Senator to pay a registration fee. Morse filed suit contending that the fee violated the Voting Rights Act including the provision that changes in voting requirements in particular jurisdictions be submitted to the Attorney General for preclearance. The Republican Party denied the application of the statute to the fee requirement, but,

---

8. Even in a system that allows fusion, a candidate for election must assemble majority support, so the State's concern cannot logically be about risks to political stability in the particular election in which the fusion candidate is running.

12. The experience in New York with fusion politics provides considerable evidence that neither political stability nor the ultimate strength of the two major parties is truly risked by the existence of successful minor parties.

argued, alternatively, that such an interpretation would violate the right of political association.

MORSE v. REPUBLICAN PARTY OF VIRGINIA, 517 U.S. 186, 116 S.Ct. 1186, 134 L.Ed.2d 347 (1996), held that application of the preclearance requirement did not violate political association rights. STEVENS, J., joined by Ginsburg, J., announcing the judgment of the Court, recognized that curtailment of party association rights must be subject to the "closest scrutiny." Nonetheless, he observed that the Act's purpose was to prevent racial discrimination and that Morse had not argued that immunity from the particular fee was protected under the first amendment: "We leave consideration of hypothetical concerns for another day."

BREYER, J., joined by O'Connor and Souter, JJ., concurring, concluded that the fees at issue were "well outside the area of greatest 'associational' concern."

SCALIA, J., joined by Thomas, J., dissenting, not only faulted the majority for ignoring vagueness and overbreadth doctrine, but also argued that the case involved a "classic prior restraint" because the party could make no changes affecting a voter's capacity to elect a candidate without governmental clearance: "A freedom of political association that must await the Government's favorable response to a 'Mother, may I?' is no freedom of political association at all."

THOMAS, J., joined by Rehnquist, C.J., and Scalia, J., dissenting, argued that the act was inapplicable, but further contended that charging each delegate a fee rather than funding the convention with major donors was a constitutionally protected choice. Moreover, to refuse preclearance "would in effect be requiring the Party to include persons who could not, or would not, pay the registration fee for its convention," violating the right to decide with whom to associate.[a]

WEALTH AND THE POLITICAL PROCESS: CONCERNS FOR EQUALITY

CON LAW: P. 1023, after note 4

AMER CON: P. 1008, after note 4

RTS & LIB: P. 930, after note 4

5. *Expenditure limitations and political parties.* COLORADO REPUBLICAN FEDERAL CAMPAIGN COMMITTEE v. FEDERAL ELECTION COMMITTEE, 518 U.S. 604, 116 S.Ct. 2309, 135 L.Ed.2d 795 (1996), ruled that the Federal Election Campaign Act's limitation on independent expenditures by political parties was unconstitutional. BREYER, J., joined by O'Connor and Souter, JJ., announced the judgment of the Court, but did not reach the question whether the Act's prohibition of expenditures coordinated with the candidate were similarly unconstitutional.

KENNEDY, J., joined by Scalia, J., concurring in part and dissenting in part, argued that the prohibition on coordinated expenditures between political parties and their candidates was also unconstitutional: "We have a constitutional tradition of political parties and their candidates engaging in joint first amendment activity. [Congress] may have authority, consistent with the first amendment, to restrict undifferentiated political party contributions [as discussed in] *Buckley*, but that type of regulation is not at issue here." Kennedy, J., dissented from the

a. Kennedy, J., joined by Rehnquist, C.J., dissenting, argued that first amendment and other concerns justified a narrow construction of the statute.

judgment's failure to reach the question of coordinated expenditures.[k]

Stevens, J., joined by Ginsburg, J., dissenting, maintained that independent expenditures by parties were contributions and that federal limits were justified by the need to level "the electoral playing field," and to avoid corruption or its appearance.

CON LAW: P. 1030, add to note 1(b)

AMER CON: P. 1015, add to note 1(b)

RTS & LIB: P. 937, add to note 1(b)

See also *Buckley v. American Constitutional Law Foundation*, ___ U.S. ___, 119 S.Ct. 636, ___ L.Ed.2d ___ (1999) (extending *Meyer* to a requirement that paid circulators be registered voters).

---

k. Thomas, J., joined by Rehnquist, C.J., and Scalia, J., would also have reached the question, arguing that *Buckley*'s anti-corruption rationale did not apply to associations between political parties and candidates. Thomas, J., on his own, additionally argued that the distinction between contributions and expenditures was generally unsatisfactory and that both should receive first amendment protection.

FREEDOM OF RELIGION

ESTABLISHMENT CLAUSE

FINANCIAL AID TO RELIGION

CON LAW: P. 1076, add at end of fn. b

AMER CON: 1053, add at end of fn. b

RTS & LIB: P. 983, add at end of fn. b

See *Agostini v. Felton,* below, holding that "later Establishment Clause cases have so undermined *Aguilar* that it is no longer good law."

CON LAW: P. 1077, at end

AMER CON: P. 1054, after *Zobrest*

RTS & LIB: P. 984, at end

AGOSTINI v. FELTON, 521 U.S. 203, 117 S.Ct. 1997, 138 L.Ed.2d 391 (1997), per O'CONNOR, J., "overruled *Aguilar* and those portions of *Grand Rapids* inconsistent with our most recent decisions." The case involved Title I of the Elementary and Secondary Education Act of 1965, the statute at issue in *Aguilar*. Congress enacted Title I "to 'provid[e] full educational opportunity to every child regardless of economic background.' Toward that end, Title I channels federal funds, through the States, to 'local educational agencies' (LEA's). The LEA's spend these funds to provide remedial education, guidance, and job counseling to eligible students. An eligible student is one (i) who resides within the attendance boundaries of a public school located in a low-income area; and (ii) who is failing, or is at risk of failing, the State's student performance standards. [T]he LEA must retain complete control over Title I funds; retain title to all materials used to provide Title I services; and provide those services through public employees or other persons independent of the private school and any religious institution. The Title I services themselves must be 'secular, neutral, and nonideological,' and must 'supplement, and in no case supplant, the level of services' already provided by the private school."

The plan in *Aguilar* "called for the provision of Title I services on private school premises during school hours. Under the plan, only public employees could serve as Title I instructors and counselors. Assignments to private schools were made on a voluntary basis and without regard to the religious affiliation of the employee or the wishes of the private school. [A] large majority of Title I teachers worked in nonpublic schools with religious affiliations different from their own [and] moved among the private schools, spending fewer than five days a week at the same school. [All] religious symbols were to be removed from classrooms used for Title I services. The rules acknowledged that it might be necessary for Title I teachers to consult with a student's regular classroom teacher to assess the student's particular needs and progress, but admonished instructors to limit those consultations to mutual professional concerns regarding the student's education. To ensure compliance with these rules, a publicly employed field supervisor was to attempt to make at least one unannounced visit to each teacher's classroom every month. * * *

"Our more recent cases have undermined the assumptions upon which *Grand Rapids* and *Aguilar* relied [respecting] whether aid to religion has an impermissible effect. * * * First, we have abandoned the presumption erected in *Meek* and *Grand Rapids* that the placement of public employees on parochial school grounds inevitably results in the impermissible effect of state-sponsored indoctrination [a] or constitutes a symbolic union between government and religion. [*Zobrest*] [b] Second, we have departed from the rule relied on in *Grand Rapids* that all government aid that directly aids the educational function of religious schools is invalid. [*Witters*] [Moreover,] as in *Zobrest,* Title I services are by law supplemental to the regular curricula [and] do not, therefore, 'reliev[e] sectarian schools of costs they otherwise would have borne in educating their students.' [Further, no] Title I funds ever reach the coffers of religious schools. [Finally], where the aid is allocated on the basis of neutral, secular criteria that neither favor nor disfavor religion, and is made available to both religious and secular beneficiaries on a nondiscriminatory basis[, the] aid is less likely to have the effect of advancing religion. See *Widmar.*"

SOUTER, J., joined by Stevens, Ginsburg and Breyer, JJ., dissented: "Instead of aiding isolated individuals within a school system, New York City's Title I program before *Aguilar* served about 22,000 private school students, all but 52 of whom attended religious schools. Instead of serving individual blind or deaf students, as such, Title I as administered in New York City before *Aguilar* (and as now to be revived) funded instruction in core subjects (remedial reading, reading skills, remedial mathematics, English as a second language) and provided guidance services. Instead of providing a service the school would not otherwise furnish, the Title I services necessarily relieved a religious school of 'an expense that it otherwise would have assumed,' and freed its funds for other, and sectarian uses.

"Finally, [in] *Zobrest* and *Witters,* it was fair to say that individual students were themselves applicants for individual benefits on a scale that could not amount to a systemic supplement. But under Title I, a local educational agency (which in New York City is the Board of Education) may receive federal funding by proposing programs approved to serve individual students who meet the criteria of need, which it then uses to provide such programs at the religious schools.'"

a. "Since we have abandoned the assumption that properly instructed public employees will fail to discharge their duties faithfully, we must also discard the assumption that pervasive monitoring of Title I teachers is required. [Moreover,] we have not found excessive entanglement in cases in which States imposed far more onerous burdens on religious institutions than the monitoring system at issue here."

b. "We do not see any perceptible (let alone dispositive) difference in the degree of symbolic union between a student receiving remedial instruction in a classroom on his sectarian school's campus and one receiving instruction in a van parked just at the school's curbside. To draw this line based solely on the location of the public employee is neither 'sensible' nor 'sound.'"

FREE EXERCISE CLAUSE AND
RELATED PROBLEMS

CONFLICT WITH STATE REGULATION

CON LAW: P. 1121, at end of 1st ¶

AMER CON: P. 1086, at end of 2d full ¶

RTS & LIB: P. 1028, at end of 1st ¶

[In *Boerne v. Flores,* p. 136 of this Supplement, O'Connor, J., joined by Breyer, J., argued that "the historical evidence [bears] out the conclusion that, at the time the Bill of Rights was ratified, it was accepted that government should, when possible, accommodate religious practice." Scalia, J., joined by Stevens, J., disagreed: "The historical evidence put forward by the dissent does nothing to undermine the conclusion we reached in *Smith.*" For an extensive review, see Michael W. McConnell, *Freedom From Persecution or Protection of the Rights of Conscience?: A Critique of Justice Scalia's Historical Arguments,* 39 Wm. & M. L. Rev. 819 (1998)].

CON LAW: P. 1126, at end of note 3

AMER CON: P. 1090, at end of note 2

RTS & LIB: P. 1033, at end of note 3

FRFA was held unconstitutional in *Boerne v. Flores,* p. 136 of this Supplement.

EQUAL PROTECTION

RACE AND ETHNIC ANCESTRY

DE JURE VS. DE FACTO DISCRIMINATION

CON LAW: P. 1184, before note 1(b)

AMER CON: P. 1091, before note 1(b)

RTS & LIB: P. 1138, before note 1(b)

Selective prosecution. In order to make out a prima facie case of intentional racial discrimination, UNITED STATES v. ARMSTRONG, 517 U.S. 456, 116 S.Ct. 1480, 134 L.Ed.2d 687 (1996), per REHNQUIST, C.J., reasoned that "the claimant must show that similarly situated individuals of a different race were not prosecuted." The fact (among several) [a] that all 24 defendants in "crack" cocaine cases closed by the Federal Public Defender in the previous year were black did not establish the defendants' "entitlement to discovery." STEVENS, J., dissented: "I am persuaded that the District Judge did not abuse her discretion when she concluded that the factual showing was sufficiently disturbing to require some response from the United States Attorney's Office."

REPEALS OF REMEDIES AND RESTRUCTURINGS OF THE POLITICAL PROCESS THAT BURDEN MINORITIES

CON LAW: P. 1226, after note 2

AMER CON: P. 1173, after note 2

RTS & LIB: P. 1133, after note 2

3. *Applicability to non-suspect classes.* *Romer v. Evans*, 517 U.S. 620, 116 S.Ct. 1620, 134 L.Ed.2d 855 (1996), included as a principal case p. 119 of this Supplement, invalidated an amendment to the Colorado constitution that forbade the state and its subdivisions to "enact, adopt or enforce any statute, regulation, ordinance or policy" protecting homosexuals against public or private discrimination. The amendment had the effect of nullifying several local ordinances and an executive order by the governor of Colorado, and the Colorado Supreme Court, whose judgement the Court affirmed, had relied on "precedents involving discriminatory restructuring of governmental decisionmaking" such as *Hunter v. Erickson* and *Washington v. Seattle School District No. 1*. But the Court, per KENNEDY, J., without further discussion of the Colorado Supreme Court's ground for decision, rested on the different rationale that the challenged amendment, which "declar[ed] that in general it shall be more difficult for one group of citizens than

a. Defendants also submitted "an affidavit alleging that an intake coordinator at a drug treatment center had told her that there are 'an equal number of caucasian users and dealers to minority users and dealers,' [an] affidavit from a criminal defense attorney alleging that in his experience many nonblacks are prosecuted in state court for crack offenses, and a newspaper article reporting that Federal 'crack criminals [are] being punished far more severely than if they had been caught with powder cocaine, and almost every single one of them is black.' "

for all others to seek aid from the government," was too broad and undifferentiated to be rationally related to any legitimate state purpose. The amendment's very
breadth "raise[d] the inevitable inference that the disadvantage imposed is born of
animosity toward the class of persons affected." Scalia, J., joined by Rehnquist,
C.J., and Thomas, J., dissented.

AFFIRMATIVE ACTION AND "BENIGN" DISCRIMINATION

CON LAW: P. 1244, at the end of note 7

AMER CON: P. 1190, at the end of note 7

RTS & LIB: P. 1151, at the end of note 7

In *Hopwood v. Texas*, 78 F.3d 932 (5th Cir.1996), the court of appeals, in
invalidating an affirmative action plan implemented by the University of Texas
Law School, explicitly rejected Justice Powell's *Bakke* opinion and held that the
use of race as a factor in law school admissions was "per se proscribed."
According to the two-judge majority, "Justice Powell's view in *Bakke* is not
binding precedent," because much of his opinion "was joined by no other justice,"
and his argument in *Bakke* never garnered a majority. Did the court of appeals
fail to account for the significance of Part V–C of Powell, J.'s *Bakke* opinion,
which a majority of the Court did join?

The Supreme Court denied certiorari in *Hopwood* on the last day of its 1995
Term. 518 U.S. 1033, 116 S.Ct. 2580, 135 L.Ed.2d 1094 (1996). In a statement
accompanying the denial, Ginsburg, J., joined by Souter, J., noted that the
University of Texas Law School had announced its abandonment of the affirmative action program challenged in the lower courts, under which it evaluated
minority applicants under separate processes and standards from those used to
evaluate others. Although the Law School had propounded a new policy, which
considers the race of minority applicants on a more individualized basis, that
policy had not been a specific subject of the court of appeals' judgment. Although
Texas officials challenged "the rationale relied on by the Court of Appeals," the
Court "reviews judgments, not opinions." "Accordingly, we must await a final
judgment on a program genuinely in controversy before addressing the important
issue raised in this petition."

DISCRIMINATIONS BASED ON GENDER

DEFINING THE LEVEL OF SCRUTINY

CON LAW: P. 1279, after note 3

AMER CON: P. 1216, after note 3

RTS & LIB: P. 1186, after note 3

4. *Requirement of "an exceedingly persuasive justification."* In *United States
v. Virginia*, 518 U.S. 515, 116 S.Ct. 2264, 135 L.Ed.2d 735 (1996), p. 112 of this
Supplement, the Court, per Ginsburg, J., quoted the *Craig* formulation that
gender-based classifications must serve "important governmental objectives" and
be "substantially related to the achievement of those objectives." But the Court
preceded its recitation of that standard with what it identified as the "core
instruction of this Court's pathmarking decisions in *J.E.B. v. Alabama ex rel. T.B.*,
[CON LAW, p. 1289, RTS & LIB, p. 1196] and *Mississippi Univ. for Women*, [CON
LAW, p. 1295; AMER CON, p. 1226, RTS & LIB, p. 1202]: Parties who seek to
defend gender-based government action must demonstrate an 'exceedingly persua-

sive justification' for that action." In holding that Virginia violated the Equal Protection Clause by excluding women from the Virginia Military Institute, the Court repeatedly invoked the "exceedingly persuasive justification" requirement. Rehnquist, C.J., who concurred in the judgment only, specifically objected that the Court introduced "an element of uncertainty" in equal protection doctrine by relying on this new formulation. Scalia, J., who dissented, protested that no authority supported departure from the *Craig* standard—which, he argued, the state of Virginia had met, since provision of all-male education via the "adversative" method was "substantially related" to the "important" state interest in educational diversity.[a]

DIFFERENCES—REAL AND IMAGINED

CON LAW: P. 1288, at the end of note 5

AMER CON: P. 1221, after Geduldig v. Aiello

RTS & LIB: P. 1195, at the end of note 5

MILLER v. ALBRIGHT, 523 U.S. 420, 118 S.Ct. 1428, 140 L.Ed.2d 575 (1998), upheld a provision of the Immigration and Naturalization Act that provides automatic naturalization for illegitimate children who are born abroad to mothers who are American citizens, but establishes various procedural requirements, which must be completed before the child turns 18 or 21, for the illegitimate children of citizen fathers and non-citizen mothers, such as the plaintiff Miller, to become American citizens. STEVENS, J., announcing the judgment of the Court in an opinion that was joined only by Rehnquist, C.J, found that the statute distinguished unmarried fathers from unmarried mothers based on gender, but was justified by important governmental interests. Although Stevens, J., concluded that deference to the political branches' immigration powers dictated a narrow standard of review, he believed that the statute would also survive "the heightened scrutiny that normally governs gender discrimination claims." SCALIA, J., joined by Thomas, J., concurred that the plaintiff's claim must fail, but did not reach the question whether the statute worked an unconstitutional discrimination: "The complaint must be dismissed because the Court has no power to provide the relief requested: conferral of citizenship on a basis other than that prescribed by Congress." O'CONNOR, J., joined by Kennedy, J., also concurred in the judgment, on the ground that the statutory distinction between children of illegitimate mothers and children of illegitimate fathers was supported by a rational basis. According to O'Connor, J., rational basis review applied because the plaintiff—an illegitimate child claiming citizenship—lacked standing to assert the rights of fathers of illegitimate children to be free from gender-based discrimination in transferring citizenship to their offspring. Although upholding the provision under a rational basis standard, O'Connor and Kennedy, JJ., did "not share Justice Stevens' assessment that the [challenged] provision withstands heightened scrutiny." BREYER, J., joined by Souter and Ginsburg, JJ., believed that the statute did discriminate on the basis of gender, reasoned that heightened scrutiny therefore applied, and concluded that the statutory discrimination should be invalidated. Noting that O'Connor and Kennedy, JJ., had also opined that the statute could not withstand heightened scrutiny (if heightened scrutiny were properly brought to bear), Breyer, J., concluded that "a majority of the Court agrees [that] '[i]t is unlikely [that] any gender classifications based on stereotypes

---

a. Thomas, J., took no part.

can survive heightened scrutiny.' '' If Breyer, J., is correct, have *Caban v. Mohammed* and *Lehr v. Robertson* ceased to be good law?

CON LAW: P. 1291, after J.E.B.
AMER CON: P. 1221, after Notes and Questions
RTS & LIB: P. 1178, after J.E.B.

UNITED STATES v. VIRGINIA

518 U.S. 515, 116 S.Ct. 2264, 135 L.Ed.2d 735 (1996).

JUSTICE GINSBURG delivered the opinion of the Court.

Virginia's public institutions of higher learning include an incomparable military college, Virginia Military Institute (VMI). The United States maintains that the Constitution's equal protection guarantee precludes Virginia from reserving exclusively to men the unique educational opportunities VMI affords. We agree.

Founded in 1839, VMI is today the sole single-sex school among Virginia's 15 public institutions of higher learning. VMI's distinctive mission is to produce "citizen-soldiers." [Assigning] prime place to character development, VMI uses an "adversative method" modeled on English public schools and once characteristic of military instruction. [This model] features "physical rigor, mental stress, absolute equality of treatment, absence of privacy, minute regulation of behavior, and indoctrination in desirable values." [VMI] cadets live in spartan barracks where surveillance is constant and privacy nonexistent. [Entering] students are incessantly exposed to the rat line, "an extreme form of the adversative model," [which] bonds new cadets to their fellow sufferers and, when they have completed the 7–month experience, to their former tormentors.

In 1990, prompted by a complaint filed with the Attorney General by a female high-school student seeking admission to VMI, the United States sued the Commonwealth of Virginia and VMI, alleging that VMI's exclusively male admission policy violated the Equal Protection Clause of the Fourteenth Amendment. [The district court upheld the policy, but the court of appeals reversed, finding an equal protection violation. Following the remand, the state of Virginia proposed a remedial plan, under which the state would adopt] a parallel program for women: Virginia Women's Institute for Leadership (VWIL). The 4–year, state-sponsored undergraduate program would be located at Mary Baldwin College, a private liberal arts school for women, and would be open, initially, to about 25 to 30 students. Although VWIL would share VMI's mission—to produce "citizen-soldiers"—the VWIL program would differ, as does Mary Baldwin College, from VMI in academic offerings, methods of education, and financial resources.

The average combined SAT score of entrants at Mary Baldwin is about 100 points lower than the score for VMI freshmen. [While] VMI offers degrees in liberal arts, the sciences, and engineering, Mary Baldwin, at the time of trial, offered only bachelor of arts degrees. [Under the proposed remedial plan,] VWIL students would participate in ROTC programs [but in] lieu of VMI's adversative method, [VWIL would offer] "a cooperative method which reinforces self-esteem."

Virginia represented that it will provide equal financial support for in-state VWIL students and VMI cadets, and the VMI Foundation agreed to supply a $5.4625 million endowment for the VWIL program. Mary Baldwin's own endowment is about $19 million; VMI's is $131 million. Mary Baldwin will add $35 million to its endowment based on future commitments; VMI will add $220 million.

[Both the district court and the court of appeals held that the proposed remedial plan satisfied the Equal Protection Clause.]

The cross-petitions in this case present two ultimate issues. First, does Virginia's exclusion of women from the educational opportunities provided by VMI—extraordinary opportunities for military training and civilian leadership development—deny to women "capable of all of the individual activities required of VMI cadets," the equal protection of the laws guaranteed by the Fourteenth Amendment? Second, if VMI's "unique" situation—as Virginia's sole single-sex public institution of higher education—offends the Constitution's equal protection principle, what is the remedial requirement?

We note, once again, the core instruction of this Court's pathmarking decisions in *J.E.B. v. Alabama ex rel. T.B.,* [CON LAW p. 1289, RTS & LIB. p. 1196] and *Mississippi Univ. for Women,* [CON LAW p. 1295, AMER CON p. 1226, RTS & LIB p. 1202]: Parties who seek to defend gender-based government action must demonstrate an "exceedingly persuasive justification" for that action. [The] burden of justification is demanding and it rests entirely on the State. The State must show "at least that the [challenged] classification serves 'important governmental objectives and that the discriminatory means employed' are 'substantially related to the achievement of those objectives.' " The justification must be genuine, not hypothesized or invented post hoc in response to litigation. And it must not rely on overbroad generalizations about the different talents, capacities, or preferences of males and females.

The heightened review standard our precedent establishes does not make sex a proscribed classification. Supposed "inherent differences" are no longer accepted as a ground for race or national origin classifications. See *Loving v. Virginia.* Physical differences between men and women, however, are enduring. [Sex] classifications may be used to compensate women "for particular economic disabilities [they have] suffered," *Califano v. Webster,* [CON LAW p. 1293, AMER CON p. 1223, RTS & LIB p. 1200], to "promote equal employment opportunity," see *California Federal Sav. & Loan Assn. v. Guerra,* [CON LAW p. 1298, AMER CON p. 1228, RTS & LIB p. 1205], [and] to advance full development of the talent and capacities of our Nation's people.[7] But such classifications may not be used, as they once were, to create or perpetuate the legal, social, and economic inferiority of women. [Measuring] the record in this case against the review standard just described, we conclude that Virginia has shown no "exceedingly persuasive justification" for excluding all women from the citizen-soldier training afforded by VMI.

[Single-sex] education affords pedagogical benefits to at least some students, Virginia emphasizes, and that reality is uncontested in this litigation. Similarly, it is not disputed that diversity among public educational institutions can serve the public good. But Virginia has not shown that VMI was established, or has been maintained, with a view to diversifying, by its categorical exclusion of

---

7. Several amici have urged that diversity in educational opportunities is an altogether appropriate governmental pursuit and that single-sex schools can contribute importantly to such diversity. Indeed, it is the mission of some single-sex schools "to dissipate, rather than perpetuate, traditional gender classifications." We do not question the State's prerogative evenhandedly to support diverse educational opportunities. We address specifically and only an educational opportunity recognized by the District Court and the Court of Appeals as "unique," an opportunity available only at Virginia's premier military institute, the State's sole single-sex public university or college.

women, educational opportunities within the State. In cases of this genre, our precedent instructs that "benign" justifications proffered in defense of categorical exclusions will not be accepted automatically; a tenable justification must describe actual state purposes, not rationalizations for actions in fact differently grounded.

[Neither] recent nor distant history bears out Virginia's alleged pursuit of diversity through single-sex educational options. In 1839, when the State established VMI, a range of educational opportunities for men and women was scarcely contemplated. [In] admitting no women, VMI followed the lead of [the] University of Virginia, founded in 1819. [Beginning in 1894,] Virginia eventually provided for several women's seminaries and colleges. [By] the mid–1970's, [however,] all [had] become coeducational. [The] University of Virginia introduced coeducation [in 1970] and, in 1972, began to admit women on an equal basis with men.

Virginia describes the current absence of public single-sex higher education for women as "an historical anomaly." But the historical record indicates action more deliberate than anomalous: First, protection of women against higher education; next, schools for women far from equal in resources and stature to schools for men; finally, conversion of the separate schools to coeducation. [In] sum, we find no persuasive evidence in this record that VMI's male-only admission policy "is in furtherance of a state policy of 'diversity.' "

[Virginia] next argues that VMI's adversative method of training provides educational benefits that cannot be made available, unmodified, to women. Alterations to accommodate women would necessarily be "radical," so "drastic," Virginia asserts, as to transform, indeed "destroy," VMI's program. [The] District Court [found] that coeducation would materially affect "at least these three aspects of VMI's program—physical training, the absence of privacy, and the adversative approach." And it is uncontested that women's admission would require accommodations, primarily in arranging housing assignments and physical training programs for female cadets. It is also undisputed, however, that "the VMI methodology could be used to educate women."

The notion that admission of women would downgrade VMI's stature, destroy the adversative system and, with it, even the school, is a judgment hardly proved, a prediction hardly different from other "self-fulfilling prophecies" once routinely used to deny rights or opportunities. [Women's] successful entry into the federal military academies, and their participation in the Nation's military forces, indicate that Virginia's fears for the future of VMI may not be solidly grounded. [Virginia], in sum, "has fallen far short of establishing the 'exceedingly persuasive justification' " that must be the solid base for any gender-defined classification.

In the second phase of the litigation, Virginia presented its remedial plan— maintain VMI as a male-only college and create VWIL as a separate program for women.

[Having] violated the Constitution's equal protection requirement, Virginia was obliged to show that its remedial proposal "directly addressed and related to" the violation, i.e., the equal protection denied to women ready, willing, and able to benefit from educational opportunities of the kind VMI offers. Virginia described VWIL as a "parallel program," and asserted that VWIL shares VMI's mission of producing "citizen-soldiers" and VMI's goals of providing "education, military training, mental and physical discipline, character * * * and leadership development." [But] VWIL affords women no opportunity to experience the rigorous military training for which VMI is famed. Instead, the VWIL program "deemphasizes" military education, and uses a "cooperative method" of education "which reinforces self-esteem."

[Virginia] maintains that these methodological differences are "justified pedagogically," based on "important differences between men and women in learning and developmental needs," "psychological and sociological differences" Virginia describes as "real" and "not stereotypes." [As] earlier stated, [however], generalizations about "the way women are," estimates of what is appropriate for most women, no longer justify denying opportunity to women whose talent and capacity place them outside the average description. "[S]ome women, at least, would want to attend [VMI] if they had the opportunity"; "some women are capable of all of the individual activities required of VMI cadets" and "can meet the physical standards [VMI] now imposes on men". It is [for] these women [that] a remedy must be crafted.[19]

[In] myriad respects other than military training, VWIL does not qualify as VMI's equal. VWIL's student body, faculty, course offerings, and facilities hardly match VMI's. Nor can the VWIL graduate anticipate the benefits associated with VMI's 157–year history, the school's prestige, and its influential alumni network.

[Virginia's] VWIL solution is reminiscent of the remedy Texas proposed 50 years ago, in response to a state trial court's 1946 ruling that, given the equal protection guarantee, African Americans could not be denied a legal education at a state facility. See *Sweatt v. Painter,* [CON LAW p. 1172, AMER CON p. 1129, RTS & LIB p. 1079]. Reluctant to admit African Americans to its flagship University of Texas Law School, the State set up a separate school for Herman Sweatt and other black law students. [This] Court contrasted resources at the new school with those at the school from which Sweatt had been excluded [and held that] the Equal Protection Clause required Texas to admit African Americans to the University of Texas Law School. In line with *Sweatt,* we rule here that Virginia has not shown substantial equality in the separate educational opportunities the State supports at VWIL and VMI. * * *

JUSTICE THOMAS took no part in the consideration or decision of this case.

CHIEF JUSTICE REHNQUIST, concurring in the judgement.

Two decades ago in *Craig v. Boren,* we announced that "to withstand constitutional challenge, * * * classifications by gender must serve important governmental objectives and must be substantially related to achievement of those objectives." [While] the majority adheres to this test today, it also says that the State must demonstrate an " 'exceedingly persuasive justification' " to support a gender-based classification. [To] avoid introducing potential confusion, I would have adhered more closely to our traditional [standard].

[I] agree with the Court that there is scant evidence in the record that [diversity] was the real reason that Virginia decided to maintain VMI as men only. [Even] if diversity in educational opportunity were the State's actual objective, [however,] the State's position would still be problematic. The difficulty [is] that the diversity benefited only one sex.

[Virginia] offers a second justification for the single-sex admissions policy: maintenance of the adversative method. [But a] State does not have substantial interest in the adversative methodology unless it is pedagogically beneficial. While considerable evidence shows that a single-sex education is pedagogically

---

19. Admitting women to VMI would undoubtedly require alterations necessary to afford members of each sex privacy from the other sex in living arrangements, and to adjust aspects of the physical training programs. Experience [at the United States military academies] shows such adjustments are manageable.

beneficial for some students, and hence a State may have a valid interest in promoting that methodology, there is no similar evidence in the record that an adversarial method is pedagogically beneficial or is any more likely to produce character traits than other methodologies.

The Court defines the constitutional violation in this case as "the categorical exclusion of women from an extraordinary educational opportunity afforded to men." By defining the violation in this way, [the] Court necessarily implies that the only adequate remedy would be the admission of women to the all-male institution. [I] would not define the violation in this way; it is not the "exclusion of women" that violates the Equal Protection Clause, but the maintenance of an all-men school without providing any—much less a comparable—institution for women. * * *

JUSTICE SCALIA, dissenting.

* * * Much of the Court's opinion is devoted to deprecating the closed-mindedness of our forebears with regard to women's education, and even with regard to the treatment of women in areas that have nothing to do with education. Closed-minded they were—as every age is, including our own, with regard to matters it cannot guess, because it simply does not consider them debatable. The virtue of a democratic system with a First Amendment is that it readily enables the people, over time, to be persuaded that what they took for granted is not so, and to change their laws accordingly. That system is destroyed if the smug assurances of each age are removed from the democratic process and written into the Constitution. So to counterbalance the Court's criticism of our ancestors, let me say a word in their praise: they left us free to change. The same cannot be said of this most illiberal Court, which has embarked on a course of inscribing one after another of the current preferences of the society (and in some cases only the counter-majoritarian preferences of the society's law-trained elite) into our Basic Law. Today it enshrines the notion that no substantial educational value is to be served by an all-men's military academy—so that the decision by the people of Virginia to maintain such an institution denies equal protection to women who cannot attend that institution but can attend others.

[In] my view the function of this Court is to preserve our society's values regarding (among other things) equal protection, not to revise them. [Whatever] abstract tests we may choose to devise, they cannot supersede—and indeed ought to be crafted so as to reflect—those constant and unbroken national traditions that embody the people's understanding of ambiguous constitutional texts. More specifically, it is my view that "when a practice not expressly prohibited by the text of the Bill of Rights bears the endorsement of a long tradition of open, widespread, and unchallenged use that dates back to the beginning of the Republic, we have no proper basis for striking it down."

The all-male constitution of VMI comes squarely within such a governing tradition. For almost all of VMI's more than a century and a half of existence, its single-sex status reflected the uniform practice for government-supported military colleges.

[To] reject the Court's disposition today, however, it is [only] necessary to apply honestly the test the Court has been applying to sex-based classifications for the past two decades. [Only] the amorphous "exceedingly persuasive justification" phrase, and not the standard elaboration of intermediate scrutiny, can be made to yield [the] conclusion that VMI's single-sex composition is unconstitutional because there exist several women (or, one would have to conclude under the Court's reasoning, a single woman) willing and able to undertake VMI's program. Intermediate scrutiny has never required a least-restrictive-means analysis, but only a "substantial relation" between the classification and the state interests that it serves.

[It] is beyond question that Virginia has an important state interest in providing effective college education for its citizens. That single-sex instruction is an approach substantially related to that interest should be evident enough from the long and continuing history in this country of men's and women's colleges. But beyond that, [there was] "virtually uncontradicted" [expert evidence introduced in this case tending to show the benefits of single-sex education].

[Besides] its single-sex constitution, VMI [employs] a "distinctive educational method," sometimes referred to as the "adversative, or doubting, model of education." [It] was uncontested that "if the state were to establish a women's VMI-type [i.e., adversative] program, the program would attract an insufficient number of participants to make the program work"; and it was found by the District Court that if Virginia were to include women in VMI, the school "would eventually find it necessary to drop the adversative system altogether." Thus, Virginia's options were an adversative method that excludes women or no adversative method at all.

There can be no serious dispute that single-sex education and a distinctive educational method "represent legitimate contributions to diversity in the Virginia higher education system." As a theoretical matter, Virginia's educational interest would have been best served (insofar as the two factors we have mentioned are concerned) by six different types of public colleges—an all-men's, an all-women's, and a coeducational college run in the "adversative method," and an all-men's, an all-women's, and a coeducational college run in the "traditional method." But as a practical matter, of course, Virginia's financial resources, like any State's, are not limitless, and the Commonwealth must select among the available options. [In] these circumstances, Virginia's election to fund one public all-male institution and one on the adversative model—and to concentrate its resources in a single entity that serves both these interests in diversity—is substantially related to the State's important educational interests.

[The] Court argues that VMI would not have to change very much if it were to admit women. The principal response to that argument is that it is irrelevant: If VMI's single-sex status is substantially related to the government's important educational objectives, as I have demonstrated above and as the Court refuses to discuss, that concludes the inquiry. [But] if such a debate were relevant, the Court would certainly be on the losing side.

[Finally], the absence of a precise "all-women's analogue" to VMI is irrelevant. [VWIL] was carefully designed by professional educators who have long experience in educating young women. [None] of the United States' own experts in the remedial phase of this case was willing to testify that VMI's adversative method was an appropriate methodology for educating women.

[The] Court's decision today will have consequences that extend far beyond the parties to the case. [Under] the constitutional principles announced and applied today, single-sex public education is unconstitutional. [Although] the

Court [purports] to have said nothing of relevance to other public schools [and to have considered] only an educational opportunity recognized * * * as "unique," [footnote 7, supra] * * * I suggest that the single-sex program that will not be capable of being characterized as "unique" is not only unique but nonexistent.

[A broader] potential of today's decision for widespread disruption of existing institutions lies in its application to private single-sex education. Government support is immensely important to private educational institutions. [When government funding is challenged, the] issue will be not whether government assistance turns private colleges into state actors, but whether the government itself would be violating the Constitution by providing state support to single-sex colleges. For example, in *Norwood v. Harrison*, [CON LAW p. 1446, AMER CON p. 1364, RTS & LIB p. 1353], we saw no room to distinguish between state operation of racially segregated schools and state support of privately run segregated schools. [The] only hope for state-assisted single-sex private schools is that the Court will not apply in the future the principles of law it has applied today. * * *

"BENIGN"—"COMPENSATORY"—"REMEDIAL" DISCRIMINATION

CON LAW: P. 1295, at end of note 3

AMER CON: P. 1225, at end of note 3

RTS & LIB: P. 1202, at end of note 3

Consider the relevance to these questions of *United States v. Virginia*, p. 112 of this Supplement.

CON LAW: P. 1298, at end of note 1

AMER CON: P. 1228, at end of note 1

RTS & LIB: P. 1204, at end of note 1

Does *United States v. Virginia*, p. 112 of this Supplement, establish that single-gender education is never permissible? Compare footnote 7 of the majority opinion with the assertions of Scalia, J., dissenting.

SPECIAL SCRUTINY FOR OTHER CLASSIFICATIONS

OTHER, CHALLENGED BASES FOR DISCRIMINATION

CON LAW: P. 1306, at the end of note 5(a)

AMER CON: P. 1237, at the end of note 5(a)

RTS & LIB: P. 1213, at the end of note 5(a)

See also *Reno v. American–Arab Anti–Discrimination Committee*, ___ U.S. ___, 119 S.Ct. 936, 142 L.Ed.2d 940 (1999) (finding that no constitutional issue was presented by a statute denying illegal aliens a forum in which to challenge their impending deportations on "selective enforcement" grounds, because "an alien unlawfully in this country [generally] has no constitutional right" to freedom from selective enforcement).

CON LAW: P. 1321, after note 2
AMER CON: P. 1251, after note 2
RTS & LIB: P. 1228, after note 2

ROMER v. EVANS

517 U.S. 620, 116 S.Ct. 1620, 134 L.Ed.2d 855 (1996).

Justice Kennedy delivered the opinion of the Court.

* * * The enactment challenged in this case is an amendment to the Constitution of the State of Colorado, adopted in a 1992 statewide referendum [and referred to] as "Amendment 2," its designation when submitted to the voters. [The] amendment reads: "No Protected Status Based on Homosexual, Lesbian, or Bisexual Orientation. Neither the State of Colorado, through any of its branches or departments, nor any of its agencies, political subdivisions, municipalities or school districts, shall enact, adopt or enforce any statute, regulation, ordinance or policy whereby homosexual, lesbian or bisexual orientation, conduct, practices or relationships shall constitute or otherwise be the basis of or entitle any person or class of persons to have or claim any minority status, quota preferences, protected status or claim of discrimination. This Section of the Constitution shall be in all respects self-executing."

[The] State's principal argument in defense of Amendment 2 is that it puts gays and lesbians in the same position as all other persons. So, the State says, the measure does no more than deny homosexuals special rights. This reading of the amendment's language is implausible. We rely not upon our own interpretation of the amendment but upon the authoritative construction of Colorado's Supreme Court, [which held that] "The immediate objective of Amendment 2 is, at a minimum, to repeal existing statutes, regulations, ordinances, and policies of state and local entities that barred discrimination based on sexual orientation." [Under Amendment 2 as thus construed, homosexuals], by state decree, are put in a solitary class with respect to transactions and relations in both the private and governmental spheres. The amendment withdraws from homosexuals, but no others, specific legal protection from the injuries caused by discrimination, and it forbids reinstatement of these laws and policies.

The change that Amendment 2 works in the legal status of gays and lesbians in the private sphere is far-reaching, both on its own terms and when considered in light of the structure and operation of modern antidiscrimination laws. That structure is well illustrated by contemporary statutes and ordinances prohibiting discrimination by providers of public accommodations. "At common law, innkeepers, smiths, and others who 'made profession of a public employment,' were prohibited from refusing, without good reason, to serve a customer." The duty was a general one and did not specify protection for particular groups. The common law rules, however, proved insufficient in many instances, and [most] States have chosen to counter discrimination by enacting detailed statutory schemes.

Colorado's state and municipal laws typify this emerging tradition of statutory protection and follow a consistent pattern. The laws first enumerate the persons or entities subject to a duty not to discriminate. The list goes well beyond the entities covered by the common law. The Boulder ordinance, for example, has a comprehensive definition of entities deemed places of "public accommodation." They include "any place of business engaged in any sales to the general public and any place that offers services, facilities, privileges, or advantages to the general public or that receives financial support through solicitation of the general public or through governmental subsidy of any kind.''

These statutes and ordinances also depart from the common law by enumerating the groups or persons within their ambit of protection. [In] following this approach, Colorado's state and local governments have not limited anti-discrimination laws to groups that have so far been given the protection of heightened equal protection scrutiny under our cases. Rather, they set forth an extensive catalogue of traits which cannot be the basis for discrimination, including age, military status, marital status, pregnancy, parenthood, custody of a minor child, political affiliation, physical or mental disability of an individual or of his or her associates—and, in recent times, sexual orientation.

Amendment 2 bars homosexuals from securing protection against the injuries that these public-accommodations laws address. That in itself is a severe consequence, but there is more. Amendment 2, in addition, nullifies specific legal protections for this targeted class in all transactions in housing, sale of real estate, insurance, health and welfare services, private education, and employment.

[Not] confined to the private sphere, Amendment 2 also operates to repeal and forbid all laws or policies providing specific protection for gays or lesbians from discrimination by every level of Colorado government. The State Supreme Court cited two examples of protections in the governmental sphere that are now rescinded and may not be reintroduced. The first is [an] Executive Order which forbids employment discrimination against '' 'all state employees, classified and exempt' on the basis of sexual orientation.'' Also repealed, and now forbidden, are ''various provisions prohibiting discrimination based on sexual orientation at state colleges.''

Amendment 2's reach may not be limited to specific laws passed for the benefit of gays and lesbians. It is a fair, if not necessary, inference from the broad language of the amendment that it deprives gays and lesbians even of the protection of general laws and policies that prohibit arbitrary discrimination [such as statutes subjecting agency action to judicial review under the arbitrary and capricious standard and making it a criminal offense for a public servant knowingly, arbitrarily, or capriciously to refrain from performing a duty imposed by law]. At some point in the systematic administration of these laws, an official must determine whether homosexuality is an arbitrary and thus forbidden basis for decision. Yet a decision to that effect would itself amount to a policy prohibiting discrimination on the basis of homosexuality, and so would appear to be no more valid under Amendment 2 than the specific prohibitions against discrimination the state court held invalid.

[The] state court did not decide whether the amendment has this effect, however, and neither need we. [Even] if, as we doubt, homosexuals could find some safe harbor in laws of general application, we cannot accept the view that Amendment 2's prohibition on specific legal protections does no more than deprive homosexuals of special rights. To the contrary, the amendment imposes a special disability upon those persons alone. Homosexuals are forbidden the safeguards that others enjoy or may seek without constraint. They can obtain specific protection against discrimination only by enlisting the citizenry of Colorado to amend the state constitution or perhaps, on the State's view, by trying to pass helpful laws of general applicability. This is so no matter how local or discrete the harm, no matter how public and widespread the injury. We find nothing special in the protections Amendment 2 withholds. These are protections taken for granted by most people either because they already have them or do not need them; these are protections against exclusion from an almost limitless number of transactions and endeavors that constitute ordinary civic life in a free society.

[If] a law neither burdens a fundamental right nor targets a suspect class, we will uphold the legislative classification so long as it bears a rational relation to some legitimate end. Amendment 2 fails, indeed defies, even this conventional inquiry. [Even] in the ordinary equal protection case calling for the most deferential of standards, we insist on knowing the relation between the classification adopted and the object to be attained. [By] requiring that the classification bear a rational relationship to an independent and legitimate legislative end, we ensure that classifications are not drawn for the purpose of disadvantaging the group burdened by the law.

Amendment 2 confounds this normal process of judicial review. It is at once too narrow and too broad. It identifies persons by a single trait and then denies them protection across the board. [It] is not within our constitutional tradition to enact laws of this sort. Central both to the idea of the rule of law and to our own Constitution's guarantee of equal protection is the principle that government and each of its parts remain open on impartial terms to all who seek its assistance. [Respect] for this principle explains why laws singling out a certain class of citizens for disfavored legal status or general hardships are rare. A law declaring that in general it shall be more difficult for one group of citizens than for all others to seek aid from the government is itself a denial of equal protection of the laws in the most literal sense. * * *

Davis v. Beason, 133 U.S. 333, 10 S.Ct. 299, 33 L.Ed. 637 (1890), not cited by the parties but relied upon by the dissent, is not evidence that Amendment 2 is within our constitutional tradition, and any reliance upon it as authority for sustaining the amendment is misplaced. In *Davis*, the Court approved an Idaho territorial statute denying Mormons, polygamists, and advocates of polygamy the right to vote and to hold office. [To] the extent *Davis* held that persons advocating a certain practice may be denied the right to vote, it is no longer good law. *Brandenburg v. Ohio*, [CON LAW p. 656, AMER CON p. 666, RTS & LIB p. 563]. To the extent it held that the groups designated in the statute may be deprived of the right to vote because of their status, its ruling could not stand without surviving strict scrutiny, a most doubtful outcome. *Dunn v. Blumstein*, [CON LAW p. 1375, AMER CON p. 1305, RTS & LIB p. 1282].

[A] second and related point is that laws of the kind now before us raise the inevitable inference that the disadvantage imposed is born of animosity toward the class of persons affected. "[I]f the constitutional conception of 'equal protection of the laws' means anything, it must at the very least mean that a bare * * * desire to harm a politically unpopular group cannot constitute a *legitimate* governmental interest." *Moreno*, [CON LAW p. 1158, AMER CON p. 1119, RTS & LIB, p. 1065]. Even laws enacted for broad and ambitious purposes often can be explained by reference to legitimate public policies which justify the incidental disadvantages they impose on certain persons. Amendment 2, however, in making a general announcement that gays and lesbians shall not have any particular protections from the law, inflicts on them immediate, continuing, and real injuries that outrun and belie any legitimate justifications that may be claimed for it.

[The] primary rationale the State offers for Amendment 2 is respect for other citizens' freedom of association, and in particular the liberties of landlords or employers who have personal or religious objections to homosexuality. Colorado also cites its interest in conserving resources to fight discrimination against other groups. The breadth of the Amendment is so far removed from these particular justifications that we find it impossible to credit them. [It] is a status-based enactment divorced from any factual context from which we could discern a relationship to legitimate state interests; it is a classification of persons undertaken for its own sake, something the Equal Protection Clause does not permit. * * *

JUSTICE SCALIA, with whom THE CHIEF JUSTICE and JUSTICE THOMAS join, dissenting.

[In] rejecting the State's arguments that Amendment 2 "puts gays and lesbians in the same position as all other persons," and "does no more than deny homosexuals special rights," [the] Court considers it unnecessary to decide the validity of the State's argument that Amendment 2 does not deprive homosexuals of the "protection [afforded by] general laws and policies that prohibit arbitrary discrimination in governmental and private settings." I agree that we need not resolve that dispute, because the Supreme Court of Colorado has resolved it for us. [The] Colorado court stated: "[I]t is significant to note that Colorado law currently proscribes discrimination against persons who are not suspect classes, including discrimination based on age, marital or family status, veterans' status, and for any legal, off-duty conduct such as smoking tobacco. *Of course Amendment 2 is not intended to have any effect on this legislation, but seeks only to prevent the adoption of antidiscrimination laws intended to protect gays, lesbians, and bisexuals.*" (emphasis added). [This] analysis, which is fully in accord with (indeed, follows inescapably from) the text of the constitutional provision, lays to rest such horribles [as] the prospect that assaults upon homosexuals could not be prosecuted. The amendment prohibits *special treatment* of homosexuals, and nothing more. It would not affect, for example, a requirement of state law that pensions be paid to all retiring state employees with a certain length of service; homosexual employees, as well as others, would be entitled to that benefit. But it would prevent the State or any municipality from making death-benefit payments to the "life partner" of a homosexual when it does not make such payments to the long-time roommate of a nonhomosexual employee.

[Despite] all of its hand-wringing about the potential effect of Amendment 2 on general antidiscrimination laws, the Court's opinion ultimately does not dispute all this, but assumes it to be true. The only denial of equal treatment it contends homosexuals have suffered is this: They may not obtain *preferential* treatment without amending the state constitution. That is to say, the principle underlying the Court's opinion is that one who is accorded equal treatment under the laws, but cannot as readily as others obtain *preferential* treatment under the laws, has been denied equal protection of the laws. If merely stating this alleged "equal protection" violation does not suffice to refute it, our constitutional jurisprudence has achieved terminal silliness.

The central thesis of the Court's reasoning is that any group is denied equal protection when, to obtain advantage (or, presumably, to avoid disadvantage), it must have recourse to a more general and hence more difficult level of political decisionmaking than others. The world has never heard of such a principle, which is why the Court's opinion is so long on emotive utterance and so short on relevant legal citation. And it seems to me most unlikely that any multilevel democracy can function under such a principle. For *whenever* a disadvantage is imposed, or conferral of a benefit is prohibited, at one of the higher levels of democratic decisionmaking (*i.e.*, by the state legislature rather than local government, or by the people at large in the state constitution rather than the legislature), the affected group has (under this theory) been denied equal protection. To take the simplest of examples, consider a state law prohibiting the award of municipal contracts to relatives of mayors or city councilmen. Once such a law is passed, the group composed of such relatives must, in order to get the benefit of city contracts, persuade the state legislature—unlike all other citizens, who need only persuade the municipality. It is ridiculous to consider this a denial of equal protection, which is why the Court's theory is unheard of. * * *

I turn next to whether there was a legitimate rational basis for the substance of the constitutional amendment—for the prohibition of special protection for homosexuals.[1] It is unsurprising that the Court avoids discussion of this question, since the answer is so obviously yes. The case most relevant to the issue before us today is not even mentioned in the Court's opinion: In *Bowers v. Hardwick*, [CON LAW p. 516, AMER CON p. 591, RTS & LIB p. 422], we held that the Constitution does not prohibit what virtually all States had done from the founding of the Republic until very recent years—making homosexual conduct a crime. [If] it is constitutionally permissible for a State to make homosexual conduct criminal, surely it is constitutionally permissible for a State to enact other laws merely *disfavoring* homosexual conduct. [And] a fortiori it is constitutionally permissible for a State to adopt a provision *not even* disfavoring homosexual conduct, but merely prohibiting all levels of state government from bestowing *special protections* upon homosexual conduct. Respondents (who, unlike the Court, cannot afford the luxury of ignoring inconvenient precedent) counter *Bowers* with the argument that a greater-includes-the-lesser rationale cannot justify Amendment 2's application to individuals who do not engage in homosexual acts, but are merely of homosexual "orientation."

[Assuming] that, in Amendment 2, a person of homosexual "orientation" is someone who does not engage in homosexual conduct but merely has a tendency or desire to do so, *Bowers* still suffices to establish a rational basis for the provision. If it is rational to criminalize the conduct, surely it is rational to deny special favor and protection to those with a self-avowed tendency or desire to engage in the conduct. Indeed, where criminal sanctions are not involved, homosexual "orientation" is an acceptable stand-in for homosexual conduct. A State "does not violate the Equal Protection Clause merely because the classifications made by its laws are imperfect." Just as a policy barring the hiring of methadone users as transit employees does not violate equal protection simply because *some* methadone users pose no threat to passenger safety, see *New York City Transit Authority v. Beazer*, [CON LAW p. 1157, AMER CON p. 1118, RTS & LIB p. 1064], [Amendment] 2 is not constitutionally invalid simply because it could have been drawn more precisely so as to withdraw special antidiscrimination protections only from those of homosexual "orientation" who actually engage in homosexual conduct.

[The] Court's opinion contains grim, disapproving hints that Coloradans have been guilty of "animus" or "animosity" toward homosexuality, as though that has been established as Unamerican. Of course it is our moral heritage that one should not hate any human being or class of human beings. But I had thought

---

1. The Court evidently agrees that "rational basis"—the normal test for compliance with the Equal Protection Clause—is the governing standard. The trial court rejected respondents' argument that homosexuals constitute a "suspect" or "quasi-suspect" class, and respondents elected not to appeal that ruling to the Supreme Court of Colorado. And the Court implicitly rejects the Supreme Court of Colorado's holding that Amendment 2 infringes upon a "fundamental right" of "independently identifiable class[es]" to "participate equally in the political process."

that one could consider certain conduct reprehensible—murder, for example, or polygamy, or cruelty to animals—and could exhibit even "animus" toward such conduct. Surely that is the only sort of "animus" at issue here: moral disapproval of homosexual conduct, the same sort of moral disapproval that produced the centuries-old criminal laws that we held constitutional in *Bowers*.

[But] though Coloradans are, as I say, *entitled* to be hostile toward homosexual conduct, the fact is that the degree of hostility reflected by Amendment 2 is the smallest conceivable. The Court's portrayal of Coloradans as a society fallen victim to pointless, hate-filled "gay-bashing" is so false as to be comical. Colorado not only is one of the 25 States that have repealed their antisodomy laws, but was among the first to do so. But the society that eliminates criminal punishment for homosexual acts does not necessarily abandon the view that homosexuality is morally wrong and socially harmful; often, abolition simply reflects the view that enforcement of such criminal laws involves unseemly intrusion into the intimate lives of citizens.

There is a problem, however, which arises when criminal sanction of homosexuality is eliminated but moral and social disapprobation of homosexuality is meant to be retained. [Because] those who engage in homosexual conduct tend to reside in disproportionate numbers in certain communities, and of course care about homosexual-rights issues much more ardently than the public at large, they possess political power much greater than their numbers, both locally and statewide. Quite understandably, they devote this political power to achieving not merely a grudging social toleration, but full social acceptance, of homosexuality.

By the time Coloradans were asked to vote on Amendment 2, [three] Colorado cities—Aspen, Boulder, and Denver—had enacted ordinances that listed "sexual orientation" as an impermissible ground for discrimination, equating the moral disapproval of homosexual conduct with racial and religious bigotry[, and] the Governor of Colorado had signed an executive order [directing] state agency-heads to "ensure non-discrimination" in hiring and promotion based on, among other things, "sexual orientation." [I] do not mean to be critical of these legislative successes; homosexuals are as entitled to use the legal system for reinforcement of their moral sentiments as are the rest of society. But they are subject to being countered by lawful, democratic countermeasures as well.

That is where Amendment 2 came in. It sought to counter both the geographic concentration and the disproportionate political power of homosexuals by (1) resolving the controversy at the statewide level, and (2) making the election a single-issue contest for both sides. [The] Court today asserts that this most democratic of procedures is unconstitutional. Lacking any cases to establish that facially absurd proposition, it simply asserts that it *must* be unconstitutional, because it has never happened before. [But, as] I have noted above, this is proved false every time a state law prohibiting or disfavoring certain conduct is passed, because such a law prevents the adversely affected group—whether drug addicts, or smokers, or gun owners, or motorcyclists—from changing the policy thus established in "each of [the] parts" of the State.

[But] there is a much closer analogy, one that involves precisely the effort by the majority of citizens to preserve its view of sexual morality statewide, against the efforts of a geographically concentrated and politically powerful minority to undermine it. The constitutions of the States of Arizona, Idaho, New Mexico, Oklahoma, and Utah *to this day* contain provisions stating that polygamy is "forever prohibited." Polygamists, and those who have a polygamous "orientation," have been "singled out" by these provisions for much more severe treatment than merely denial of favored status; and that treatment can only be changed by achieving amendment of the state constitutions. The Court's disposition today suggests that these provisions are unconstitutional, and that polygamy must be permitted in these States on a state-legislated, or perhaps even local-option, basis—unless, of course, polygamists for some reason have fewer constitutional rights than homosexuals.

[Has] the Court concluded that the perceived social harm of polygamy is a "legitimate concern of government," and the perceived social harm of homosexuality is not? [I] strongly suspect that the answer [to the last question is] yes, which leads me to the last point I wish to make: [To] suggest [that] this constitutional amendment springs from nothing more than " 'a bare * * * desire to harm a politically unpopular group,' " is nothing short of insulting. (It is also nothing short of preposterous to call "politically unpopular" a group which enjoys enormous influence in American media and politics, and which, as the trial court here noted, though composing no more than 4% of the population had the support of 46% of the voters on Amendment 2.) [When] the Court takes sides in the culture wars, it tends to be with the knights rather than the villeins—and more specifically with the Templars, reflecting the views and values of the lawyer class from which the Court's Members are drawn. How that class feels about homosexuality will be evident to anyone who wishes to interview job applicants at virtually any of the Nation's law schools. The interviewer may refuse to offer a job because the applicant is a Republican; because he is an adulterer; [or] because he went to the wrong prep school or belongs to the wrong country club. But if the interviewer should wish not to be an associate or partner of an applicant because he disapproves of the applicant's homosexuality, *then* he will have violated the pledge which the Association of American Law Schools requires all its member-schools to exact from job interviewers: "assurance of the employer's willingness" to hire homosexuals. This law-school view of what "prejudices" must be stamped out may be contrasted with the more plebeian attitudes that apparently still prevail in the United States Congress, which has been unresponsive to repeated attempts to extend to homosexuals the protections of federal civil rights laws.

[Today's] opinion has no foundations in American constitutional law, and barely pretends to. The people of Colorado have adopted an entirely reasonable provision which does not even disfavor homosexuals in any substantive sense, but merely denies them preferential treatment. Amendment 2 is designed to prevent piecemeal deterioration of the sexual morality favored by a majority of Coloradans, and is not only an appropriate means to that legitimate end, but a means that Americans have employed before. Striking it down is an act, not of judicial judgment, but of political will.   * * *

"FUNDAMENTAL RIGHTS"

VOTING

"DILUTION" OF THE RIGHT: APPORTIONMENT

CON LAW: P. 1368, before notes and questions

AMER CON: P. 1298, before notes and questions

RTS & LIB: P. 1275, before notes and questions

On remand in *Miller,* the plaintiffs amended their complaint to challenge a second of the majority-black districts. The district court held that the district violated *Miller* standards. When the Georgia legislature was unable to produce a plan of its own, the district court produced a plan with only one majority-black district. The plaintiffs did not defend the original district, but protested the failure of the district court to include another majority-black district.

ABRAMS v. JOHNSON, 521 U.S. 74, 117 S.Ct. 1925, 138 L.Ed.2d 285 (1997), per KENNEDY, J., upheld the district court. He found "ample basis in the record" to support the district court's conclusion that a second majority-black district could not have been drawn without allowing race to predominate over traditional districting principles such as protecting incumbents from contests with each other and preserving (1) county lines where possible; (2) district cores; (3) four traditional districts in the corners of the state; and (4) a majority-black district in the center of Atlanta.[a]

Kennedy, J., therefore, found that strict scrutiny applied. He assumed, but did not decide, that a need to comply with section two of the Voting Rights Act would meet the standard, but concluded that there was no such need.

BREYER, J., joined by Stevens, Souter, and Ginsburg, JJ., dissenting, argued on the facts that a second majority-black district would not have interfered with other important districting objectives and contended that the district court should have deferred to the legislature's reasonable belief that the failure to have a second majority-black district would violate section two of the Voting Rights Act.[b]

CON LAW: P. 1369, after note 4

AMER CON: P. 1299, after note 4

RTS & LIB: P. 1276, after note 4

5. BUSH v. VERA, 517 U.S. 952, 116 S.Ct. 1941, 135 L.Ed.2d 248 (1996), struck down congressional districts crafted to meet what Texas argued was needed to meet the requirements of the Voting Rights Act. Although race was a factor in drawing the lines, Texas argued that the predominant factor was the protection of incumbents. O'CONNOR, J., joined by Rehnquist, C.J., and Kennedy, J., agreed that avoiding contests between incumbents was a legitimate districting consideration,[a] and she emphasized that the "decision to create majority-minority districts

a. In the same term, *Lawyer v. Department of Justice*, 521 U.S. 567, 117 S.Ct. 2186, 138 L.Ed.2d 669 (1997), per Souter, J., upheld the constitutionality of a Florida state senate district that had been approved as a part of a judicial settlement. The district was produced as a replacement for another district that had been challenged on racial grounds, and the lower court found a substantial evidentiary and legal basis for the challenge of the prior district. A non-settling defendant challenged the new district on the ground that it too was motivated by predominantly racial considerations. The new district included two counties, crossed a body of water, was not compact, and was irregular in shape. In addition, it contained a percentage of black voters significantly higher than the percentage in the counties from which the district was drawn. Souter, J., upheld the lower court's determination that the new district was in traditional respects in line with other districts in the state. Moreover, he denied the principle that black residents in a district may not exceed the percentage of black residents in the political subdivisions from which the district is produced.

Scalia, J., joined by O'Connor, Kennedy, and Thomas, JJ., dissenting, did not reach the issue, arguing instead that the district court should have determined the merits of the law suit—as opposed to finding a substantial basis for it—and should also have given the state legislature an opportunity to reapportion before proceeding with the settlement.

b. Souter, J., found this belief reasonable because of the presence of at least two majority-black districts in the plans that had previously been produced by the Georgia legislature in this census period. Kennedy, J., replied that the presence of such districts represented a response to Justice Department pressure, not the legislature's true preference. Souter, J., did not deny the pressure, but offered what he believed to be independent legislative testimony of a desire for a second or third black-majority district and evidence of a section two violation.

a. The "incumbents" were members of the Texas legislature who had declared their intention to run for Congress. Is protection of these persons a legitimate state interest? Should

was not objectionable in and of itself." She concluded on the facts, however, that strict scrutiny was appropriate because race had predominated over legitimate districting considerations. Among the findings weighing in favor of the application of strict scrutiny were "that the State substantially neglected traditional districting criteria such as compactness, that it was committed from the outset to creating majority-minority districts, and that it manipulated district lines to exploit unprecedentedly detailed racial data." She observed that none of the findings would independently justify strict scrutiny. O'Connor, J., also concluded that the Texas districts were not narrowly tailored to meet the requirements of the Voting Rights Act because the act does not require a state to create districts that are not reasonably compact:[b] "If, because of the dispersion of the minority population, a reasonably compact majority-minority district cannot be created, the [Voting Rights Act] does not require a majority-minority district; if a reasonably compact district can be created, nothing in [the Voting Rights Act] requires the race-based creation of a district that is far from compact."[c]

In a separate concurring opinion, O'CONNOR, J., summarized "the rules governing the States consideration of race in the districting process[:] First, so long as they do not subordinate traditional districting criteria to the use of race for its own sake or as a proxy, States may intentionally create majority-minority districts,[d] and may otherwise take race into consideration, without coming under strict scrutiny. See ante, at ___-___ (plurality opinion); (Stevens, J., dissenting); (Souter, J., dissenting). Only if traditional districting criteria are neglected and that neglect is predominantly due to the misuse of race does strict scrutiny apply. (plurality opinion).

"Second, where voting is racially polarized, § 2 [of the Voting Rights Act] prohibits States from adopting districting schemes that would have the effect that minority voters 'have less opportunity than other members of the electorate to * * * elect representatives of their choice.' § 2(b). That principle may require a State to create a majority-minority district where the three Gingles factors are present—viz., (i) the minority group 'is sufficiently large and geographically compact to constitute a majority in a single-member district,' (ii) 'it is politically

---

incumbent protection be a legitimate state interest? In a state where racially polarized voting is prominent, under what circumstances is it possible to protect incumbents without taking race into account in drawing district lines?

b. The Court reached the same conclusion in the companion case, *Shaw v. Hunt*, 517 U.S. 899, 116 S.Ct. 1894, 135 L.Ed.2d 207 (1996)(districts described in *Shaw v. Reno* not narrowly tailored to meet a compelling state interest even assuming that compliance with the Voting Rights Act was compelling).

c. Thomas, J., joined by Scalia, J., concurring, argued that the intentional creation of majority-minority district should be enough to invoke strict scrutiny. Kennedy, J., concurring, strongly suggested he would join Thomas and Scalia, JJ., on that point if the issue were presented. Stevens, J., joined by Ginsburg and Breyer, JJ., dissenting, denied that race was a predominant consideration in the formation of the Texas districts, maintained that the creation of districts not reasonably compact was consistent with the Voting Rights Act (though

he conceded that liability could be imposed only if the state could have created a majority-minority reasonably compact district), and he continued to question *Shaw*. Souter, J., joined by Ginsburg and Breyer, JJ., dissenting, continued to question *Shaw* and argued that the post-*Shaw* cases had failed to provide a manageable standard.

d. *Hunt v. Cromartie*, ___ U.S. ___, 119 S.Ct. 1545, ___ L.Ed.2d ___ (1999), per Thomas, J., stated that the intentional use of race to create districts with slightly less than a majority of minority citizens could also be subject to an equal protection challenge, but found that summary judgment as to the legislature's intent was inappropriate under the circumstances because there was controversy whether the intent was political or racial. Stevens, J., joined by Souter, Ginsburg and Breyer, JJ., concurring, argued that the inclusion of black voters may well have been motivated by the desire to create a Democratic district, not by a desire to create a district with a black representative.

cohesive,' and (iii) 'the white majority votes sufficiently as a bloc to enable it * * * usually to defeat the minority's preferred candidate.'

"Third, the state interest in avoiding liability under [§ 2] is compelling.[e] If a State has a strong basis in evidence for concluding that the Gingles factors are present, it may create a majority-minority district without awaiting judicial findings. Its 'strong basis in evidence' need not take any particular form, although it cannot simply rely on generalized assumptions about the prevalence of racial bloc voting.

"Fourth, if a State pursues that compelling interest by creating a district that 'substantially addresses' the potential liability, and does not deviate substantially from a hypothetical court-drawn § 2 district for predominantly racial reasons, its districting plan will be deemed narrowly tailored. Cf. (plurality opinion)(acknowledging this possibility); (Souter, J., dissenting)(same); (Stevens, J., dissenting)(contending that it is applicable here).

"Finally, however, districts that are bizarrely shaped and non-compact, and that otherwise neglect traditional districting principles and deviate substantially from the hypothetical court-drawn district, for predominantly racial reasons, are unconstitutional. (plurality opinion)."

TRAVEL

CON LAW: P. 1380

AMER CON: P. 1310

RTS & LIB: P. 1286

SAENZ v. ROE, ___ U.S. ___, 119 S.Ct. 1518, ___ L.Ed.2d ___ (1999), per STEVENS, J., shifted equality analysis in right to travel cases from the equal protection to the privilege and immunities and citizenship clauses in section one of the fourteenth amendment: "In 1992, California enacted a statute limiting the maximum welfare benefits available to newly arrived residents. The scheme limits the amount payable to a family that has resided in the State for less than 12 months to the amount payable by the State of the family's prior residence. The questions presented by this case are whether the 1992 statute was constitutional when it was enacted and, if not, whether an amendment to the Social Security Act enacted by Congress in 1996 affects that determination.

"The word 'travel' is not found in the text of the Constitution. Yet the 'constitutional right to travel from one State to another' is firmly embedded in our jurisprudence. [The] 'right to travel' discussed in our cases embraces at least three different components. It protects the right of a citizen of one State to enter and to leave another State, the right to be treated as a welcome visitor rather than an unfriendly alien when temporarily present in the second State, and, for those travelers who elect to become permanent residents, the right to be treated like other citizens of that State.* * *

"What is at issue in this case [is the] third aspect of the right to travel—the right of the newly arrived citizen to the same privileges and immunities enjoyed by other citizens of the same State. That right is protected not only by the new arrival's status as a state citizen, but also by her status as a citizen of the United

---

e. The four dissenters in *Vera* (who also dissented in *Hunt*) together with O'Connor J., supported this proposition.

States. That additional source of protection is plainly identified in the opening words of the Fourteenth Amendment:

"Despite fundamentally differing views concerning the coverage of the Privileges or Immunities Clause of the Fourteenth Amendment, most notably expressed in the majority and dissenting opinions in the *Slaughter-House Cases*, it has always been common ground that this Clause protects the third component of the right to travel. Writing for the majority in the *Slaughter-House Cases*, Justice Miller explained that one of the privileges conferred by this Clause 'is that a citizen of the United States can, of his own volition, become a citizen of any State of the Union by a bona fide residence therein, with the same rights as other citizens of that State.' * * *

"Neither mere rationality nor some intermediate standard of review should be used to judge the constitutionality of a state rule that discriminates against some of its citizens because they have been domiciled in the State for less than a year. The appropriate standard may be more categorical than that articulated in *Shapiro*, but it is surely no less strict. * * *

"It is undisputed that respondents and the members of the class that they represent are citizens of California and that their need for welfare benefits is unrelated to the length of time that they have resided in California. We thus have no occasion to consider what weight might be given to a citizen's length of residence if the bona fides of her claim to state citizenship were questioned. Moreover, because whatever benefits they receive will be consumed while they remain in California, there is no danger that recognition of their claim will encourage citizens of other States to establish residency for just long enough to acquire some readily portable benefit, such as a divorce or a college education, that will be enjoyed after they return to their original domicile. See, e.g., *Sosna v. Iowa*; *Vlandis v. Kline*.

"Disavowing any desire to fence out the indigent, California has instead advanced an entirely fiscal justification for its [scheme]. The enforcement of § 11450.03 will save the State approximately $10.9 million a year. The question is not whether such saving is a legitimate purpose but whether the State may accomplish that end by the discriminatory means it has chosen. An evenhanded, across-the-board reduction of about 72 cents per month for every beneficiary would produce the same result. But our negative answer to the question does not rest on the weakness of the State's purported fiscal justification. It rests on the fact that the Citizenship Clause of the Fourteenth Amendment expressly equates citizenship with residence: 'That Clause does not provide for, and does not allow for, degrees of citizenship based on length of residence.' *Zobel*. * * *

"The question that remains is whether congressional approval of durational residency requirements in the 1996 amendment to the Social Security Act somehow resuscitates the constitutionality of § 11450.03. That question is readily answered, for we have consistently held that Congress may not authorize the States to violate the Fourteenth Amendment."

REHNQUIST, C.J., joined by Thomas, J., dissented: "The Court today breathes new life into the previously dormant Privileges or Immunities Clause of the Fourteenth Amendment—a Clause relied upon by this Court in only one other decision, *Colgate v. Harvey*, 296 U.S. 404, 56 S.Ct. 252, 80 L.Ed. 299 (1935), overruled five years later by *Madden v. Kentucky*, 309 U.S. 83, 60 S.Ct. 406, 84 L.Ed. 590 (1940). It uses this Clause to strike down what I believe is a reasonable measure falling under the head of a "good-faith residency requirement." Because I do not think any provision of the Constitution—and surely not a provision relied upon for only the second time since its enactment 130 years ago—requires this result, I dissent. * * *

"I agree with the proposition that a 'citizen of the United States can, of his own volition, become a citizen of any State of the Union by a bona fide residence therein, with the same rights as other citizens of that State.' *Slaughter-House Cases*. But I cannot see how the right to become a citizen of another State is a necessary 'component' of the right to travel, or why the Court tries to marry these separate and distinct rights. A person is no longer 'traveling' in any sense of the word when he finishes his journey to a State which he plans to make his home. Indeed, under the Court's logic, the protections of the Privileges or Immunities Clause recognized in this case come into play only when an individual *stops* traveling with the intent to remain and become a citizen of a new State. [At] most, restrictions on an individual's right to become a citizen indirectly affect his calculus in deciding whether to exercise his right to travel in the first place, but such an attenuated and uncertain relationship is no ground for folding one right into the other.

"No doubt the Court has, in the past 30 years, essentially conflated the right to travel with the right to equal state citizenship in striking down durational residence requirements similar to the one challenged here.* * *

"The Court today tries to clear much of the underbrush created by these prior right-to-travelcases, abandoning its effort to define what residence requirements deprive individuals of 'important rights and benefits' or 'penalize' the right to travel. Under its new analytical framework, a State, outside certain ill-defined circumstances, cannot classify its citizens by the length of their residence in the State without offending the Privileges or Immunities Clause of the Fourteenth Amendment. The Court thus departs from *Shapiro* and its progeny, and, while paying lipservice to the right to travel, the Court does little to explain how the right to travel is involved at all. Instead, as the Court's analysis clearly demonstrates, this case is only about respondents' right to immediately enjoy all the privileges of being a California citizen in relation to that State's ability to test the good-faith assertion of this right. * * *

"In unearthing from its tomb the right to become a state citizen and to be treated equally in the new State of residence, however, the Court ignores a State's need to assure that only persons who establish a bona fide residence receive the benefits provided to current residents of the State.[T]he Court has consistently recognized that while new citizens must have the same opportunity to enjoy the privileges of being a citizen of a State, the States retain the ability to use bona fide residence requirements to ferret out those who intend to take the privileges and run.* * *

"If States can require individuals to reside in-state for a year before exercising the right to educational benefits, the right to terminate a marriage, or the right to vote in primary elections that all other state citizens enjoy, then States may surely do the same for welfare benefits. Indeed, there is no material difference between a 1–year residence requirement applied to the level of welfare benefits given out by a State, and the same requirement applied to the level of tuition subsidies at a state university. The welfare payment here and in-state tuition rates are cash subsidies provided to a limited class of people, and California's standard of living and higher education system make both subsidies quite attractive. Durational residence requirements were upheld when used to regulate the provision of higher education subsidies, and the same deference should be given in the case of welfare payments.

"The Court today recognizes that States retain the ability to determine the *bona fides* of an individual's claim to residence, but then tries to avoid the issue. It asserts that because respondents' need for welfare benefits is unrelated to the length of time they have resided in California, it has 'no occasion to consider what weight might be given to a citizen's length of residence if the bona fides of her claim to state citizenship were questioned.' But I do not understand how the absence of a link between need and length of residency bears on the State's ability to objectively test respondents' resolve to stay in California. There is no link between the need for an education or for a divorce and the length of residence, and yet States may use length of residence as an objective yardstick to channel their benefits to those whose intent to stay is legitimate. * * *

"The Court tries to distinguish education and divorce benefits by contending that the welfare payment here will be consumed in California, while a college education or a divorce produces benefits that are 'portable' and can be enjoyed after individuals return to their original domicile. But this 'you can't take it with you' distinction is more apparent than real, and offers little guidance to lower courts who must apply this rationale in the future. Welfare payments are a form of insurance, giving impoverished individuals and their families the means to meet the demands of daily life while they receive the necessary training, education, and time to look for a job. The cash itself will no doubt be spent in California, but the benefits from receiving this income and having the opportunity to become employed or employable will stick with the welfare recipient if they stay in California or go back to their true domicile. Similarly, tuition subsidies are 'consumed' in-state but the recipient takes the benefits of a college education with him wherever he goes. A welfare subsidy is thus as much an investment in human capital as is a tuition subsidy, and their attendant benefits are just as 'portable.' More importantly, this foray into social economics demonstrates that the line drawn by the Court borders on the metaphysical, and requires lower courts to plumb the policies animating certain benefits like welfare to define their 'essence' and hence their 'portability.' * * *

"I therefore believe that the durational residence requirement challenged here is a permissible exercise of the State's power to 'assur[e] that services provided for its residents are enjoyed only by residents.' "

THOMAS, J., joined by Rehnquist, C.J., dissented: "Unlike the Equal Protection and Due Process Clauses, which have assumed near-talismanic status in modern constitutional law, the Court all but read the Privileges or Immunities Clause out of the Constitution in the *Slaughter-House Cases*. * * *

"Unlike the majority, I would look to history to ascertain the original meaning of the Clause. At least in American law, the phrase (or its close approximation) appears to stem from the 1606 Charter of Virginia, which provided that 'all and every the Persons being our Subjects, which shall dwell and inhabit within every or any of the said several Colonies * * * shall HAVE and enjoy all Liberties, Franchises, and Immunities * * * as if they had been abiding and born, within this our Realme of England.' [The] colonists' repeated assertions that they maintained the rights, privileges and immunities of persons 'born within the realm of England' and 'natural born' persons suggests that, at the time of the founding, the terms 'privileges' and 'immunities' (and their counterparts) were understood to refer to those fundamental rights and liberties specifically enjoyed by English citizens, and more broadly, by all persons. * * * Justice Bushrod Washington's landmark opinion in *Corfield v. Coryell* reflects this historical understanding. * * * Justice Washington's opinion in *Corfield* indisputably influenced the Members of Congress who enacted the Fourteenth Amendment. When Congress gathered to debate the Fourteenth Amendment, members frequently, if not as a matter of course, appealed to *Corfield*, arguing that the Amendment was necessary to guarantee the fundamental rights that Justice Washington identified in his opinion. * * *

"That Members of the 39th Congress appear to have endorsed the wisdom of Justice Washington's opinion does not, standing alone, provide dispositive insight into their understanding of the Fourteenth Amendment's Privileges or Immunities Clause. Nevertheless, their repeated references to the *Corfield* decision, combined with what appears to be the historical understanding of the Clause's operative terms, supports the inference that, at the time the Fourteenth Amendment was adopted, people understood that 'privileges or immunities of citizens' were fundamental rights, rather than every public benefit established by positive law. Accordingly, the majority's conclusion—that a State violates the Privileges or Immunities Clause when it 'discriminates' against citizens who have been domiciled in the State for less than a year in the distribution of welfare benefit appears contrary to the original understanding and is dubious at best.

"As The Chief Justice points out, it comes as quite a surprise that the majority relies on the Privileges or Immunities Clause at all in this case. [Although] the majority appears to breathe new life into the Clause today, it fails to address its historical underpinnings or its place in our constitutional jurisprudence. Because I believe that the demise of the Privileges or Immunities Clause has contributed in no small part to the current disarray of our Fourteenth Amendment jurisprudence, I would be open to reevaluating its meaning in an appropriate case. Before invoking the Clause, however, we should endeavor to understand what the framers of the Fourteenth Amendment thought that it meant. We should also consider whether the Clause should displace, rather than augment, portions of our equal protection and substantive due process jurisprudence. The majority's failure to consider these important questions raises the specter that the Privileges or Immunities Clause will become yet another convenient tool for inventing new rights, limited solely by the 'predilections of those who happen at the time to be Members of this Court.' "

ACCESS TO THE COURTS

CON LAW: P. 1386, addition to fn. c
AMER CON: P. 1316, addition to fn. c
RTS & LIB: P. 1293, addition to fn. c

To what extent should prisons be required to provide law library facilities for inmates? If a right to adequate law library facilities exists, is it founded in equal protection, due process, or the right to petition the courts for redress of grievances? See *Lewis v. Casey*, 518 U.S. 343, 116 S.Ct. 2174, 135 L.Ed.2d 606 (1996).

CON LAW: P. 1388, before notes and questions
AMER CON: P. 1318, before notes and questions
RTS & LIB: P. 1295, before notes and questions

A Mississippi chancery court terminated M.L.B.'s parental rights to her two young children. M.L.B. tried to appeal, but Mississippi required that she pay record preparation fees of $22,352.36 in advance. She could not afford to do so, and her appeal was dismissed.

M.L.B. v. S.L.J., 519 U.S. 102, 117 S.Ct. 555, 136 L.Ed.2d 473 (1996), per GINSBURG, J., held that "just as the State may not block an indigent petty offender's access to an appeal afforded others, so Mississippi may not deny M.L.B., because of her poverty, appellate review of the sufficiency of the evidence on which the trial court found her unfit to be a parent. [A]s *Ortwein* underscored, this Court has not extended *Griffin* to the broad array of civil cases. But tellingly, the Court has consistently set apart from the mine run of cases those involving state controls or intrusions on family relationships. * * * [T]he Court's decisions concerning access to judicial processes * * * reflect both equal protection and due process concerns. * * * The equal protection concern relates to the legitimacy of fencing out would-be appellants based solely on their inability to pay core costs. The due process concern hones in on the essential fairness of the state-ordered proceedings anterior to adverse state action. * * * Nevertheless, '[m]ost decisions in this area,' we have recognized, 'res[t] on an equal protection framework, * * * for [due] process does not independently require that the State provide an appeal.

"[Unlike *Washington v. Davis*,] the Mississippi prescription here at issue [is] not merely *disproportionate* in impact. Rather [it is] wholly contingent on one's ability to pay, and thus 'visi[ts] different consequences on two categories of persons;' [it applies] to all indigents and do[es] not reach anyone outside that class. In sum, under [a broad] reading of *Washington v. Davis,* our overruling of the *Griffin* line of cases would be two decades overdue. It suffices to point out that this Court has not so conceived the meaning and effect of our 1976 'disproportionate impact precedent.'

"Respondents and the dissenters urge that we will open floodgates if we do not rigidly restrict *Griffin* to cases typed 'criminal.' But we have repeatedly noticed what sets parental status termination decrees apart from [the] mine run [of] civil actions, even from other domestic relations matters such as divorce, paternity, and child custody. To recapitulate, termination decrees 'wor[k] a unique kind of deprivation.' In contrast to matters modifiable at the parties' will or based on changed circumstances, termination adjudications involve the awesome authority of the State 'to destroy permanently all legal recognition of the parental relationship.' Our [decisions], recognizing that parental termination decrees are among the most severe forms of state action have not served as precedent in other areas. We are therefore satisfied that the label 'civil' should not entice us to leave undisturbed the Mississippi courts' disposition of this case.

"For the reasons stated, we hold that Mississippi may not withhold from M.L.B. 'a "record of sufficient completeness" to permit proper [appellate] consideration of [her] claims.' "[a]

T[HOMAS], J., joined by Scalia, J., and Rehnquist, C.J., in part, dissented: "[M.L.B.] defended against the 'destruction of her family bonds' in the Chancery Court hearing at which she was accorded all the process this Court has required of the States in parental termination cases. She now desires 'state aid to subsidize [her] privately initiated' appeal—an appeal that neither petitioner nor the majority claims Mississippi is required to provide—to overturn the determination that resulted from that hearing. I see no principled difference between a facially neutral rule that serves in some cases to prevent persons from availing themselves of state employment, or a state-funded education, or a state-funded abortion—each of which the State may, but is not required to, provide—and a facially

---

a. Kennedy, J., concurring, would have rested on the due process clause "given the existing appellate structure in Mississippi" though he also observed that "the authorities do not hold that an appeal is required even in a criminal case."

neutral rule that prevents a person from taking an appeal that is available only because the State chooses to provide it.[1]

"The *Griffin* line of cases ascribed to—one might say announced—an equalizing notion of the Equal Protection Clause that would, I think, have startled the Fourteenth Amendment's Framers. In those cases, the Court did not find, nor did it seek, any purposeful discrimination on the part of the state defendants. That their statutes had disproportionate effect on poor persons was sufficient for us to find a constitutional violation. In *Davis,* among other cases, we began to recognize the potential mischief of a disparate impact theory writ large, and endeavored to contain it. In this case, I would continue that enterprise. Mississippi's requirement of prepaid transcripts in civil appeals seeking to contest the sufficiency of the evidence adduced at trial is facially neutral; it creates no classification. The transcript rule reasonably obliges would-be appellants to bear the costs of availing themselves of a service that the State chooses, but is not constitutionally required, to provide. Any adverse impact that the transcript requirement has on any person seeking to appeal arises not out of the State's action, but out of factors entirely unrelated to it.[b]

1. *Harper v. Virginia Bd. of Elections,* struck down a poll tax that directly restricted the exercise of a right found in that case to be fundamental—the right to vote in state elections. The fee that M.L.B. is unable to pay does not prevent the exercise of a fundamental right directly: The fundamental interest identified by the majority is not the right to a civil appeal, it is rather the right to maintain the parental relationship.

b. In another section of his opinion, Thomas, J., argued that he would overrule *Griffin* in a proper case, but would, in any event, confine *Griffin* to criminal cases. Rehnquist, C.J., did not join that section of the opinion.

THE CONCEPT OF STATE ACTION

"GOVERNMENT FUNCTION"

CON LAW: P. 1416, add to fn. b

RTS & LIB: P. 1323, add to fn. b

Would it be "state action" if one of the major political parties imposed a registration fee in order to attend its convention to nominate candidates (assuming this would be barred by the 24th amendment if done by a state)? See *Morse v. Republican Party of Virginia*, p. 103 of this Supplement. Suppose the party excluded African Americans?

CONGRESSIONAL ENFORCEMENT
OF CIVIL RIGHTS

MODERN DEVELOPMENTS

CON LAW: P. 1473, before Notes & Questions

AMER CON: P. 1384, before *Guest*

RTS & LIB: P. 1380, before Notes & Questions

LOPEZ v. MONTEREY COUNTY, ___ U.S. ___, 119 S.Ct. 693, 142 L.Ed.2d 728 (1999), per O'CONNOR, J., held that Congress had power under § 2 of the fifteenth amendment to suspend voting regulations in a California county which was "covered" under the Voting Rights Act of 1965 even though the state legislature of California, which was not "covered," had passed a statute requiring the new voting regulations.

Kennedy, joined by Rehnquist, C.J., concurring, and Thomas, J., dissenting, avoided deciding the constitutional issue, but expressed "grave constitutional concerns."

CON LAW: P. 1498, at end

AMER CON: P. 1405, before *Jones*

RTS & LIB: P. 1405, at end

BOERNE v. FLORES

521 U.S. 507, 117 S.Ct. 2157, 138 L.Ed.2d 624 (1997).

JUSTICE KENNEDY delivered the opinion of the Court.

A decision by local zoning authorities to deny a church a building permit was challenged under the Religious Freedom Restoration Act of 1993 (RFRA). * * *

Congress enacted RFRA in direct response to the Court's decision in *Employment Div. v. Smith,* [CON LAW, P. 1113; AMER CON P. 1079; RTS & LIB, P. 1020]. *Smith* held that neutral, generally applicable laws may be applied to religious practices even when not supported by a compelling governmental interest. [Many] criticized the Court's reasoning, and this disagreement resulted in the passage of RFRA. * * *

RFRA prohibits "[g]overment" from "substantially burden[ing]" a person's exercise of religion even if the burden results from a rule of general applicability unless the government can demonstrate the burden "(1) is in furtherance of a compelling governmental interest; and (2) is the least restrictive means of furthering that compelling governmental interest." * * *

Congress relied on its Fourteenth Amendment enforcement power in enacting the most far reaching and substantial of RFRA's provisions, those which impose its requirements on the States. [W]e agree with respondent, of course, that

Congress can enact legislation under § 5 enforcing the constitutional right to the free exercise of religion. * * *

Congress' power under § 5, however, extends only to "enforc[ing]" the provisions of the Fourteenth Amendment. The Court has described this power as "remedial," *South Carolina v. Katzenbach.* The design of the Amendment and the text of § 5 are inconsistent with the suggestion that Congress has the power to decree the substance of the Fourteenth Amendment's restrictions on the States. Legislation which alters the meaning of the Free Exercise Clause cannot be said to be enforcing the Clause. Congress does not enforce a constitutional right by changing what the right is. It has been given the power "to enforce," not the power to determine what constitutes a constitutional violation. Were it not so, what Congress would be enforcing would no longer be, in any meaningful sense, the "provisions of [the Fourteenth Amendment]."

While the line between measures that remedy or prevent unconstitutional actions and measures that make a substantive change in the governing law is not easy to discern, and Congress must have wide latitude in determining where it lies, the distinction exists and must be observed. There must be a congruence and proportionality between the injury to be prevented or remedied and the means adopted to that end. Lacking such a connection, legislation may become substantive in operation and effect. * * *

The Fourteenth Amendment's history confirms the remedial, rather than substantive, nature of the Enforcement Clause. [The] objections to the [Joint] Committee's first draft of the Amendment ["The Congress shall have power to make all laws which shall be necessary and proper to secure to the citizens of each State all privileges and immunities of citizens in the several States, and to all persons in the several States equal protection in the rights of life, liberty, and property."] have a direct bearing on the central issue of defining Congress' enforcement power. * * * Members of Congress from across the political spectrum criticized the Amendment, and the criticisms had a common theme: The proposed Amendment gave Congress [a] power to intrude into traditional areas of state responsibility, a power inconsistent with the federal design central to the Constitution. [Under] the revised Amendment, Congress' power was no longer plenary but remedial [and] did not raise the concerns expressed earlier regarding broad congressional power to prescribe uniform national laws with respect to life, liberty, and property.[a] * * *

The design of the Fourteenth Amendment has proved significant also in maintaining the traditional separation of powers between Congress and the Judiciary. The first eight Amendments to the Constitution set forth self-executing prohibitions on governmental action, and this Court has had primary authority to interpret those prohibitions. The [first] draft, some thought, departed from that tradition by vesting in Congress primary power to interpret and elaborate on the meaning of the new Amendment through legislation. Under it, "Congress, and not the courts, was to judge whether or not any of the privileges or immunities were not secured to citizens in the several States." Horace E. Flack, *The Adoption of the Fourteenth Amendment* 64 (1908). While this separation of powers aspect did not occasion the widespread resistance which was caused by the proposal's threat to the federal balance, it nonetheless attracted the attention of

a. Compare Douglas Laycock, *Conceptual Gulfs in City of Boerne v. Flores*, 39 Wm. & M. L. Rev. 743, 766 (1998): "Senators and representatives argued [that] the enforcement power would add nothing if it were confined to the judicially enforceable meaning of the Amendment."

various Members. As enacted, the Fourteenth Amendment confers substantive rights against the States which, like the provisions of the Bill of Rights, are self-executing. The power to interpret the Constitution in a case or controversy remains in the Judiciary.[b] * * *

There is language in our opinion in *Morgan* which could be interpreted as acknowledging a power in Congress to enact legislation that expands the rights contained in § 1 of the Fourteenth Amendment. This is not a necessary interpretation, however, or even the best one. [As] Justice Stewart explained in *Mitchell*, interpreting *Morgan* to give Congress the power to interpret the Constitution "would require an enormous extension of that decision's rationale."

If Congress could define its own powers by altering the Fourteenth Amendment's meaning, no longer would the Constitution be "superior paramount law, unchangeable by ordinary means." It would be "on a level with ordinary legislative acts, and, like other [acts,] alterable when the legislature shall please to alter it." *Marbury v. Madison.* Under this approach, it is difficult to conceive of a principle that would limit congressional power. Shifting legislative majorities could change the Constitution and effectively circumvent the difficult and detailed amendment process contained in Article V. * * *

Respondent contends that RFRA is a proper exercise of Congress' remedial or preventive power. The Act, it is [said,] prevents and remedies laws which are enacted with the unconstitutional object of targeting religious beliefs and practices. See *Church of the Lukumi Babalu Aye, Inc. v. Hialeah,* [CON LAW P. 1124, AMER CON P. 1088, RTS & LIB P. 1031] To avoid the difficulty of proving such violations, it is said, Congress can simply invalidate any law which imposes a substantial burden on a religious practice unless it is justified by a compelling interest and is the least restrictive means of accomplishing that interest. If Congress can prohibit laws with discriminatory effects in order to prevent racial discrimination in violation of the Equal Protection Clause, then it can do the same, respondent argues, to promote religious liberty.

While preventive rules are sometimes appropriate remedial measures, there must be a congruence between the means used and the ends to be achieved. * * * Strong measures appropriate to address one harm may be an unwarranted response to another, lesser one.

A comparison between RFRA and the Voting Rights Act is instructive. In contrast to the record which confronted Congress and the judiciary in the voting rights cases, RFRA's legislative record lacks examples of modern instances of generally applicable laws passed because of religious bigotry. [Rather,] the emphasis of the hearings was on laws of general applicability which place incidental burdens on religion. * * *

Regardless of the state of the legislative record, RFRA [is] so out of proportion to a supposed remedial or preventive object that it cannot be understood as responsive to, or designed to prevent, unconstitutional behavior. It appears, instead, to attempt a substantive change in constitutional protections. Preventive measures prohibiting certain types of laws may be appropriate when there is reason to believe that many of the laws affected by the congressional enactment have a significant likelihood of being unconstitutional. See *Rome.* * * *

b. Scalia, J., did not join the material in the two preceding paragraphs from the Court's opinion.

RFRA is not so confined. Sweeping coverage ensures its intrusion at every level of government, displacing laws and prohibiting official actions of almost every description and regardless of subject matter. [Any] law is subject to challenge at any time by any individual who alleges a substantial burden on his or her free exercise of religion.

The reach and scope of RFRA distinguish it from other measures passed under Congress' enforcement power, even in the area of voting rights. In *South Carolina v. Katzenbach,* the challenged provisions were confined to those regions of the country where voting discrimination had been most flagrant, and affected a discrete class of state laws, i.e., state voting laws. Furthermore, to ensure that the reach of the Voting Rights Act was limited to those cases in which constitutional violations were most likely (in order to reduce the possibility of overbreadth), the coverage under the Act would terminate "at the behest of States and political subdivisions in which the danger of substantial voting discrimination has not materialized during the preceding five years." The provisions restricting and banning literacy tests, upheld in *Morgan* attacked a particular type of voting qualification, one with a long history as a "notorious means to deny and abridge voting rights on racial grounds." [This] is not to say, of course, that § 5 legislation requires termination dates, geographic restrictions or egregious predicates. Where, however, a congressional enactment pervasively prohibits constitutional state action in an effort to remedy or to prevent unconstitutional state action, limitations of this kind tend to ensure Congress' means are proportionate to ends legitimate under § 5. * * *

The substantial costs RFRA exacts, both in practical terms of imposing a heavy litigation burden on the States and in terms of curtailing their traditional general regulatory power, far exceed any pattern or practice of unconstitutional conduct under the Free Exercise Clause as interpreted in *Smith.* [In] addition, the Act imposes in every case a least restrictive means requirement—a requirement that was not used in the pre-*Smith* jurisprudence RFRA purported to codify—which also indicates that the legislation is broader than is appropriate if the goal is to prevent and remedy constitutional violations.

When [the] Court has interpreted the Constitution, it has acted within the province of the Judicial Branch, which embraces the duty to say what the law is. When the political branches of the Government act against the background of a judicial interpretation of the Constitution already issued, it must be understood that in later cases and controversies the Court will treat its precedents with the respect due them under settled principles, including stare decisis, and contrary expectations must be disappointed. RFRA was designed to control cases and controversies, such as the one before us; but as the provisions of the federal statute here invoked are beyond congressional authority, it is this Court's precedent, not RFRA, which must control. * * *

JUSTICE STEVENS, concurring.

In my opinion, RFRA is a "law respecting an establishment of religion" that violates the First Amendment * * *.[b]

JUSTICE O'CONNOR, with whom JUSTICE BREYER joins except as to [the first two sentences below].

b. The concurring opinion of Scalia, J., joined by Stevens, J., both of whom joined the Court's opinion, is omitted.

* * * I agree with much of the reasoning set forth in [the] Court's opinion. Indeed, if I agreed with the Court's standard in *Smith,* I would join the opinion. [But] I remain of the view that *Smith* was wrongly decided, and I would use this case to reexamine the Court's holding there. Therefore, I would direct the parties to brief the question whether *Smith* represents the correct understanding of the Free Exercise Clause and set the case for reargument. If the Court were to correct the misinterpretation of the Free Exercise Clause set forth in *Smith,* it would simultaneously put our First Amendment jurisprudence back on course and allay the legitimate concerns of a majority in Congress who believed that *Smith* improperly restricted religious liberty. We would then be in a position to review RFRA in light of a proper interpretation of the Free Exercise Clause. * * *

JUSTICE SOUTER, dissenting.

* * * Justice O'Connor's opinion [raises] very substantial issues about the soundness of the *Smith* rule. [In] order to provide full adversarial consideration, this case should be set down for reargument permitting plenary reexamination of the issue. Since the Court declines to follow that course, our free-exercise law remains marked by an "intolerable tension," *Lukumi,* and the constitutionality of the Act of Congress to enforce the free-exercise right cannot now be soundly decided. I would therefore dismiss the writ of certiorari as improvidently granted * * *.

———

FLORIDA PREPAID POSTSECONDARY EDUCATION EXPENSE BOARD v. COLLEGE SAVINGS BANK, __ U.S. __, 119 S.Ct. 2199, __ L.Ed.2d __ (1999), per REHNQUIST, C.J., explored *Boerne's* scope in the context of Congress' exercising its § 5 power—which may be used to abrogate the states' immunity from suits in federal court guaranteed by the eleventh amendment—to expressly make states subject to federal court actions for patent infringement: Although patents "have long been considered a species [of] 'property' of which no person may be deprived by a State without due process of law [, *Boerne*] held that for Congress to invoke § 5, it must identify conduct transgressing the Fourteenth Amendment's substantive provisions, and must tailor its legislative scheme to remedying or preventing such conduct. * * *

"In enacting the Patent Remedy Act, however, Congress identified no pattern of patent infringement by the States, let alone a pattern of constitutional violations. Unlike the undisputed record of racial discrimination confronting Congress in the voting rights cases, Congress came up with little evidence of infringing conduct on the part of the States. [At] most, Congress heard testimony that patent infringement by States might increase in the future* * *.

"[U]nder the plain terms of the [Due Process] Clause [, only] where the State provides no remedy, or only inadequate remedies, to injured patent owners for its infringement of their patent could a deprivation of property without due process result.

"Congress, however, barely considered the availability of state remedies for patent infringement and hence whether the States' conduct might have amounted to a constitutional violation under the Fourteenth Amendment. It did hear a limited amount of testimony to the effect that the remedies available in some States were uncertain.

"The primary point made by these witnesses, however, was not that state remedies were constitutionally inadequate, but rather that they were less convenient than federal remedies, and might undermine the uniformity of patent law.[9] [The] need for uniformity in the construction of patent law is undoubtedly important, but that is a factor which belongs to the Article I patent-power calculus, rather than to any determination of whether a state plea of sovereign immunity deprives a patentee of property without due process of law.* * *

"The legislative record thus suggests that the Patent Remedy Act does not respond to a history of 'widespread and persisting deprivation of constitutional rights' of the sort Congress has faced in enacting proper prophylactic § 5 legislation. [Though] the lack of support in the legislative record is not determinative, identifying the targeted constitutional wrong or evil is still a critical part of our § 5 calculus because '[s]trong measures appropriate to address one harm may be an unwarranted response to another, lesser one.' *Boerne.* Here, the record at best offers scant support for Congress' conclusion that States were depriving patent owners of property without due process of law by pleading sovereign immunity in federal-court patent actions.

"Because of this lack, the provisions of the Patent Remedy Act are 'so out of proportion to a supposed remedial or preventive object that [they] cannot be understood as responsive to, or designed to prevent, unconstitutional behavior.' *Boerne.* Congress did nothing to limit the coverage of the Act to cases involving arguable constitutional violations, such as where a State refuses to offer any state-court remedy for patent owners whose patents it had infringed. Nor did it make any attempt to confine the reach of the Act by limiting the remedy to certain types of infringement, such as nonnegligent infringement or infringement authorized pursuant to state policy; or providing for suits only against States with questionable remedies or a high incidence of infringement."

STEVENS, J., joined by Souter, Ginsburg and Breyer, JJ., dissented: "Sound reasons support both Congress' authority over patents and its subsequent decision in 1800 to vest exclusive jurisdiction over patent infringement litigation in the federal courts. [The] principle that undergirds all aspects of our patent system: national uniformity [supports] the congressional decision in 1982 to consolidate appellate jurisdiction of patent appeals in the Court of Appeals for the Federal Circuit [which] would be undermined by any exception that allowed patent infringement claims to be brought in state court.* * *

"It is quite unfair for the Court to strike down Congress' Act based on an absence of findings supporting a requirement this Court had not yet articulated. * * *

"It is true that, when considering the Patent Remedy Act, Congress did not review the remedies available in each State for patent infringements and surmise what kind of recovery a plaintiff might obtain in a tort suit in all 50 jurisdictions. But, [g]iven that Congress had long ago pre-empted state jurisdiction over patent infringement cases, it was surely reasonable for Congress to assume that such remedies simply did not exist. Furthermore, it is well known that not all States have waived their sovereign immunity from suit, and among those States that have, the contours of this waiver vary widely.

"Even if such remedies might be available in theory, it would have been 'appropriate' for Congress to conclude that they would not guarantee patentees due process in infringement actions against state defendants. State judges have

---

9. It is worth mentioning that the State of Florida provides remedies to patent owners for alleged infringement on the part of the State. Aggrieved parties may pursue a legislative remedy through a claims bill for payment in full, or a judicial remedy through a takings or conversion claim.

never had the exposure to patent litigation that federal judges have experienced for decades, and, unlike infringement actions brought in federal district courts, their decisions would not be reviewable in the Court of Appeals for the Federal Circuit. * * *

"Even if state courts elected to hear patent infringement cases against state entities, the entire category of such cases would raise questions of impartiality. This concern underlies both the constitutional authorization of diversity jurisdiction and the statutory provisions for removal of certain cases from state to federal [courts.]

"Finally, this Court has never mandated that Congress must find 'widespread and persisting deprivation of constitutional rights,' in order to employ its § 5 authority. It is not surprising, therefore, that Congress did not compile an extensive legislative record analyzing the due process (or lack thereof) that each State might afford for a patent infringement suit retooled as an action in tort. In 1992, Congress had no reason to believe it needed to do such a thing; indeed, it should not have to do so today.

[The] Court's opinion today threatens to read Congress' power to pass prophylactic legislation out of § 5 altogether; its holding is unsupported by *Boerne* and in fact conflicts with our reasoning in that case. * * *

"The difference between the harm targeted by RFRA and the harm that motivated the enactment of the Patent Remedy Act is striking. In RFRA Congress sought to overrule this Court's interpretation of the First Amendment. The Patent Remedy Act, however, was passed to prevent future violations of due process, based on the substantiated fear that States would be unable or unwilling to provide adequate remedies for their own violations of patent-holders' rights. Congress' 'wide latitude' in determining remedial or preventive measures, see *Boerne*, has suddenly become very narrow indeed.

"[In *Boerne*,] the sweeping coverage of the statute ensured 'its intrusion at every level of government, displacing laws and prohibiting official actions of almost every description and regardless of subject matter.' [Here, the Act] has no impact whatsoever on any substantive rule of state law, but merely effectuates settled federal policy to confine patent infringement litigation to federal judges. There is precise congruence between 'the means used' (abrogation of sovereign immunity in this narrow category of cases) and 'the ends to be achieved' (elimination of the risk that the defense of sovereign immunity will deprive some patentees of property without due process of law).

"That congruence is equally precise whether infringement of patents by state actors is rare or frequent. If they are indeed unusual, the statute will operate only in those rare cases. But if such infringements are common, or should become common as state activities in the commercial arena increase, the impact of the statute will likewise expand in precise harmony with the growth of the problem that Congress anticipated and sought to prevent. In either event the statute will have no impact on the States' enforcement of their own laws. None of the concerns that underlay our decision in *Boerne* are even remotely implicated in this case."

LIMITATIONS ON JUDICIAL POWER AND REVIEW

STANDING

THE STRUCTURE OF STANDING DOCTRINE

CON LAW: P. 1517, at the end note 3

AMER CON: P. 1416, at the end of note 3

RTS & LIB: P. 1419, at the end of note 3

The Court again emphasized the linkage between standing and the separation of powers in LEWIS v. CASEY, 518 U.S. 343, 116 S.Ct. 2174, 135 L.Ed.2d 606 (1996), which held that prison inmates lack standing to challenge denials of access to law libraries and other forms of legal assistance unless they can show that denial impedes the presentation of non-frivolous legal claims. The district court had granted a broad injunction, which was affirmed by the court of appeals. Reversing, the Court, per SCALIA, J., observed that the distinction between the judicial role and that of the political branches "would be obliterated if, to invoke intervention of the courts, no actual or imminent harm were needed, but merely the status of being subject to a governmental institution that was not organized or managed properly." Souter, J., joined by Ginsburg and Breyer, J.J., concurred in part and dissented in part. Stevens, J., dissented.

If prisoners lack access to prison libraries or other sources of legal advice, how can they be expected to establish—as a requirement of standing—that their legal claims are non-frivolous?

CON LAW: P. 1518, at the end of footnote i

AMER CON: P. 1416, at the end of footnote i

RTS & LIB: P. 1419, at the end of footnote i

United Food & Commercial Workers Union Local 751 v. Brown Group, Inc., 517 U.S. 544, 116 S.Ct. 1529, 134 L.Ed.2d 758 (1996), held that Congress may override the third requirement of the *Hunt* test for organizational standing and authorize a union to sue for damages on behalf of its members.

TAXPAYER STANDING AND OTHER STATUS–BASED STANDING ISSUES

CON LAW: P. 1528, at the end of note 2

AMER CON: P. 1426, at the end of note 2

RTS & LIB: P. 1429, at the end of note 2

The Court returned to the issues involving "generalized grievances" that are inadequate to support standing in FEC v. AKINS, 524 U.S. 11, 118 S.Ct. 1777, 141 L.Ed.2d 10 (1998). The Court per BREYER, J., upheld the standing of a group of voters to challenge a determination by the Federal Election Commission ("FEC") that the American Israel Public Affairs Committee ("AIPAC") is not a "political committee" as defined by the Federal Election Campaign Act of 1971 and, accordingly, that AIPAC had not violated the Act and was not required to make disclosures concerning its membership, contributions, and expenditures. "The FEC's strongest argument," the Court said, is "that this lawsuit involves only a 'generalized grievance' " inadequate to ground standing. But the "language [disclaiming the justiciability of generalized grievances] to which the FEC points * * * invariably appears in cases where the harm at issue is not only widely shared, but is also of an abstract and indefinite nature—for example, harm to the 'common concern for obedience to law.' " By contrast, the Court concluded, the injury of which the plaintiffs complained, that of being denied information through AIPAC's failure to make disclosures allegedly mandated by the statute, though "widely shared," was nonetheless concrete and specific; the case was analogous to those "where large numbers of voters suffer interference with voting rights" but all affected persons have standing.

SCALIA, J., joined O'Connor and Thomas, JJ., dissented. He thought that *United States v. Richardson* was not distinguishable: "[T]he Court is wrong to think that generalized grievances have only concerned us when they are abstract. One need go no further than *Richardson* to prove that—unless the Court believes that deprivation of information is an abstract injury, in which event this case could be disposed of on that much broader ground." Justice Scalia continued: "What is noticeably lacking in the Court's discussion of our generalized-grievance jurisprudence is all reference to two words that have figured in it prominently: 'particularized' and 'undifferentiated'. 'Particularized' means that 'the injury must affect the plaintiff in a personal and individual way.' If the effect is 'undifferentiated and common to all members of the public,' the plaintiff has a 'generalized grievance' that must be pursued by political rather than judicial means." The harm of being deprived of information fit that description: "The harm caused to Mr. Richardson [and Mr. Akins] * * * was precisely the same as the harm caused to everyone else."

CON LAW: P. 1530, at end of note 5

AMER CON: P. 1427, at end of note 5

RTS & LIB: P. 1430, at end of note 5

See also *Shaw v. Hunt,* 517 U.S. 899, 116 S.Ct. 1894, 135 L.Ed.2d 207 (1996)(holding that plaintiffs lack standing to challenge districting legislation as an unconstitutional racial gerrymander when they neither reside within the challenged district nor present specific evidence that they personally have been subjected to a racial classification). Stevens, J., dissenting, again would have denied standing more generally.

CON LAW: P. 1531, at the end of note 6

AMER CON: P. 1427, at the end of note 6

RTS & LIB: P. 1430, at the end of note 6

RAINES v. BYRD, 521 U.S. 811, 117 S.Ct. 2312, 138 L.Ed.2d 849 (1997), per REHNQUIST, C.J., distinguished *Coleman v. Miller,* which had upheld the standing of state legislators who complained that their votes against a proposed constitutional amendment were rendered nullities when the lieutenant governor impermissibly broke a tie by casting an affirmative vote, and held that members of Congress lacked standing to challenge the constitutionality of the Line Item Veto Act ("the Act"), which authorizes the President to "cancel" certain spending and tax benefit measures after signing them into law: *Coleman* "stands (at most * * *) for the proposition that legislators whose votes would have been sufficient to defeat (or enact) a specific legislative act have standing to sue if that legislative action goes into effect (or does not go into effect), on the ground that their votes have been completely nullified." Although plaintiffs alleged that the Line Item Veto Act diluted the significance of their votes for bills that are subject to presidential cancellation, there was a "vast difference" between the "level of vote nullification" in this case and that in *Coleman*. "We attach some significance to the fact that appellees have not been authorized to represent their respective Houses of Congress, and indeed both Houses actively oppose their suit. [N]or [does the decision] foreclose[ ] the Act from constitutional challenge (by someone who suffers judicially cognizable injury as a result of the Act). Whether the case would be different if any of these circumstances were different we need not now decide."

Souter, J., joined by Ginsburg, J., agreed that the plaintiffs lacked standing. Stevens, J., dissented, as did Breyer, J.

CONGRESSIONAL POWER TO CREATE STANDING

CON LAW: P. 1536, at the end of note 2

AMER CON: P. 1421, at the end of note 8

RTS & LIB: P. 1424, at the end of note 8

In FEC v. AKINS, 524 U.S. 11, 118 S.Ct. 1777, 141 L.Ed.2d 10 (1998), the Court, per BREYER, J., upheld the power of Congress to confer standing on any "aggrieved" person who suffers the harm of "inability to receive information" as a result of a decision by the FEC that reporting and disclosure requirements are not applicable to a private party. Although the interest in acquiring information was not protected at common law, and although "prudential" considerations might have precluded recognition of standing to sue based on so widespread an injury in the absence of a statute, Congress had specifically authorized suit under the Federal Election Campaign Act. Judicially imposed "prudential" limitations on standing therefore had to give way; the "failure to obtain relevant information" is a "concrete" enough injury to satisfy the requirements of Article III.

SCALIA, J., joined by O'Connor and Thomas, JJ., dissented. The asserted injury was too generalized and undifferentiated to support standing, and a statute could not cure the constitutional defect. "If today's decision is correct, it is within the power of Congress to authorize any interested person to manage (through the courts) the Executive's enforcement of any law that includes a requirement for the filing and public availability of a piece of paper. This is not the system we have had, and it is not the system we should desire."

†